Effective Requirements Practices

Addison-Wesley Information Technology Series
Capers Jones and David S. Linthicum, Consulting Editors

The information technology (IT) industry is in the public eye now more than ever before because of a number of major issues in which software technology and national policies are closely related. As the use of software expands, there is a continuing need for business and software professionals to stay current with the state of the art in software methodologies and technologies. The goal of the Addison-Wesley Information Technology Series is to cover any and all topics that affect the IT community: These books illustrate and explore how information technology can be aligned with business practices to achieve business goals and support business imperatives. Addison-Wesley has created this innovative series to empower you with the benefits of the industry experts' experience.

For more information point your browser to http://www.awl.com/cseng/series/it/

Sid Adelman, Larissa Terpeluk Moss, *Data Warehouse Project Management.* ISBN: 0-201-61635-1

Wayne Applehans, Alden Globe, and Greg Laugero, *Managing Knowledge: A Practical Web-Based Approach.* ISBN: 0-201-43315-X

Michael H. Brackett, *Data Resource Quality: Turning Bad Habits into Good Practices.* ISBN: 0-201-71306-3

Frank Coyle, *Wireless Web: A Manager's Guide.* ISBN: 0-201-72217-8

James Craig and Dawn Jutla, *e-Business Readiness: A Customer-Focused Framework.* ISBN: 0-201-71006-4

Gregory C. Dennis and James R. Rubin, *Mission-Critical Java™ Project Management: Business Strategies, Applications, and Development.* ISBN: 0-201-32573-X

Kevin Dick, *XML: A Manager's Guide.* ISBN: 0-201-43335-4

Jill Dyché, *e-Data: Turning Data into Information with Data Warehousing.* ISBN: 0-201-65780-5

Dr. Nick V. Flor, *Web Business Engineering: Using Offline Activites to Drive Internet Strategies.* ISBN: 0-201-60468-X

David Garmus and David Herron, *Function Point Analysis: Measurement Practices for Successful Software Projects.* ISBN: 0-201-69944-3

Capers Jones, *Software Assessments, Benchmarks, and Best Practices.* ISBN: 0-201-48542-7

Capers Jones, *The Year 2000 Software Problem: Quantifying the Costs and Assessing the Consequences.* ISBN: 0-201-30964-5

Ravi Kalakota and Marcia Robinson, *e-Business 2.0: Roadmap for Success.* ISBN: 0-201-72165-1

David S. Linthicum, *B2B Application Integration: e-Business-Enable Your Enterprise.* ISBN: 0-201-70936-8

Sergio Lozinsky, *Enterprise-Wide Software Solutions: Integration Strategies and Practices.* ISBN: 0-201-30971-8

Joanne Neidorf and Robin Neidorf, *e-Merchant: Retail Strategies for e-Commerce.* ISBN: 0-201-72169-4

Patrick O'Beirne, *Managing the Euro in Information Systems: Strategies for Successful Changeover.* ISBN: 0-201-60482-5

Mai-lan Tomsen, *Killer Content: Strategies for Web Content and E-Commerce.* ISBN: 0-201-65786-4

Bill Wiley, *Essential System Requirements: A Practical Guide to Event-Driven Methods.* ISBN: 0-201-61606-8

Ralph R. Young, *Effective Requirements Practices.* ISBN: 0-201-70912-0

Bill Zoellick, *Web Engagement: Connecting to Customers in e-Business.* ISBN: 0-201-65766-X

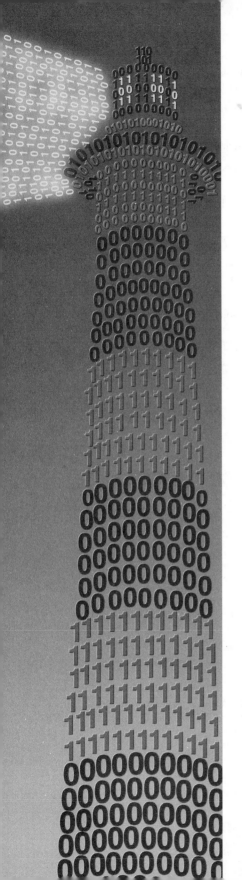

Effective
Requirements
Practices

Ralph R. Young

Addison-Wesley

Boston • San Francisco • New York • Toronto • Montreal
London • Munich • Paris • Madrid
Capetown • Sydney • Tokyo • Singapore • Mexico City

Many of the designations used by manufacturers and sellers to distinguish their products are claimed as trademarks. Where those designations appear in this book, and Addison-Wesley was aware of a trademark claim, the designations have been printed with initial capital letters or in all capitals.

The views expressed in this book are the author's and not necessarily those of Litton PRC or any affiliates.

Capability Maturity Model and CMM are registered in the U.S. Patent and Trademark Office.

Capability Maturity Model Integration (CMMI), Personal Software Process (PSP), and Team Software Process (TSP) are service marks of Carnegie Mellon University.

The Software Engineering Institute (SEI) is a federally funded research and development center sponsored by the U.S. Department of Defense.

DOORS is a registered trademark and DOORSnet and DOORSrequireIT are trademarks of Quality Systems & Software Inc., acquired by Telelogic on 9/15/00.

Credits for many of the figures provided in this book are given in the Credits Section located on pp. 321–324.

The author and publisher have taken care in the preparation of this book but make no expressed or implied warranty of any kind and assume no responsibility for errors or omissions. No liability is assumed for incidental or consequential damages in connection with or arising out of the use of the information or programs contained herein.

The publisher offers discounts on this book when ordered in quantity for special sales. For more information, please contact

Pearson Education Corporate Sales Division
One Lake Street
Upper Saddle River, NJ 07458
(800) 382-3419
corpsales@pearsontechgroup.com

Visit AW on the Web: www.awl.com/cseng/

Library of Congress Cataloging-in-Publication Data

Young, Ralph Rowland.
    Effective requirements practices / Ralph R. Young.
        p.   cm.—(Addison-Wesley information technology series)
    Includes bibliographical references and index.
    ISBN 0-201-70912-0
    1. Software engineering.   2. Computer software—Development.   I. Title.   II. Series.
    QA76.758.Y68 2001
    005.1—dc21   00-066511

ISBN 0-201-70912-0
Text printed on recycled paper
1 2 3 4 5 6 7 8 9 10—MA—0504030201
First printing, March 2001

This book is dedicated to the systems and software engineering professionals who have devoted their life's work to serving others.

Contents at a Glance

Contents

CHAPTER 5   USE AND CONTINUALLY IMPROVE A REQUIREMENTS PROCESS   97

CHAPTER 9 PERFORM REQUIREMENTS VERIFICATION AND VALIDATION 201

CHAPTER 10 PROVIDE AN EFFECTIVE MECHANISM TO ACCOMMODATE REQUIREMENTS CHANGES 217

CHAPTER 11 **PERFORM THE DEVELOPMENT EFFORT USING KNOWN, FAMILIAR PROVEN INDUSTRY, ORGANIZATIONAL, AND PROJECT BEST PRACTICES   231**

PART III WHAT TO DO NEXT   271

List of Figures

Foreword

It's your worst nightmare. A customer walks into your office, sits down, looks you straight in the eye, and says, "I know you think you understand what I said, but what you don't understand is what I said is not what I mean." Invariably, this happens late in the project, after deadline commitments have been made, reputations are on the line, and serious money is at stake.

All of us who have worked in the systems and software business for more than a few years have lived this nightmare, and yet, few of us have learned to make it go away. We struggle when we try to elicit requirements from our customers. We have trouble understanding the information that we do acquire. We often record requirements in a disorganized manner, and we spend far too little time verifying what we do record. We allow change to control us, rather than establishing mechanisms to control change. In short, we fail to establish a solid foundation for the system or software that we intend to build. Each of these problems is challenging. When they are combined, the outlook is daunting for even the most experienced managers and practitioners. But solutions do exist.

In this book, Ralph Young presents a comprehensive requirements process that identifies the key steps necessary to gather, understand, record, and verify the things that customers require when they request systems and software solutions. His treatment of the subject addresses the three critical elements that make a process work: (1) the tasks required to implement the process, (2) practical guidance required to implement the tasks, and (3) a strategy that helps to improve the process continually.

An experienced industry practitioner and manager, Dr. Young recognizes that effective requirements practices demand effective people practices. He provides pragmatic guidelines for creating requirements teams that meld the skills and knowledge of both customers and contractors. He recommends practical methods for eliciting requirements and at the same time understanding real customer needs. He proposes step-by-step suggestions for maintaining communication between the customer and all engineering groups as the project proceeds. He suggests indispensable techniques for verifying that the requirements we do record accurately reflect the customer's needs. He discusses the impact of change on requirements and offers practical steps for managing change. In short, Ralph Young has written an excellent guide for those who must understand and manage their customers' requirements. And this means just about everyone in the systems and software world.

Roger S. Pressman, Ph.D.
Consultant and Author
President, R.S. Pressman
& Associates, Inc.

Preface

Dealing effectively with requirements tops the list of the challenges to managers and practitioners developing systems and software. Improving the effectiveness of requirements practices has been a focus for me throughout my career. My vision of this book is to help you in your life's work by providing practical, useful, effective requirements practices.

This book describes ten requirements practices that provide a framework for overcoming current industry problems. Although systems and software development efforts have been going on for five decades, the industry has major difficulty worldwide in delivering products that meet customer needs. By applying effective requirements practices, one can remove causes of project failure. The reasons for failure are well documented (see Chapter 1). The needed improvement activities can be financed via the one third of total project costs now wasted. This book is full of suggestions concerning how to transform this waste into productive use.

The theme of this book is that practitioners should insist on using effective requirements practices. The use of effective requirements practices will reduce costs, improve the quality of work products, and increase customer satisfaction. The practices, ideas, suggestions, and recommendations provided in this book can be used individually or collectively, and not all have to be implemented to achieve progress. One can gradually implement some good practices quickly, with good payback, and then continue to work toward a more sophisticated, high-performance set of requirements practices.

This book provides a baseline for managers and project leaders to use to ensure that they are doing what is necessary to make a project successful. The practices, methods, techniques, and the requirements process itself have been filtered through experience, so the ideas are practical, cost-effective, and proven.

This book deals with the practical difficulties of requirements elicitation and management from a pragmatic, organizational, and project perspective. Attention is given to the pitfalls, costs, and risks as well as to the benefits of these practices. Unfortunately, many good practices never get implemented because the benefits are oversold, and the costs and risks aren't recognized. Political realities of organizations and projects must also be considered.

Application of the practices in this book will result in more productive, healthier, and happier organizations for systems and software development. The analysis extends beyond the technical issues to human issues and values. This book emphasizes the need for a shared vision of project success and advises how to obtain the required customer and supplier commitment.

The effective requirements practices described in this book will help you whether you are in a small organization or a large one, whether you build systems or software. Advice is provided for the information technology executive, consultant, manager, architect, systems or software engineer, systems integrator, developer, tester, process improvement engineer, member of the quality assurance group, or one responsible for configuration management. This book is invaluable for systems and software engineering courses, at both the undergraduate and graduate levels, and also for venues relating practical, useful guidance such as industry association and corporate courses concerning management of systems, requirements, as well as systems and software process engineering.

Although one frequently sees references to "requirements management," let's be clear that the challenge to system and software developers extends far beyond simply managing requirements. The requirements process is a full life cycle systems engineering process. It requires special effort and practices at the beginning of a project or system to identify what I refer to as *the real requirements*. Because the world changes while we are developing systems and software, it's essential to address new and changed requirements within the requirements process.

The requirements process requires mechanisms, for example, to achieve a shared vision, to ensure joint customer and supplier responsibility for the requirements, and to enable effective project coordination. The requirements process impacts every other activity performed in developing systems and software. One needs an automated requirements tool that provides for attributes such as the priority of each requirement, how it is linked to the design, where it is met in the code, how it is verified and tested, and so forth. It should be apparent already that we as an industry do not spend enough time and effort on the requirements process, and that this itself is a root cause of our problems.

The requirements comprise the basis for all the development work that follows. If you don't get the requirements right, you are in for a long, hard, and expensive pull. Your chances of "finishing" are small, and the probability of satisfying the users of the planned system is nil. We know from industry experience that customers don't know their "real requirements" (even though they may have spent a lot of time defining them and believe they know them). Suppliers and system developers don't know them either. Identifying the real requirements requires an *interactive* requirements process, supported by effective mechanisms, methods, techniques, and tools. The requirements process need not be complicated or expensive. However, a requirements process is *required* for a project of any size. It's more important that a project or organization *have* a requirements process than the nature of its specific components.

This leads to another fundamental premise of this book: Continuous improvement and a quality ethic within a project or organization lead to repeatable processes and reuse that save time and money. My commitment to these values comes from my work experiences and also from my study under Dr. W. Edwards Deming. Dr. Deming clarified for me that many of the root causes of problems are not technical issues. Rather, the root causes concern our responsibility as organizational and project executives, managers, and leaders to provide the environment in which "the workers" can be effective, productive, and fulfilled. Management must empower its work force to unleash its incredible capabilities.

The systems and software development environment needs attention, as we all can attest, based on our experience. The effective practices advocated in this book will facilitate your creation of the needed environment and will empower and enable your development team. I have witnessed (as I hope you have too) the power and the results of effective teams in positive environments. My experience is that an empowered team can accomplish anything it sets out to do. We must work to create the needed environment for success.

To benefit from the information in this book, you need bring only your involvement in systems and software-related activities coupled with a desire to improve. If you are a customer or client of the system or software provider indus-try, you will be particularly interested in Chapters 1 through 5 and 12. If you are a practitioner already familiar with the issues and problems, you may proceed directly to whichever of Chapters 2 through 11 relate most closely to your spe-cific work activities, noting the references to additional information and sources. If you are an executive or manager, you may want to focus on Chapters 1, 7, and 12 to gain added insight into the issues, to garner a high-level understanding, and to formulate some ideas concerning candidate improvement actions. If you are a student of systems or software engineering, you'll likely find it worth your time to proceed deliberately through the book. If you are participating in a require-ments-related course, you'll find the entire book insightful and provocative.

A rich collection of suggested references is provided in the footnotes, the Key References and Suggested Readings sections provided for each chapter, and the bibliography. No source is included just because it provides related information. Rather, each and every one is noted because it provides additional insights, more detailed suggestions and ideas, a recommended technique/approach, or an alter-native concept you might want to consider.

Primary Features of This Book

- Provides a practical organizational and project perspective.
- Emphasizes the need for a partnership approach and explains how to obtain commitment.
- Focuses on specific improvement activities.
- Explains how to evolve the real requirements.
- Considers the human dimension.
- Emphasizes the importance of effective communication.
- Provides sample templates (for example, for a requirements process and a requirements plan).
- Discusses the need to iterate the requirements and the architecture.
- Recommends how to deal with changing requirements.
- Explains requirements verification and validation.
- Suggests several mechanisms to facilitate self-correction and to help main-tain momentum.
- Stresses the need for an automated requirements tool.
- Provides advice and recommendations for executives, project managers, and leaders.

- Enables organizations and projects to utilize their resources better.
- Includes a rich set of references.

I am very grateful to a large number of reviewers for the material presented in this book. They have been helping me for 28 years to understand what works. Some I've come to know only recently, and many of them are industry experts in requirements, systems, or software engineering. The publisher tasked some industry experts to review these materials, and their review comments were invaluable. Others provided informal reviews because they are experts in particular areas or because they are professionally interested. Addison-Wesley's publishing professionals have made an invaluable contribution to the final product.

All of the reviewers have reinforced something I already knew: These practices are urgently needed today on projects and efforts of all sizes in all systems and software efforts. My hope is that they will help you. Of course, different practices work well in different environments. This is something we all understand from our experience, no matter where that experience was acquired or what fields it concerned. So you will need to select appropriate practices, recommendations, and suggestions, and apply them with a large measure of common sense—always a great guide!

I hope that you take the time and effort to share with me your experiences in applying the practices, recommendations, and suggestions in this book. This will help me further strengthen and improve my own insights and understandings and, God willing, allow me to share them again with others. Please write to me at *ryoungrr@aol.com.*

Ralph Young
February 2001

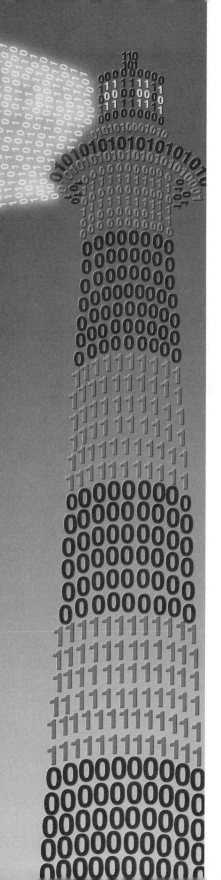

Acknowledgments

Every author knows that writing a book is a team effort. Families sacrifice time together. Publishing professionals work miracles. Friends and associates are asked to review work, make comments, validate ideas from their experience, perhaps even write something. Industry experts are contacted and asked to confirm their views, suggest additional references, and provide insights. Librarians search diligently for needed references.

Thank you to my wife, Judy, for her incredible patience and understanding. Thank you to Addison-Wesley (A-W), particularly to my editor, Debbie Lafferty, and also to Kristin Erickson whose enthusiasm, support, and encouragement led me to write this book. Patrick Peterson of the A-W production department made this part of the effort easy, Catherine Ohala did a magnificent job as copy editor, and Steve Katigback created extremely useable indexes. Friends and associates who lent a hand (and mind) include Stephen Bachanan, Cora Carmody, Pete Carroll, Barb Dreon, Jim Faust, Jim Fowler, Bob Fox, Steven Gaffney, Tom Gilb, Sharon Guenterberg, Jack Hayes, Alice Hill-Murray, Craig Hollenbach, Ivy Hooks, Earl Hoovler, Ray Huber, Barbara Kopp, Dan Marchegiani, Charles Markert, Andy Meadow, Hal Miller, John Moore, Matt Noah, Mark Paulk, Christina Pringle, Rich Raphael, John ("Mike") Reeves, Olga Rosario, Bette Rutherford, Dora Schield, Doug Smith, John Waters, Penny Waugh, Beth Werner, Doug Whall, and Don Young.

Additional industry experts who helped include Dennis Beude, Jeff Grady, Rita Hadden, Watts Humphrey, Capers Jones, Dean Leffingwell, Steve McConnell, Fergus O'Connell, Roger Pressman, Pete Sawyer, Jerry Weinberg, Neal Whitten, Karl Wiegers, Ed Yourdon, and Richard Zultner.

Thanks are also due to many individuals, organizations, and companies that provided permission to reuse their materials, including Al Pflugrad and Litton PRC, Addison-Wesley, Rational Corporation, the Software Engineering Institute, Charles Markert, Litton Applied Technology, Compliance Automation, the Institute of Electrical and Electronics Engineers, Litton-TASC, Telelogic, John Wiley & Sons, The Open Group, Microsoft Press, McGraw-Hill, Software Productivity Research, International Thomson Computer Press, The Neal Whitten Group, AMACOM (publishing arm of The American Management Association), American Programmer, Prentice-Hall, Prentice-Hall Europe, ETP Inc., Dorset House, and the International Council on Systems Engineering.

My writings and insights have been strengthened by the reviewers, including Len Bass, Gary Chastek, Sholom Cohen, Jack Hayes, Ivy Hooks, John Moore, Joseph Morin, Mark Paulk, Daniel Rawsthorne, Rob Sabourin, Karl Weigers, Bill Wiley, and Neil Williams.

Prayer works. Thanks to Art Banks, Tom Foss, Craig Hollenbach, and Joe Matney. Family support buoys the spirit. Thanks to Kim Wallace, Jeff Young, and Matt Young.

Errors and omissions are my responsibility. God willing, I'll have opportunities to fix them.

PART I

Background

Part I consists of Chapter 1, which explains the reason for this book. It defines a process and explains why there has been increased emphasis on process improvement in recent years. It defines the activities that should be included in a requirements process, reports on the benefits of using processes, and identifies pitfalls concerning the use of a process-oriented approach. It suggests that the use of ten recommended effective requirements practices will have a significant impact on results. Part I also provides information that will maximize your use of the book. Key roles and terms are defined. The different types of requirements are described. Insights are provided concerning system and software engineers. A "mind-set" to use while reading the book is suggested.

CHAPTER ONE

Introduction

Chapter 1 characterizes the current state of the systems and software engineering industry and explains why effective requirements **practices** need to be deployed and used. The typical project reflects unmet **requirements**, cost and schedule overruns, and customer dissatisfaction. The use of ineffective requirements practices is a root cause of project failure. My experience shows that the use of effective requirements practices has a *huge* positive impact on program costs, schedule, and success. The value of a **requirements process** is introduced. Several topics that help in using this book are discussed.

I've written this book because I wish to share ten effective requirements practices and related ideas, suggestions, and recommendations that I've found helpful in performing requirements-related activities concerning software and **systems engineering** and project management. My intent is to provide practical, useful ideas that you can use quickly and with a good return on investment. I hope that they prove useful to you.

The State of the Industry Today

Systems and software development efforts have enabled unprecedented achievements such as landing a man on the moon, medical breakthroughs that ensure longer life, and the technological advances used by organizations (networks, spreadsheets, and **databases**, to name a few). Yet, industry reports and analyses concerning systems and software development activities describe unmet **customer needs**, foiled **user** expectations, and extensive waste of resources.

In 1994, *Scientific American* reported there exists a chronic crisis despite 50 years of "progress," suggesting that we are decades short of the mature engineering discipline required to meet the needs of our information age.[1] Among the examples cited were the baggage system at the Denver International Airport, California's Department of Motor Vehicles driver and vehicle registration systems, and the Federal Aviation Administration's Advanced Automation System, all of which were dismal failures.

The Standish Group publishes oft-quoted CHAOS and COMPASS reports concerning industry efforts.[2] A 1998 report indicated that 26% of **projects** are successful, 46% are challenged, and 28% failed.[3] Other findings show that the average cost overrun is 89%, the average schedule overrun is 122%, and 45% of the functions provided in newly developed systems are never used. Fortune 1000 companies spent more than $275 *billion* on application development projects in 1996, and 58% or $145 billion of this investment was a casualty of cost overruns and failed projects. Why does this occur? According to the Standish Group, five of the top eight reasons why projects fail are related to requirements:[4]

1. Incomplete requirements
2. Lack of user involvement
3. Unrealistic **customer** expectations
4. Changing requirements and **specifications**
5. No longer need the capabilities provided

---

[1]W. Wayt Gibbs, "Trends in Computing: Software's Chronic Crisis." Available at http://www.di. ufpe.br/~java/graduacao/referencias/SciAmSept1994.html.

[2]Available at http://standishgroup.com/msie.htm.

[3]*Standish Group Report 1998*. See also *Software Runaways* by Robert Glass, which provides some good insights. Grady Booch has stated that many projects fail for the simple reason that the developers fail to build the right thing. Either they deliver a system that does not meet the expectations of its intended users, or they deliver a system that focuses on secondary functions at the expense of its primary use (comments extracted from Booch's review of Wiegers' *Managing Software Requirements*). Capers Jones believes a major contributing factor is failure to use formal estimating tools. See his article titled "Software Project Management in the 21st Century."

[4]CHAOS Report, 1995

Other factors relate to project management, such as lack of executive management support, too few competent staff members, the scope of the milestones used, the experience of the **project manager**, and the competence of project planning activities.

A comment from CHAOS University participant Sanjiv was, "If you don't nail the requirements, you fail the project. If you nail the requirements, you'll deliver."

Steve McConnell[5] reports that as of 1998,

- Approximately two million people were working on roughly 300,000 software projects in the United States
- Between one third and two thirds of those projects will exceed their schedule and budget targets before they are delivered
- Of the most expensive projects, approximately half will eventually be cancelled for being out of control, whereas others will be cancelled in more subtle ways.

Bill Curtis and colleagues[6] found that the three most important problems in software development are (1) the thin spread of **application** domain knowledge, (2) changes in and conflicts between requirements, and (3) communication and coordination problems. It's necessary to address all three of these problems in the requirements process.[7]

Progress in **requirements engineering** has been painfully slow.[8] System and software **development** efforts continue to be plagued with requirements-related problems. Given this, one would expect systems and software development companies and organizations to

- Identify the problems
- Analyze their root causes
- Plan and implement improvements
- Measure results
- Achieve progress

---

[5]Steve McConnell, *Software Project Survival Guide*, p. vii.

[6]Bill Curtis, Herb Krasner, and N. Iscoe, "A Field Study of the Software Design Process for Large Systems."

[7]See "Tales of Terror," Cover Feature, in *Software Development Magazine*, October 2000, for several recent examples of failures.

[8]Alan M. Davis, Foreward to *Software Requirements Engineering*, p. vii.

This has not happened.

As a result, we still see projects that skip requirements engineering entirely, or call their design a requirements specification just so it looks like they care about requirements. . . . The progress that has occurred can best be described as "back to basics." Projects that practice "back to basics" do several simple things. They maintain lists of their requirements in databases (where annotating, sorting, filtering, and cross-referencing are easy). They prototype systems before baselining requirements. They involve customers and users in the requirements process. They strive to find ways of reducing complexity and computer jargon in their requirements. They avoid approaches that claim to be panaceas.[9]

Root causes of requirements problems include the following:

1. The requirements provided by customers (**stated requirements**) are not the **real requirements**. Additional analysis is required to determine real customer needs and expectations. Then, the requirements need to be clarified and re-stated. Capers Jones[10] notes that customers vary widely in their understanding of fundamental business processes and their ability to explain the requirements.
2. **Suppliers** (developers of systems) contribute to the problems by using ineffective requirements and project management practices.
3. There is a lack of emphasis on joint customer/supplier responsibility for the success of the project.

The Need to Use Effective Requirements Practices

Practical on-the-job experience and study of the industry literature lead me to conclude that the use of ten effective requirements practices has the potential to achieve

- An understanding of the customer's real needs
- Clarification of the customer's stated requirements
- Good communication and a good relationship between the customer and the supplier

---

[9]*Ibid.*

[10]Capers Jones, *Estimating Software Costs,* pp. 435–436.

- A strong commitment of all parties to project objectives
- **Design**, deployment, and use of a repeatable requirements process that is continuously improved
- A system **architecture** that accommodates the customer's current and planned needs
- The ability to accommodate changes in requirements
- High **quality** of the system and its products
- Monetary savings
- Accurate schedules
- Customer satisfaction

The Requirements Process

What Is a Process?

A **process** is a set of activities that results in the accomplishment of a task and the achievement of an outcome. Organizations and projects have processes for what they do. The processes may not be defined or documented; nevertheless, there are tasks that are performed to achieve outcomes.[11] As shown in Figure 1-1, a process integrates people and **tools** as well as procedures and **methods**.

In recent years, there has been much emphasis on process. We realize that when we define and document our processes for doing things, we can save time and money by *reusing* the same process when we have to do the same thing on our own project, or in another organization or project. There is the opportunity for *repeatability* in using processes that saves the effort, time, and money of recreating the process. We often hear our peers talk about "not reinventing the wheel"—a reference to efficiencies of process and work product reuse.

The opportunity for *continuous improvement* is another advantage of having a defined, documented process. The users of any process are likely to have some ideas and suggestions about the current process to make it even better. If we take the time and trouble to capture their ideas and suggestions, update the process, and provide training for the revised process, the results produced will be better, not only for us, but for others who reuse it. We may measure some aspects of the

---

[11]Steve McConnell has provided a good analysis of projects that pay no attention to process compared with those that do. See his article titled "The Power of Process." He also notes that the criticism that systematic processes limit developers' creativity is not valid.

Figure 1-1   Process Integrates People, Tools, Procedures, and Methods

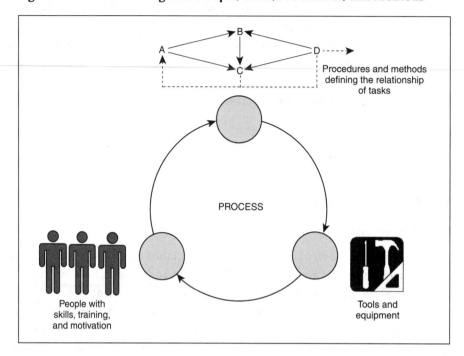

performance of the process prior to applying the ideas and suggestions, and again after they are applied. The difference (or *delta*) is a measure of the value of process improvement.

A process typically has a high-level or "macro" view and component steps or efforts. A process typically has several customers (more than we normally think at the outset), each of whom has specific, valid requirements they expect from the performance or completion of the process. Here we differentiate between the customer's *stated* requirements and those that are really *valid. An example of a stated requirement that is* not *valid is a requirement that is not understandable, measurable, or achievable.* Often customers have requirements that are not valid. It's important to evaluate each stated requirement based on a set of defined criteria (see Chapter 4 for suggested criteria).

A process typically involves several different groups, departments, or organizations. Some of the component steps or efforts in a high-level process may require a defined subprocess or "micro" process. A process typically is initiated by a customer need and is completed by the satisfaction of that need.

One way of describing a process is to draw a flowchart depicting the steps and actions involved and to write a narrative (**process description**) providing the information needed to explain and to perform or execute the process. The **process flowchart** should indicate the names of the process and the customer, state the customer's "valid" requirements, and provide the flow of activities and steps of the process. The process description may provide information such as the process identification, process purpose, related standards, related processes, version number, customer description, customer requirements, entrance criteria, inputs, outputs, exit criteria, responsibilities, tasks, tools, resources, quality indicators, and process indicators. More information on how to design a process is provided in Chapter 5. A process flowchart template and a process description template are provided there.

What Is the Requirements Process?

Any system or software effort starts with a set of requirements the planned system is intended to meet. *A requirement is a necessary* **attribute** *in a system. It may also be defined as a statement that identifies a capability, characteristic, or quality factor of a system in order for it to have value and utility to a user.* Developers address the requirements for the systems they build by performing activities or work tasks in support of a project. This may involve developing in-house software, identifying and licensing **commercial-off-the-shelf** (COTS) software that meets part or all of the requirements, or subcontracting the development effort to a third party. This may be done informally, with no defined or documented process to address the requirements, or the developers may have a defined and documented process based on their experience, or one provided by the organization or the project they are supporting.

A requirements process should address the following aspects of system activities:

Identifying requirements—This involves stating requirements in simple sentences and providing them as a set. **Business requirements** are the essential activities of an enterprise. They are derived from business goals (the objectives of the enterprise). **Business scenarios** may be used as a technique for understanding business requirements. A key factor in the success of a system is the extent to which it supports the business requirements and facilitates an organization in achieving them.

Understanding the customers' needs—This is often referred to as *requirements elicitation*. Note that the requirements can include several types, such as business requirements, quality requirements, performance requirements, interface requirements, and functional (or behavioral or operational) requirements. Another type is the nonbehavioral requirements addressed in the system engineering of the planned system, such as designability, **portability**, reliability, efficiency, human engineering, testability, understandability, and modifiability.

Clarifying and restating the requirements—The requirements must describe the customer's real needs.

Analyzing the requirements—For example, using a set of criteria to ensure that the requirements are "valid."

Defining the requirements—The requirements must be defined in a way that means the same thing to all of the **stakeholders** (those who have an interest in the system). Note that each stakeholder has a significantly different perspective of the system and the system's requirements. Sometimes this requires investing significant time learning a special vocabulary or project lexicon.

Specifying the requirements—This requires including all the precise details of each requirement so that they can be included in a specification document.

Prioritizing the requirements—All requirements are not of equal importance to the customers and users of the planned system. Some are critical, some are of relatively high priority, some are of "normal" or average priority, and some have lower priority. It is important to prioritize because there is never enough time or money to do *everything* we'd like to do in our developed systems. Prioritizing the requirements gives the opportunity to address the highest priority first and possibly to provide a later release of a product that addresses lower priority needs.

Deriving requirements—There are some requirements that come about because of the design of a system but do not provide a direct benefit to the end user. A requirement for disk storage may result from the need to have a lot of data stored, for example.

Partitioning requirements—For example, we categorize requirements into those that can be met by hardware, by software, through training, and in documentation.

Allocating requirements—We allocate requirements to different subsystems or components of the system.

Tracking requirements—We need the capability to trace or track where in the system each requirement is addressed and satisfied.

Managing requirements—We need to be able to add, delete, and modify requirements during all phases of system design, development, **integration and test**, deployment, and operation.

Testing and verifying requirements—This is the formal process of checking requirements, designs, code, test plans, and system products to ensure that the requirements are met.

Validating requirements—This is the process for proving that design **risks** presented by the requirements are minimized before excess money is spent doing the design. The order of **validation** of requirements should be prioritized because there is a limited amount of funding available for this activity.

It's clear from this list of requirements-related activities that the requirements process spans the full **system life cycle**. It is not just an activity that one needs to address at the beginning of a project. Nor is it limited to **requirements management**. There are many other activities that need to be addressed by the requirements process in addition to *managing* the requirements. All projects have a requirements process because they must deal with most or all of the previously listed aspects of systems activities to develop a system or software product. This list of requirements-related activities suggests the need for a defined, documented, reusable process that can be continuously improved over time by a project or organization.

Benefits of a Process Approach

Figure 1-2 provides benchmark data for organizations that have maintained a focus on process improvement for five years. These data are consistent with the improvements achieved by PRC projects that have achieved Capability Maturity Model (CMM) level 3 or higher. (PRC is a systems integration company with headquarters in McLean, Virginia. It is a wholly owned subsidiary of Litton Industries [Litton PRC]).

**Figure 1-2   Benchmark Data on Improvements for CMM Level 3
                Organizations**

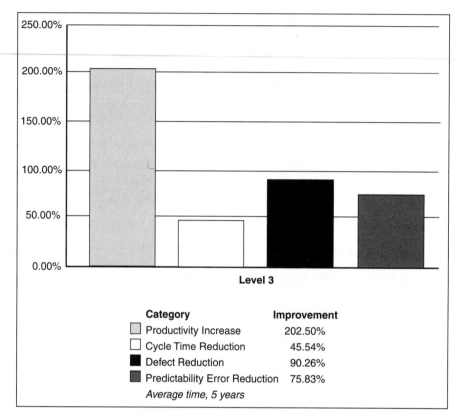

Category	Improvement
Productivity Increase	202.50%
Cycle Time Reduction	45.54%
Defect Reduction	90.26%
Predictability Error Reduction	75.83%

Average time, 5 years

Pitfalls of Using a Process Approach

Listed here are a few roadblocks one may run into, along with some suggestions
for dealing with them:

1. Many managers and developers aren't convinced of the value of developing
   and using processes. Either the concepts of reuse, repeatability, continuous
   improvement, and measurement are not familiar to them or they just don't
   believe in them. Therefore, one of the pitfalls is that the ability to utilize
   processes effectively requires an organizational commitment. This in turn
   requires **senior management** sponsorship and support. Mid-level and project managers are not likely to invest in process improvement in the absence
   of top-management interest and guidance to do so. The required action here

is to enlist the support of top management in the process improvement effort. This can be accomplished by providing the experiences of other companies or projects that have been successful, and through peer pressure, such as the need to keep up with the competition.

2. In many circles today, there isn't recognition that a "requirements process" is needed to build systems successfully. To be sure, any project to develop a system or software will have requirements. But an understanding that the requirements process is a full system **life cycle** effort is lacking.[12] Industry data suggest that the best results are achieved when 8% to 14% of total project cost is invested in the requirements process. An approach here would be to undertake a pilot effort, giving added emphasis and funding support to some of the requirements-related practices suggested in this book, and then compare results with other similar efforts.

3. Many organizations recognize that there is a requirements process, but they think of it as being limited to **requirements definition** and requirements management. There is a lot more to it than just these two components. Sharing information, perhaps during training sessions or during informal lunchtime meetings, can provide awareness that the requirements process is a full life cycle engineering process.

4. Many organizations and projects are content to accept the customer's stated requirements as the basis for the technical work. I've experienced a customer who stated adamantly, "This volume contains all of our requirements . . . we've been working on the requirements specification document for a year." After an investment of 40 person-years of development effort, the customer then indicated, "We do need to go back and identify the real requirements." As systems and software professionals, we owe it to our customers to share industry experience that stated requirements are never complete and that a concerted joint effort to evolve the real requirements is a valuable investment.

5. There is a tendency to want to utilize the newest methods and tools on our development projects. There seems to be an underlying mental thought

---

[12]In an e-commerce environment, development cycles are short (a few months maximum) and are becoming shorter every day. The idea is to try and implement newly defined, high-priority requirements in the next evolutionary cycle while completing the previous one. The process of managing requirements and deciding which requirements to include in which release is the key to success. It is still important to take the time to track requirements. We might think in terms of a *product requirements continuum* to clarify that requirements tracking continues even after product shipment.

process that "new is best." Somehow we have not learned that we need to use familiar, proven practices, methods, and tools. Sometimes a customer will even specify that a certain method or tool *will be used!* This statement is often made in the absence of any information concerning the practices, methods, and tools the development team is familiar with or even what industry experience is with the practice, method, or tool. We are left with two choices: Negotiate with the customer concerning the engineering environment we recommend, or hire staff with a familiarity *and a successful track record* in the method or tool being demanded. One of these choices should be selected prior to proceeding.

About This Book

A review of the following topics will assist in applying the effective requirements practices recommended in this book.

Roles

An understanding of the following **roles** facilitates use of the recommended practices:

Stakeholder—Any group, individual, or organization that is affected by or can affect the project. Customers, users, and developers are all *stakeholders* in a development effort.

User—Any stakeholder who will work with the system in some capacity, and so must understand it from the perspective of actual *use.*

Customer—The person with the funds to pay for the project or its end product. The customer is not necessarily the user.

Project managers—Individuals who are responsible for overseeing the work, assigning staff, empowering people, and enabling improvements.

Key Terms

A glossary that will help in clarifying the definitions and use of terms in this book is provided at the end of the book. Words that are bolded in the text are defined in the glossary. An understanding of the following key terms is essential to understanding and applying the effective requirements practices presented later. An example of each is provided.

A **mechanism** is a way of getting something done or achieving a result. For example, having each engineering group periodically present a brown-bag lunch session concerning its current activities to others assigned to the project is a mechanism to facilitate communication and intergroup coordination.

A *method* is a way, technique, process, plan, mechanism, body of skills or techniques, discipline, practice, system, model, **framework**, capability, or procedure for doing something. For example, an organization may utilize a particular process flowchart *method*.

A **methodology** is a body of methods, rules, and postulates employed by a discipline. For example, the set of procedures used to perform software development in a particular organization is a *methodology*.

A *practice* is the performance of work activities, performed repeatedly, to become proficient. A practice is the usual way of doing something to achieve a good result. An example is the *practice* of using a requirements process throughout an organization.

A *process* is a set of activities that results in accomplishing a task or achieving an outcome. For example, the requirements *process* is the set of activities that results in achieving development of a system that meets the customer's needs.

A *requirement* is a necessary attribute in a system. It is also a statement that identifies a capability, characteristic, or quality factor of a system in order for it to have value and utility to a user.[13]

Real requirements comprise the subset of all the requirements that reflect validated customer needs and expectations. The term *real requirements* suggests that the stated requirements should be clarified and restated until they meet the fundamental and essential needs of the users of any system.

A **technique** is a set of rules to follow to accomplish a task, a treatment of technical details, a body of technical methods, or a method of accomplishing a desired aim. An example of a software engineering *technique* is inspections, which are a more rigorous form of peer reviews.

A *tool* is something used to facilitate performing an operation or practicing a process or activity. A tool can be a checklist, a simple Microsoft Excel spreadsheet to track requirements for a tiny project, or an industry-strength automated requirements tool such as DOORS by Telelogic or RequisitePro by Rational. (See Chapter 4 for a list of commercially available requirements tools, vendors, and Web sites.)

---

[13]See "What is a Requirement" by Harwell, et al., pp. 23–29.

A Requirements Taxonomy

Figure 1-3 provides a taxonomy of different types of requirements in the form of a three-dimensional **Venn diagram**.

Grady describes his figure as follows:

> The top layer corresponds to development requirements, often called *design-to* requirements that must be clearly understood before design. The lower layer corresponds to product requirements, commonly called *build-to* requirements. The requirements above the heavy middle line correspond

Figure 1-3   Requirements Taxonomy

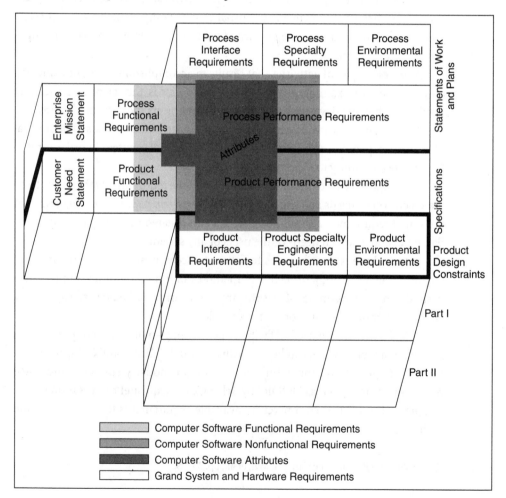

to process requirements captured in statements of work and plans. Development requirements can be further categorized as performance requirements and design constraints of three different kinds. Performance requirements tell what an item must do and how well it must do it. Constraints form boundary conditions within which the designer must remain while satisfying the performance requirements. Functional requirements are allocated to things in the evolving system physical model, commonly a hierarchical architecture, and expanded into performance requirements for that item. Verification requirements are paired with the item requirements. One could draw another dimension for design and verification requirements but it would be very hard to envision and draw in two dimensions. This approach corresponds to the fundamental notion that a design requirement should always be verified at the time the design requirement is defined. The reason for this is that it results in the definition of much better design requirements when one is forced to tell how he will determine whether or not the resultant design has satisfied that design requirement. If nothing else, it will encourage quantifying requirements because it is very difficult to tell how it will be verified without a numerical value against which one can measure product characteristics. (See Grady, *System Validation and Verification*, 1997: 24–25.)

Systems and Software Engineers

Every human being is unique and special; in my experience systems and software engineers are *very* special people. They tend to be bright, have extensive experience, are strongly committed, and are extremely persevering. They also tend to have strong views about what things are or ought to be. For example, systems engineers tend to be very careful in distinguishing the domain of systems engineering from software engineering. One gets the feeling that systems engineering is perceived by systems engineers to be better than (or more important than) software engineering—certainly very *different* from software engineering—in the view of many system engineers. One hears this tone at professional conferences, and it permeates the work of our industry everywhere. Some system engineers may consider this text primarily a resource for software engineers. On the other hand, some software engineers are likely to consider it a resource primarily for system engineers.

Intended Audience

There are ideas here that have value for *anyone* who is involved with systems in any role—customer/**client**, executive, manager, system engineer, software engineer, teacher, **configuration management** or quality assurance specialist, tester, independent verification and validation specialist, trainer, or documentation specialist. The intended audience includes customers and clients of system and software providers, practitioners, and students of requirements engineering.

Recommended Mind-set for Readers of This Book

For the purpose of this book, I invite you to have the following mind-set:

1. The skills of many disciplines are needed to get what is of value accomplished.
2. No discipline is "better than" or "more important than" another discipline. All are needed and vital.
3. Progress is often better when we graciously accept the views and ideas of the other members of the team and gradually work toward consensus, knowing that "two heads are better than one" (always).
4. Although we have well-formulated (that is, strong) views of the definitions of things, approaches toward things, methods, tools, practices, and so forth, it's not constructive to insist that "my" view is the only correct one and others are "wrong" or that there is only "one way" of doing something. We know from experience that there are *many ways* of doing just about anything, with some better in some situations and others better in different situations. I have seen much time wasted and many relationships jeopardized by a team member who insists on a specific definition of an engineering term or a specific way that something should be done.
5. Related to this is the need for patience with one another and acceptance of another's point of view. Often in the heat of battle and the pressures of our jobs, we lose sight of the fact that others are only trying to help and contribute in the best way they can.

I'm sure these concerns are very familiar. I urge that we in our professions work constructively together with an open mind and a spirit of teamwork, knowing that others' respect for our views, knowledge, and ability to contribute is a function of our respect for one another.

The "Team," the "Project," and the "Project Manager"

You will note as you read through this book that I have capitalized words such as the Team, the Project, and the Program or Project Manager in some instances, but not in others. You may feel that it's inappropriate or incorrect capitalization. Let me explain. I take the view that these and other terms, used in connection with a particular project, are very special, because they refer to *the* team or project or project manager under discussion. Accordingly, I have capitalized terms when I've used them in a context to emphasize that we are talking about a specific situation. Please don't let this distract you from the content or substance of what is being discussed.

Footnotes in This Book

Footnotes are intended to be a source of additional information and to provide insight. You'll note that many of the footnotes are written from my own particular perspective and are based on my personal experience. This is not to suggest that this is the only view or "right" view. It's just my own view (at the time of writing). I have also provided many Web addresses in situations in which I feel that you may enjoy knowing other sources of information, as well as e-mail addresses to facilitate contacting people.

Key References and Suggested Readings

At the end of each chapter, a list of key references and suggested readings is provided. These are the references I have found particularly helpful and insightful in connection with the subject of that chapter. There are many books available, and some are more useful than others. Many of these references provide information beyond the scope of this text. A reader interested in a particular area may find these to be good sources.

Upcoming Topics

The following chapters address the recommended effective requirements practices:

2—Commit to the Approach

3—Establish and Utilize a Joint Team Responsible for the Requirements

4—Define the *Real* Customer Needs

5—Use and Continually Improve a Requirements Process

6—Iterate the System Requirements and Architecture Repeatedly

7—Use a Mechanism to Maintain Project Communication

8—Select Familiar Methods and Maintain a Set of Work Products

9—Perform Requirements Verification and Validation

10—Provide an Effective Mechanism to Accommodate Requirements Changes

11—Perform the Development Effort Using Known Familiar Proven Industry, Organizational, and Project Best Practices

Summary

Although system and software providers have made enormous contributions to society, there are unmet customer needs in most systems and an extensive waste of resources. Requirements-related problems contribute to these issues. Practical experience and study of the industry literature led me to evolve ten effective requirements practices that address the root causes of requirements problems.

In recent years, there has been much emphasis on *process* because it enables reuse, repeatability, continuous improvement, and customer satisfaction. A requirements process should be developed, used, and continuously improved by every organization developing systems or software. It should address all requirements-related activities, which span the entire system life cycle.

The customer's or client's stated requirements are never complete. A concerted joint customer and supplier effort to evolve the real requirements is a valuable investment.

I anticipate that your use of the ten effective requirements practices recommended in this text will have a significant and positive impact on your results. I hope that you will take the time to share with me your experiences in applying these practices. Please send comments, suggestions, and your experiences to me at ryoungrr@aol.com.

Key References and Suggested Readings

Barry W. Boehm and Kevin J. Sullivan. *Software Economics.* **White Paper, 1999.** Boehm and Sullivan stress the importance of understanding the relationships between software development decisions and business decisions. The goal is maximal value creation. Technical software decisions should be based on value creation; therefore, software engineers, designers, and managers should base decisions on value maximization objectives. Boehm and Sullivan assert that software engineers are usually not involved in and do not understand **enterprise**-level value creation objectives, and that senior management often does not understand success criteria for software development or how investments at the technical level can contribute to value creation. It is in our enlightened self-interest to increase our understanding of and ability to deal with the economic aspects of software and its development.

Dennis M. Buede. *The Engineering Design of Systems: Models and Methods.* **New York: John Wiley & Sons, 2000.** This book provides an excellent discussion of systems engineering, with good emphasis on requirements, the design process, modeling, architecture development, and decision analysis. Buede emphasizes that requirements are the cornerstone of the systems engineering process. Case studies and problems are provided.

W. Edwards Deming. *Out of the Crisis.* **Cambridge, MA: Massachusetts Institute of Technology, Center for Advanced Engineering Study, 1986.** Dr. Deming is the father of quality in Japan and did much for the United States as we reluctantly gave more attention to it. Deming's 14 points provide a theory of management. His seven deadly diseases afflict most companies and stand in the way of progress. Deming's thesis is that American management does not enable and empower its work force, which is "only doing its best." Deming asserts that American management does not understand variation (faults of the system [common causes] and faults from fleeting **events** [special causes]). It's vital for every manager to capture the essence of Deming's perspective (see the reference to Mary Walton's book later in this section).

Donald C. Gause and Gerald M. Weinberg. *Exploring Requirements: Quality Before Design.* **New York: Dorset House Publishing, 1989.** This book is one of the classics concerning requirements elicitation. Gause and Weinberg provide a large collection of ideas and approaches based on their consulting experience in discovering what is desired in systems. They believe that meeting the following three conditions helps to ensure a successful project: (1) achieving a consistent understanding of the requirements among all participants, (2) achieving teamwork, and (3) knowing how to work effectively as a team (that is, developing the necessary skill and tools to define requirements).

Tom Gilb. *Principles of Software Engineering Management.* **Wokingham, UK: Addison-Wesley, 1988.** Gilb has made many significant contributions to the industry over the years, including his work concerning inspections, requirements-driven management, evolutionary delivery, and impact estimation. His book is an easily readable, comprehensive discussion of software engineering principles and is recommended as a good foundation for practitioner study. See Gilb's Web site for current activities and publications (http://www.Result-Planning.com).

Jeffrey O. Grady. *System Requirements Analysis.* **New York: McGraw-Hill, 1993.** Grady has devoted his career to requirements and related topics, and he teaches courses and develops tutorials. He is a founding member of the National Council on Systems Engineering (NCOSE; now the International NCOSE). This book provides a systems approach and thorough explanations of **requirements analysis,** traceability specifications, requirements integration, **requirements verification,** and explanations of techniques including structured analysis, structured **decomposition,** and architecture synthesis.

Ivy F. Hooks and Kristin A. Farry. *Customer-Centered Products: Creating Successful Products Through Smart Requirements Management.* **New York: AMACOM, 2001.** This book is a guide to how good requirements are possible when managers are involved in guiding the requirements process. It provides advice and insights based on years of experience and many suggestions for how to perform requirements-related activities. Hooks and Farry emphasize the importance of managers allocating resources, defining and enforcing processes, educating personnel, and measuring the impact of requirements on final product quality. This is recommended reading for project managers.

Capers Jones. "Software Project Management in the 21st Century." *American Programmer* **1998:11(2):24–30.** Jones notes that manual software estimating methods fail for large systems because of their **complexity**. He advocates using automated project management and software cost-estimating tools, noting that integrated management tool suites that share common **interfaces** and common data repositories will probably be developed within a few years. He suggests that a Web-based software cost estimation and planning service and a benchmarking service are likely. He indicates that the most visible and important gap in software project management capabilities concerns data and information and that there is a growing need to be able to deal with long-range estimating and measurement at the enterprise or corporate level.

Capers Jones. *What It Means To Be "Best in Class" for Software.* **Burlington, MA: Software Productivity Research, Inc. Vers. 5. February 10, 1998.** This rigorous and analytical report lists 15 key software performance goals that, if achieved, indicate that *best-in-class* status is within your grasp. The report provides qualitative and quantitative results from the top 5% of the projects of the top 10% of the clients of Software Productivity Research, Inc. (SPR). Also, quality targets for the five levels of the Software Engineering Institute CMM are suggested. The report surveys process improvement strategies and tactics that excellent software producers have utilized. The report is available from SPR at capers@spr.com.

Dean Leffingwell and Don Widrig. *Managing Software Requirements: A Unified Approach.* **Reading, MA: Addison-Wesley, 2000.** This book emphasizes the team skills that are required for the requirements process. Leffingwell and Widrig share their many years of experience and describe proven techniques for understanding needs, organizing requirements information, and managing the scope of a project.

James N. Martin. *Systems Engineering Guidebook: A Process for Developing Systems and Products.* **Boca Raton, FL: CRC Press, 1996.** This book is a comprehensive guide to the systems engineering process, application tasks, methodologies, tools, documentation, terminology, system hierarchy, synthesis of functional and performance requirements into the product architecture, integration, verification, metrics, **defects** and defect types, and programmatic application. Martin describes the systems engineering process as a multidisciplinary effort. The system life cycle and **life cycle model** are described, and the role of the systems engineering process champion is explained. An extensive set of figures and tables that describe all aspects of systems engineering is provided.

Mark C. Paulk, Bill Curtis, Mary Beth Chrissis, and Charles V. Weber. *Capability Maturity Model for Software.* **Version 1.1. Pittsburgh, PA: Software Engineering Institute, Carnegie-Mellon University, 1993.** Also available at http://www.sei. cmu.edu/publications/documents/93.reports/93.tr.024.html. The CMM for Software (SW-CMM) has been the industry model for software process improvement for more than a decade. It has provided a standard that has allowed projects and organizations to evaluate their practices, provide a basis for improvement actions, develop improvement plans, and measure improvements. This book is highly recommended for projects and organizations.

Ian Sommerville and Pete Sawyer. *Requirements Engineering: A Good Practice Guide.* **New York: John Wiley & Sons, 1997.** This book provides a set of basic, intermediate, and advanced guidelines consistent with SW-CMM levels to facilitate gaining requirements engineering process maturity, and it explains in detail how to apply these guidelines in practice. Sommerville and Sawyer define requirements elicitation as follows: The system requirements are *discovered* (emphasis added) through consultation with stakeholders, from system documents, domain knowledge, and market studies. Their Chapter 4 explains how to apply 13 guidelines to perform requirements elicitation.

Mary Walton. *The Deming Management Method.* **New York: Putnam Publishing, 1986.** This is a good summary and explanation of Dr. Deming's teachings, with a foreword by the master. Walton describes Deming's 14 points, the seven deadly diseases, and the parable of the red beads. Walton describes Deming's beliefs that management is the primary cause of the results in organizations. The "workers" (everyone else) are powerless, lacking the environment to be effective. Managers should be challenged to recognize the distinction between a stable system and an unstable one and to be able to recognize and address special causes. The conditions necessary to achieve teamwork are described. This is recommended reading for anyone who seeks a good foundation for a quality improvement ethic.

Bill Wiley. *Essential System Requirements: A Practical Guide to Event-Driven Methods.* **Reading, MA: Addison-Wesley, 2000.** Wiley provides an event-driven strategy for software development that he believes provides an intuitive, effective partitioning of the user domain and the proposed system. Events jump-start the identification and specification of system requirements with early user involvement and improved user communication. When combined with a spiral, incremental approach that dovetails with an "architected" rapid application development strategy, event-driven methods accelerate the delivery process. Wiley provides a **function point** example.

Recommended Requirements Practices

Part II consists of ten chapters, one for each of the ten effective requirements practices. Each chapter describes the practice and provides a discussion concerning how to perform it. Extensive references are provided in the footnotes and in the key references and suggested readings.

The ten effective requirements practices are the following:

1. Commit to the approach.
2. Establish and utilize a joint team responsible for the requirements.
3. Define the *real* customer needs.
4. Use and continually improve a requirements process.
5. **Iterate** the system requirements and the system architecture repeatedly.
6. Use a mechanism to maintain communication.
7. Select familiar methods and maintain a set of work products.
8. Perform requirements **verification** and validation.
9. Provide an effective mechanism to accommodate requirements changes.
10. Perform the development effort using known familiar proven industry, organizational, and project best practices.

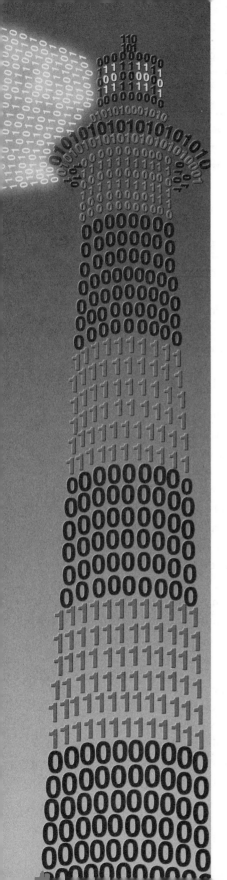

CHAPTER TWO

Commit to the Approach

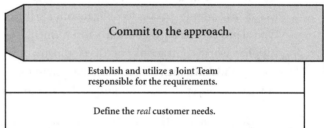

Commit to the approach.
Establish and utilize a Joint Team responsible for the requirements.
Define the *real* customer needs.
Use and continually improve a requirements process.
Iterate the system requirements and architecture repeatedly.
Use a mechanism to maintain project communication.
Select familiar methods and maintain a set of work products.
Perform requirements verification and validation.
Provide an effective mechanism to accommodate requirements changes.
Perform the development effort using known, familiar proven industry, organizational, and project best practices.

This chapter emphasizes that commitment is critical to the success of any system or software development effort. It explains what is meant by commitment and how commitment can be attained and maintained. It provides recommendations to use in evolving the suggested partnering approach.

What Do We Mean by Commitment?

Commitment means a lot of different things to different people. In its general usage, "to commit" means to obligate one's self to do something. Let's consider a typical project start-up situation. Commitment is what a customer expects from a supplier when contracting for development of a system. "We'll commit some money, and ABC, Inc., will develop the system for us." A more detailed description of what the buyer is really thinking is that the contractor will do the following:

- Determine exactly what the specifications that will meet all of the buyer's needs in a particular functional area should be.
- Design and develop a system that meets these specifications.
- Implement the system with "minimal" impact on existing business activities, using precisely the appropriate (and the most cost-effective) hardware, which certainly won't become obsolete in the "foreseeable future."
- Accommodate any and all changes that the **buyer** and any of its representatives or users have during the development process in the event, say, that not all of the buyer's needs were identified in the initial request or the buyer's business needs change during the development process or someone comes up with new technologies or futuristic ideas that they'd like to have addressed and accommodated in the new system.
- Deliver the new system per the original schedule and budget (of course!).
- Be willing and able to address any and all issues concerning the developed system once it's implemented, in a very timely manner, so as not to jeopardize any of the buyer's business activities.

Suppliers, on the other hand, have a different perspective. They want to perform the work as expeditiously as possible and get paid. They are in business, after all, to make a profit. How else could they remain in business? Suppliers develop and install systems related to buyers' needs all the time. Most likely, the supplier has developed similar systems and can reuse appropriate hardware and architecture solutions and previously developed software to accommodate a

Figure 2-1   Customer and Supplier Issues

Customer	Supplier
Doesn't understand the real need.	Doesn't understand the customer's need.
Doesn't understand what can be achieved within fiscal boundaries.	Is unwilling/unable to meet true needs within fiscal boundaries.
Doesn't communicate the need effectively.	Doesn't encourage and nurture more effective communication.
Provides overly specific specifications.	Doesn't engage the client in a process to distill real needs.
Doesn't update the statement of current user operating concepts or technology improvements.	Lacks subject matter expertise to address functional needs.

significant portion of a particular buyer's needs. In other words, suppliers can achieve economies by reusing solutions they have developed and sold previously. Figure 2-1 contrasts typical customer and supplier issues.

The issues presented in Figure 2-1 can be summarized as follows:

- The real needs (the requirements) are not defined.
- The funding envisioned by the customer won't pay for all of the work that needs to be done.
- The risk of conflict escalation is high because of poor communication.
- There is no mechanism
  - To achieve a joint vision of the project.
  - To agree to common goals and guiding principles for the project.
  - To resolve issues.
  - To conduct objective evaluations.

Accordingly, there is great potential and risk for both the customer and the supplier to become uncommitted (not obligated) to the successful completion of the project.

Thus, by commitment, I mean the following:[1]

1. An atmosphere of cooperation and collegial problem solving among the project stakeholders is created at the beginning of the project and maintained throughout its performance period.
2. The stakeholders pledge themselves to a jointly developed definition (shared vision) of project success.
3. The parties pledge to resolve issues and problems.
4. Mechanisms to maintain a joint approach are provided, such as a mutually developed vision statement, a definition of project success, a statement of common goals and guiding principles, and a procedure to resolve issues.

How Can Commitment Be Attained and Maintained?

The partnering concept is designed to create trust and communication between the customer and the supplier. It is a proven, effective method for achieving and maintaining commitment. (Clearly, partnering is not the only way to attain commitment. Honest, candid communication and a sincere desire to work toward jointly shared goals and objectives provide the basis for commitment.) A summary of the partnering concept is provided in Figure 2-2.

This approach provides both an operational definition of commitment and a context for its implementation. The approach is evolved in a partnering workshop, a one- to three-day event attended by representatives (including decision makers) of both the customer and the supplier, and it is facilitated by a trained, experienced facilitator. Frequently, customers have not thought through the details of an effort in enough detail to be able to describe what success really means! Without that definition, it is impossible to manage the project in a way that guides both the customer and the contractor in the performance of the contractual effort. It is surprising how many customers learn, for the first time, that success frequently depends on specific and timely input that they, the client, must provide. The partnering workshop defines the personal expectations and concerns of the team members. Current organizational charts are explained. Partnering is described and explained. A discussion concerning personal leadership styles is

---

[1]Harwell stresses the value of commitment and emphasizes that customer, management, and project team commitments are essential for success. See "Systems Engineering Is More Than Just a Process."

Figure 2-2   The Partnering Concept

Partnering is a structured process designed to create an atmosphere of commitment, cooperation, and collegial problem solving among organizations and individuals that work together on a project. Partnering uses mutually developed vision statements, common goals, guiding principles, issue resolution procedures, and evaluation methods to help ensure project success. The process is normally initiated at a workshop at the beginning of the project.

At the workshop, everyone is considered equal. No participant or organization should be allowed to dominate the workshop process. All parties need to recognize that partnering is the building of the team to complete the project.

Partnering does not change the parties' contract obligations. It does facilitate the manner in which the contracting parties treat each other during the course of contract performance. It creates a climate in which the interests and expectations of the contracted parties are more readily achievable. To this end, a written charter is created during the workshop that states the parties' common interests in reducing time-consuming and costly disputes, as well as improving communications to the benefit of all parties.

All contracting parties have an economic interest in the success of the project. Just as customers are concerned with getting good value for their money, suppliers are in business to make a fair profit for the services they provide. When a supplier is squeezed for profit, the quality of the work and business relationships can suffer or be destroyed, creating hostility and expensive, protracted litigation of claims. Driving good suppliers out of business is not in anyone's best interest. The long-term goal should be to keep good contractors in business so that competitive bidding is as robust as possible in the future.

Partnering should include the ultimate user of the system. Customers need to be involved in the partnering process from start to finish. They provide valuable information about their project needs and can participate in problem-solving sessions at the workshop and follow-up meetings, and may gain a better understanding of where their dollars are going

(continued)

Figure 2-2   The Partnering Concept (*continued*)

when contract modifications are required. A typical goal of the partnering team is to deliver a quality project to the customer that meets the customer's functional needs and financial constraints. Customer satisfaction is an essential ingredient in virtually all partnering efforts.

The costs for partnering generally include one to three days of the participants' time at the start of a project to conduct the workshop, and later for any follow-up sessions. There are also the facilitator's fees for these meetings. These costs are small, however, when a project is delivered within the customer's budget, at a profit for the supplier, and ahead of schedule. The time required is small in comparison to the time saved over the course of the project. At the initial workshop, many partnering teams will identify and resolve potential problems. This can prevent weeks or months of delay later in the project. During the project, the team uses partnering procedures to work together to avoid other schedule delays and to achieve project goals.

Anyone who has a direct impact in the success of the project should be a participant and attend the initial partnering workshop to become a team member. Participation in the workshop ensures an understanding of the team's common goals and mutual vision. When an individual is not present at the workshop, partnering may have no meaning to that person.

Follow-up sessions are sometimes delayed or canceled because of the pressures of project performance and completion schedules. This prevents the partnering process from effectively working when it is most needed. It takes a strong commitment to partnering to ensure that follow-up sessions take place when everyone is otherwise busy. To avoid this problem, a schedule for the follow-up sessions should be established during the initial workshop. Dates can be set to meet all team members' schedule requirements.

Subcontractors should participate to inform the other participants of their interests and value to the project. Subcontractors will, in turn, learn and appreciate what is important to the other project participants. Subcontractor participation in the workshop can help prevent disputes during performance.

> Two essential elements of a successful partnering relationship are trust and communication. If any team member feels that other team members are taking advantage of her, trust will be adversely affected. Team members should be encouraged to communicate this feeling plainly and promptly to the others when the issue arises.

held, and an exercise to facilitate cooperation and communication is provided. A discussion concerning the value of a shared vision of project success is held. Barriers to implementation and achievement of this vision are discussed. After a discussion of potential project goals, consensus concerning common goals is achieved.

The core values shared by the group are identified, and a shared vision of project success is agreed on. An *issue resolution ladder* (Figure 2-3) is developed. Figure 2-4 presents a typical action planning worksheet used to resolve issues. The value of action planning is discussed, and some initial action plans including specific actions, dates, and formats for deliverables (both client and contractor) are developed. An evaluation process is described and developed, and an implementation strategy is created. A project charter is described and developed. Figure 2-5 provides a sample project charter.

The workshop participants plan for follow-up activities to ensure that the partnering agreement remains active throughout the project performance period. They also develop and agree on a set of guiding principles for the conduct of the project. Evaluation methods to define project progress are developed. The workshop concludes with a dinner to celebrate the success of the workshop and the joint commitment to partnering.

The result of this effort is an integrated team of players who understand their roles and responsibilities to meet project objectives. Charles Markert of Mediate Tech, Inc.,[2] and Leo Brennan of Litton PRC[3] are experienced in

---

[2]Charles D. Markert, P.E., Mediate Tech, Inc., Senior Vice President and Technical Director, facilitator, and contributing author of *Partnering in Construction: A Practical Guide to Project Success,* 800-967-4555, markert@erols.com.

[3]Leo Brennan, Litton PRC, 1500 PRC Drive, McLean, VA 22102, brennan_leo@prc.com.

Figure 2-3   Issue Resolution Ladder

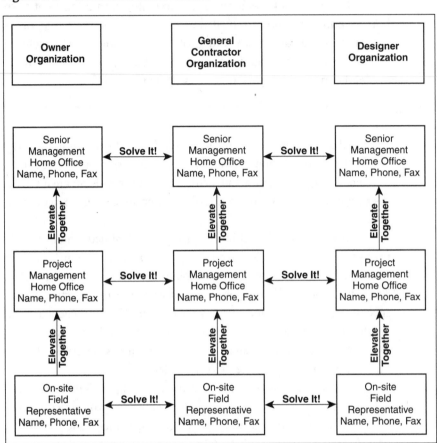

providing partnering workshops. Markert suggests the benefits and characteristics of partnering shown in Figure 2-6.

The commitment and teamwork developed in a partnering workshop can be reinforced by means of a quarterly one-day follow-up session.

Figure 2-4 Action Planning Worksheet

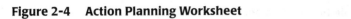

Problem Title

_____

Date/Time

Agreed-on Statement of the Problem

Possible Causes

Potential Solutions

The Proposed Solution with Justification

Responsible Team Member   Responsible Team Member   Responsible Team Member

Figure 2-5   Sample Project Charter

Partnering Agreement

Among EPA, USACE, Mass. DEP.

Baird & McGuire Task Force, OHM

We, the partners of the Baird & McGuire Superfund Site, agree to work together as a cohesive team to produce a quality project that protects and informs the surrounding community in accordance with the contract, on time, within budget, and safely, while enabling the contractor to earn a fair profit. Members of the partnering team will deal with each other in a fair, open, trusting, and professional manner. In that sprit, we are committed to the following concepts:

Communication

1. Communicate problems openly and as early as possible.
2. Establish and maintain community relations through open lines of communication by keeping the public informed and an integral part of the cleanup process.
3. Resolve problems and make decisions at the lowest possible level in a timely manner.
4. Maintain a professional atmosphere of mutual respect and resolve personal conflicts immediately.
5. Communicate problems openly before resorting to written correspondence.
6. Develop a periodic evaluation program on the partnership's effectiveness.

Performance

1. Produce a quality product the first time, through an effective and committed quality management program. (QA & QC)
2. Complete project ahead of, or on, schedule. (Avoid delays.)
3. Perform work in a safe manner, minimizing recordable lost-time injuries and maintaining the utmost concern for public safety in the surrounding community.
4. Promote pride in workmanship by all members of the partnering team.
5. Minimize formal disputes. (*No litigation.*)
6. Ensure successful project completion.

Figure 2-6   Benefits of Partnering

- Reduced litigation exposure
- Fewer cost overruns
- Better quality product
- Expedited decision making
- Expedited project
- Swifter problem resolution
- Lower administrative costs
- Increased innovation
- Fewer delays and disputes
- Increased financial success
- Reduced cycle time
- Issues are found early
- Escalation is an easy option

Recommendations to Assist in Evolving the Partnering Approach

The following four recommendations will assist in evolving the partnering approach and will help achieve and maintain commitment:

1. Involve the sponsor of the system effort and managers from several management levels of both the customer and the supplier in the partnering workshop. Provide mechanisms to maintain their sponsorship and support throughout the development effort.
2. Develop a requirements plan and gain agreement on the requirements process and approach to be used. Utilize the planning process to strengthen commitments.
3. Utilize a set of mechanisms, methods, techniques, and tools to gain an increasingly more robust understanding of the customers' real needs and expectations throughout the system development cycle. These need to be understood by the development team in order for them to be used effectively. Training most likely will be required.
4. Work toward a *quality culture*. Create a list of rules for interacting with one another and reach consensus to abide by them.

Each of these recommendations is described in the following paragraphs with suggestions on how to apply the recommendation.

Involve Managers with Authority in the Partnering Workshop

You may recall from your own experience such as conferences or sessions you've attended at which much was accomplished through discussion and dialog. Disagreements were overcome through improved understanding. Motivation to move forward with an effort or a project was achieved. Then, after the conference or session, the commitment faded and things seemed to fall apart. One mechanism to facilitate maintaining momentum and commitment is to involve key people in the partnering workshop. In particular, include managers with decision-making authority from several levels. Decision makers can learn about the project, participate in evolving the definition of success, make commitments to the project, and, most important, commit to mechanisms to resolve issues as the development effort proceeds.

Develop a Requirements Plan

A detailed requirements plan[4] should be written addressing the following areas (see Figure 2-7 for a sample table of contents):

- Roles and responsibilities
- Suggested strategy and recommended approach to elicit, identify, analyze, define, specify, prioritize, derive, partition, allocate, track, manage, verify, and validate the requirements for a proposed system
- Background concerning the project
- Use of the system engineering process
- Requirements process to be utilized
- Importance of the requirements process in leveraging project resources
- Mechanisms, methods, techniques, and tools to be used
- Integration of proven requirements best practices
- References for more information
- Appendixes (those listed here are samples; they depend on the situation)

---

[4]Practitioners are familiar with different types of plans, for example, a system engineering management plan, a project plan, a quality assurance plan, a configuration management plan, a risk management plan, a software development plan, contingency/mitigation plans, a software verification and validation plan, and so forth. However, the concept of a requirements plan is new. I wrote a requirements plan in support of a large system migration and integration effort in 1999. It provided the basis for important decisions. The topics noted here reflect its recommended organization and contents. Small projects will do well to address these topics, even if briefly. My thanks to my manager, Al Pflugrad, Executive Director, Systems & Process Engineering, Litton PRC, for suggesting this idea.

- Requirements process flowcharts
- Partnering process briefing
- Characteristics of good requirements
- Guidelines for system development based on requirements considerations
- Draft project requirements policy
- Time line
- Action plans

The Team should consider conducting a professionally facilitated two- to five-day session to help focus this plan. (Again, Charles Markert has facilitated such sessions.)

Figure 2-7   **Sample Table of Contents for a Requirements Plan**

Section
Summary of Updates to this Version of the Document
Purpose
Contract Summary
Use of the System Engineering Process
Suggested Strategy
Requirements Process
Importance of the Requirements Process
Mechanisms, Methods, and Tools
Suggested Approach
Industry Requirements Best Practices
References Consulted
Appendixes
A   Requirements Process (flowcharts and process descriptions)
B   Partnering Process Briefing
C   Characteristics of Good Requirements
Goals of Good Requirements Engineers
Before You Write Requirements
The Up-front Process
D   Guidelines for System Development Based on Requirements Considerations

Utilize a Set of Mechanisms, Methods, Techniques, and Tools

Proper use of mechanisms, methods, techniques, and tools is an important contributor to process maturity.[5] Experience has shown that developers cannot adopt or purchase methods and tools and just throw them at the development effort. Selection of methods, techniques, and tools requires study of their applicability and compatibility with the project's practices. The tools must also be compatible or interoperable with each other. A process that meets the organization's or project's needs, methods must be identified, techniques that effectively support that process must be selected, and then tools can be considered. Commitment, training, and time are required to make effective use of methods and tools. Methods, techniques, and tools are not a panacea. If selected and used properly, they can provide great benefits. If regarded as a magic solution or misused, they may prove to be an expensive failure. Figure 2-8 summarizes the advantages based on experience on a PRC project.

Work Toward a Quality Culture

Much has been written about total quality management and other expressions of and acronyms for quality programs.[6] I've had the opportunity to work for organizations that espoused no quality programs (or even a commitment to quality), for organizations that claimed emphasis on quality but lacked a real commitment to it, and for organizations that lived a real commitment to continuous improvement.

The bottom line is that an organization that is truly committed to quality has aspects of its culture that enable it to be more effective, efficient, and profitable:

- There is a willingness to invest to achieve quality, for example, in training and in process definition and improvement.
- There is an attitude toward others in the organization that reflects genuine **teamwork** and support of one another. "Your call is not an interruption to my work, but a reason I am here."

---

[5]Alan Davis's *Software Requirements: Objects, Functions, and States* focuses on the early phases of the software development life cycle and arms the reader with an understanding of many requirements techniques with emphasis that no particular technique will always be right. Ed Yourdon believes that methods lacking tool support are ineffective, and vice versa. Steve McConnell's *Rapid Development* provides a concise description of 27 best practices for software development. Gause and Weinberg, *Are Your Lights On? How to Know What the Problem REALLY Is,* address many of the difficulties encountered in the art of problem definition.

[6]See Chapter 12 by Carr et al., Partnering in Construction.

Figure 2-8   Advantages of Utilizing a Set of Mechanisms, Methods, Techniques, and Tools

Requirements are reviewed more often.

A cleaner design that implements the requirements more effectively is developed.

The documentation is more complete and accurate, and some is eliminated.

The code is tested more thoroughly.

The environment is more controlled, enabling smooth transitions from one activity to the next.

There is better insight into where the problems are occurring during development.

- There is an understanding that the term *customer* is not only those who pay for the work, but anyone who is involved in the entire work process. When we treat each other as customers and recognize that we have different needs, all of which are vital to the total effort, we honor and empower one another, and the result is improved productivity and work effectiveness.
- We agree on a methodology for process definition that becomes understood and used throughout the organization (institutionalized).
- We consider a set of rules for interacting with one another in our normal work activities. Litton PRC has adopted *rules of conduct* (Figure 2-9) that are widely deployed and enable good work practices and higher profitability.

Figure 2-9   PRC Rules of Conduct

- Respect each person.
- Share responsibility.
- Criticize ideas, not people.
- Keep an open mind.
- Question and participate.
- Arrive on time.
- Keep interruptions to a minimum.
- Manage by fact.

Summary

Commitment is critical to the success of any system or software development effort. Commitment involves the participants in the development effort obligating themselves to the success of the project. A typical project generates issues between the customer and the supplier because of their different perspectives. One technique that can be used to deal proactively with potential issues is partnering. A partnering workshop, held at the beginning of the contract performance, can be invaluable in overcoming parochial perspectives. It is a proven, effective method for developing a shared vision of project success, providing a set of guiding principles for use during contract performance, and creating an issue resolution ladder to overcome barriers and "rocks in the road." Recommendations including involving managers with authority in the partnering workshop; developing a requirements plan; utilizing a set of mechanisms, methods, techniques, and tools; and working toward a quality culture assist in evolving and implementing the partnering approach and help to achieve and maintain commitment.

Key References and Suggested Readings

Frank Carr, Kim Hurtado, Charles Lancaster, Charles Markert, and Paul Tucker. *Partnering in Construction: A Practical Guide to Project Success.* **Chicago, IL: American Bar Association Publishing, 1999.** This book is an excellent guide for implementing the partnering process. Carr and colleagues are professional facilitators with extensive experience in actual partnering efforts. They provide a practical approach that includes samples of the products of partnering workshops. Lessons learned and case studies from their experience are provided. A glossary of related terms is included.

Michael Cusumano and Richard Selby. *Microsoft Secrets: How the World's Most Powerful Software Company Creates Technology, Shapes Markets, and Manages People.* **New York: Free Press, 1995.** Cusumano and Selby performed almost two years of on-site research at Microsoft headquarters. The book is an objective, analytical, and thorough profile of an important company. It focuses on the relationship between business strategies and software development. It explains Microsoft's management model, organizational culture, technologies, and software development approach.

Richard Harwell. "System Engineering Is More Than Just a Process." In: **Martin, James N., ed.** *Systems Engineering Guidebook.* **Boca Raton, FL: CRC**

Press, 1996: 249–255. Harwell's work advocates several of the effective requirements practices recommended in this book, noting that many companies overlook them. As a result, those companies realize no apparent benefit from the system engineering process. Harwell emphasizes that today's customer and the development team must work together to achieve a successful development process.

Capers Jones. *Assessment and Control of Software Risks.* **Englewood Cliffs, NJ: Prentice Hall, 1994.** Jones cataloged 63 specific risks that affect software projects. He provides a description of each risk, severity, frequency, occurrence, root causes, cost impact, methods of prevention, methods of control, product support, and the effectiveness of known therapies. Jones discusses the risk of creeping requirements, inaccurate sizing of deliverables, and crowded office conditions, to name a few examples. His book is a valuable reference. As Jones maintains, problems don't go away by themselves, and his comprehensive treatment provides valuable insights. He provides a list of tools that he believes is an approximate 5% sample of thousands of commercially available tools.

Charles Markert. *Partnering: Unleashing the Power of Teamwork.* **1998.** Available at markert@erols.com. This marketing briefing describes partnering; its attributes, characteristics, and benefits; and why one would participate in partnering. It also provides a process for partnering: preparation, a partnering workshop, what it means to "walk the talk," getting feedback, and celebration. Keys to the partnering process are presented, and lessons learned from partnering experiences are presented.

Gerald M. Weinberg, James Bach, and Naomi Karten, eds. *Amplifying Your Effectiveness.* **New York: Dorset House, 2000.** The editors and a group of software consultants present ideas on how software engineers and managers can amplify their professional effectiveness—as individuals, as members of teams, and as members of organizations. The contributed essays are organized in the categories of empowering the individual, improving interpersonal interactions, mastering projects, and changing the organization. A theme is that we're more likely to enhance effectiveness if we start by looking within and asking ourselves what we might do better or differently. There are a lot of insights here, and they are presented in a fresh, unique way.

Karl E. Wiegers. *Software Requirements.* **Redmond, WA: Microsoft Press, 1999.** This is an excellent, easily readable book that offers practical advice on how to manage and participate in the requirements engineering process. Commitment is viewed in this book as "finding the voice of the customer." Engaging the participants in the project is considered critical to success. Wiegers's experience at Eastman Kodak and as an independent consultant indicates that customers don't know what they really need, and neither do the developers.[7]

---

[7]Karl Wiegers, *Software Requirements,* p. 110.

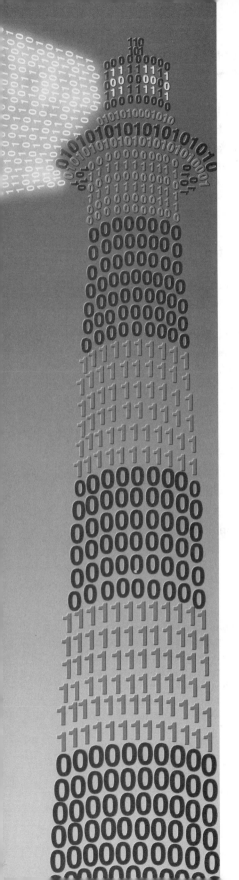

CHAPTER THREE

Establish and Utilize a Joint Team Responsible for the Requirements

Commit to the approach.
Establish and utilize a Joint Team responsible for the requirements.
Define the *real* customer needs.
Use and continually improve a requirements process.
Iterate the system requirements and architecture repeatedly.
Use a mechanism to maintain project communication.
Select familiar methods and maintain a set of work products.
Perform requirements verification and validation.
Provide an effective mechanism to accommodate requirements changes.
Perform the development effort using known, familiar proven industry, organizational, and project best practices.

This chapter recommends that a joint team that includes both customer and contractor representatives be established. The joint team is charged with the responsibility for achieving definition and agreement on all requirements throughout the entire development effort, including changes to requirements.

This chapter advises and recommends that a joint customer/supplier management and technical requirements team ("joint team") be established to be responsible for the requirements and their use for the life of the project.[1]

What Is a "Joint Team"?

The joint team is charged with the responsibility for achieving definition of and agreement on all requirements throughout the entire development effort, including changes to requirements. It is a small group of people who possess knowledge of the customer requirements or requirements engineering with the authority to make decisions concerning requirements on behalf of the project. The joint team serves as a mechanism to

- Enable and empower both the buyer and the supplier to take shared commitment (in the sense of the previous chapter) for the requirements
- Recognize that it's not possible to know all of the requirements at the beginning of an effort
- Provide the ability for an increasingly specific definition of the real requirements and the ability to control and adjust costs and schedule in a coordinated manner

---

[1]A likely scenario is that the buyer and supplier are two internal entities called *product management* and *development* (for example, in the case of shrink wrap product development). Several companies develop shrink-wrapped software with management structures inspired by the Microsoft Enterprise Application Model. A multidisciplinary team is set up to manage, as a team of peers, the product development effort through the product life cycle. These familiar roles are product management, program management, development, testing, logistics, and user education. The product manager manages customer requirements definition and acts as the customer advocate throughout development. The product manager synthesizes these requirements through product planning, market research, competitive analysis, business needs, major sales opportunities, and customer feedback. The prioritization and subsequent elaboration of requirements is done with input from all peers as partners and equal stakeholders in the products' success. The roles of product manager, as the customer advocate, and user education, as the user advocate, are distinct. The customer is the person who ultimately purchases the product; the user is the person who ultimately uses it. See http://www.microsoft.com.

- Recognize that some of the stated requirements are not "good" requirements or "real" requirements (see the next chapter for definitions of these terms)
- Recognize that requirements change during the development process
- Recognize that there are cost and schedule implications that need to be accommodated

The joint team is an **integrated product team** (IPT). An IPT is a group that includes customers and developers that blends perspectives into a functioning or united whole. In this case the focus is on requirements to achieve system objectives. You might choose to call the joint team the *requirements IPT*. A partnership relationship is established at the beginning of the project. The joint team addresses all requirements-related activities throughout the system life cycle. The joint team members commit to one another and to project success. The joint team is a vital mechanism to achieve project success. The members commit to translate customer needs and expectations into a verifiable set of requirements.

The composition of the joint team may change over the course of the system development effort as different levels of the system are defined and addressed. The joint team helps implement the commitment achieved during the partnership workshop (discussed in Chapter 2) to establish and maintain a partnership relationship throughout the system development process. Because there are schedule and cost implications of these decisions, members of the joint team must have decision authority regarding changes in cost and schedule. Impacts of the decisions are communicated to other members of both the customer and supplier organizations by one of their own employees who understands and supports the rationale for the decisions.

What Does the Joint Team Do?

The members of the joint team

- Reach consensus on a comprehensive statement of system objectives
- Review the customer's stated requirements to identify those that are
  - Not good requirements (utilizing the criteria provided in the next chapter)
  - Not real requirements (utilizing the definition provided in the next chapter)
- Revise or eliminate requirements that are not good or real
- Prioritize requirements
- Evaluate proposed requirements changes and determine whether to accept them, and decide on the version of the system in which to implement the accepted requirements changes

Thus, the joint team helps the project manager and the customer control the costs of the project. Industry experience is that actual project costs typically exceed budgeted costs by a factor of two. The *Gruehl chart* provided in Chapter 4 provides data from the National Aeronautics and Space Administration indicating the percentage of cost overrun, which ranged from 80% to 200% for programs that invested less than 5% in the requirements process. See Hooks and Farry, Customer-Centered Products, p. 10. The data from The Standish Group reports show that 53% of industry's investment on application development projects is a casualty of cost overruns and failed projects, and that the cost of rework is typically 45% of project costs. See *A Special COMPASS Report: Requirements Management Tools,* The Standish Group International, 1998. The joint team eliminates poor requirements and enforces a focus on the essential functionality. For example, it can

- Ensure that developers are trained not to add features or personal style to the code
- Enforce a discipline of control of changes to requirements
- Initiate a change to the project schedule and budget when changes are made to the requirements

How Is the Joint Team Created?

The joint team should be created as an action of the partnership workshop. The customer and supplier select their members from among participants present at the workshop so that they understand the rationale for the partnering approach and a commitment to the joint definition of "project success." An opportunity for the newly appointed joint team to caucus and provide an initial **work product**, perhaps a charter for the joint team, would be invaluable and would also serve to jump-start its efforts. This could be an evening session on day one of the partnering workshop, for example.

Who Should Be on the Joint Team?

The joint team should have the minimum number of members required to provide

- Knowledge of the requirements (technical aspects and understanding of need)
- Decision authority (management responsibility)

The joint team could consist of as few as two people (one each from the customer and supplier) for a small project, or several people for a large project. However, bear in mind that, the larger the team, the more group dynamics come into play.

Careful consideration should be given to those selected for this role. The joint team will make decisions that have major impacts on the project. Members of the joint team should

- Be knowledgeable (about the real customer and user needs, about requirements engineering, or about both)
- Be conscientious and persevering
- Have excellent interpersonal skills. It will serve neither the interests of the customers/users nor the interests of the supplier/systems developer to have members of the joint team who don't get along well with others or who are argumentative
- Respect other people and others' points of view
- Have a large measure of common sense; oftentimes, a practical, achievable approach is needed
- Be willing to achieve consensus and move on

How Often Should the Joint Team Meet?

This depends on the stage of the project and the level of the requirements volatility. Initially, the team will need to meet frequently (probably at least weekly) to develop its charter, operating procedures, and a comprehensive understanding of the system and/or software requirements. Requirements priorities and planned releases will need to be sorted out. The members of the joint team will be able to determine the needed frequency of meetings based on project considerations and activities.

What Metrics Need to Be Created and Tracked?

As in all aspects of project management, the things that are measured and tracked are the ones that improve. The time to start developing and tracking estimates of costs and benefits of various capabilities of the system is at the beginning of the project. Also, changes to requirements need to be tracked in an automated requirements tool. An important metric the joint team should track is *requirements volatility*, which should be maintained at less than 2% to stay within schedule and budget, with a target of 0.5%.[2] Requirements changes always result in concomitant changes in the project schedule and budget. However, often the schedule and budget are not adjusted accordingly. We pretend that we can provide added functionality with no cost and schedule impact! You may want to refer to How Much Can Requirements Change? in Chapter 10 for industry experience concerning requirements volatility and suggestions to control changes.

Calculating Return on Investment (ROI) from Using Effective Requirements Practices

Most of us (and our managers) accept that the requirements process has a critical effect on an organization's or project's development costs as well as product quality. We and our managers have experienced the pain resulting from poor requirements and ineffective requirements practices. How can we convince our managers to invest in effective requirements practices?

The joint team may find it useful to measure and track the ROI of various requirements-related activities. This mechanism facilitates evaluation of these activities to determine those that are most effective.

Dean Leffingwell[3] has provided a convincing estimate of rework costs and an effective approach to calculate the value of investment in improving requirements engineering practices. If, by applying more effective requirements practices, such as those recommended in this book, we can reduce rework, we can save our projects and organizations (including our customers) money. Figure 3-1 provides the assumptions, project costs, and a template for calculating rework costs for your project. It also provides a table to estimate the ROI over the life of the first project of selected requirements error reduction percentages.

Customer and Supplier Roles

Among available commercial courses concerning requirements is one provided by Telelogic titled, "Writing Better Requirements."[4] Figure 3-2 is derived from

---

[2]According to Capers Jones's data, the U.S. average is approximately 2% per month. See his book titled *Estimating Software Costs,* Chapter 17, and the extended discussion of creeping requirements in this book in Chapter 8. One way to deal with rapidly changing business requirements is to release a new version of the system every few months.

[3]Dean Leffingwell, *Calculating Your Return on Investment from More Effective Requirements Management.*

[4]For more information, visit the Telelogic Web site at http://www.telelogic.com/doors.

Figure 3-1   Calculating ROI from Effective Requirements Practices

Estimating Typical Project and Rework Costs

Consider an application that contains 50,000 lines of code and is produced by a staff of six developers supported by one program manager, two software testers, and one quality assurance person. To determine the product time line, let's assume coding is the critical path (probably a defensible assumption in most organizations!). Based on a productivity rate of 350 lines of debugged source code per month, then the project timeline is 24 months (i.e., 50,000 LOC ÷ 350 LOC/month ÷ 6 developers). If the loaded cost per developer/tester/QA personnel per month is $10,000, then that creates a total project budget of approximately $2.4 million. Of this cost, even if only 30% of the project is invested in rework (an optimistic assumption?), then the total rework budget is $720,000. If 70% of the rework is due to requirement errors, then the total rework costs related to requirement errors are over half a million dollars!

Project Cost Estimates for a Software Project

	Typical Project	Your Project
Number of lines of code	50,000	
Number of developers	6	
Person-months of coding	142.9	
Time to market	24 calendar months	
Loaded cost/team member/mo	$10,000	
Total project labor cost	$2,400,000	
Total rework costs (30%)	$720,000	
Total requirements errors rework cost (= 70%)	$504,000	

(continued)

**Figure 3-1   Calculating ROI from Effective Requirements
Practices** (*continued*)

Return on Investment of More Effective Requirements Management

	Case 1	Case 2	Case 3	Your Project
Requirements error reduction percentage	10%	20%	40%	
Cost savings on typical project	$50,400	$100,800	$201,600	
Months shaved off time to market	.5	1.0	2.0	
Payback time for investment in months	9.5	4.7	2.4	
% Return on investment over life of *first project*	153%	407%	913%	

this course, and it illustrates the roles of the customer (buyer) and the supplier (contractor) throughout the system life cycle.

It's vital to understand that both the customer and the supplier have important assignments and responsibilities concerning the requirements effort throughout the entire life cycle as shown in Figure 3-2. The joint team provides a way to manage the interface of these activities. Because it is small and empowered, the joint team can maintain good awareness of the activities. Because it's responsible and informed concerning the system objectives, it can keep the requirements (and thus the project) in control.

Figure 3-2   Customer (Buyer) and Supplier Roles Throughout the System Life Cycle

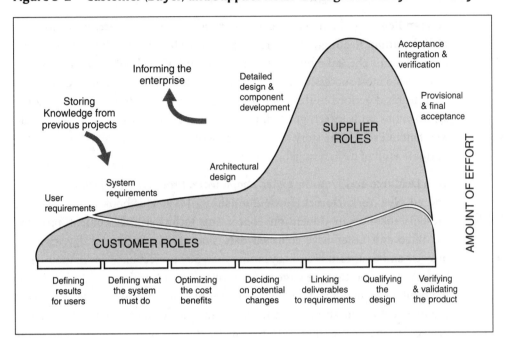

Summary

Experience has shown that a mechanism is required to be responsible for the requirements throughout the development effort. The joint team is a small group of people who are knowledgeable concerning the requirements, with the authority to make requirements decisions on behalf of the project. The customer and the contractor are represented. The members of the joint team are responsible for achieving definition of and agreement on all requirements, including changes to requirements. Because there are cost and schedule implications of these decisions, the joint team provides a mechanism to communicate the impacts of these decisions to both the customer and the contractor. The joint team can help prioritize requirements. The joint team can be created as an action of the partnering workshop discussed in Chapter 2. Requirements volatility should be tracked and managed by the joint team. A template was provided to facilitate calculating the ROI to help the joint team evaluate various requirements practices.

Key References and Suggested Readings

Warren Bennis and Patricia Ward Biederman. *Genius: The Secrets of Creative Collaboration.* **Reading, MA: Perseus Books, 1997.** This is a book about great teams. I found the "take-home lessons" at the end of the book to be apt descriptions of the most successful teams with which I have been associated. One of the great teams described in this book is The Skunk Works, a term that has become synonymous with secret, groundbreaking technological work. Another is The Manhattan Project, the story of the building of the atomic bomb. "None of us is as smart as all of us" is a valuable lesson.

Tom DeMarco and Timothy Lister. *Peopleware: Productive Projects and Teams.* **2nd ed. New York: Dorset House Publishing, 1999.** This book is a classic that presents the human dimension concerning technical development projects. DeMarco and Lister have collected data since 1977 concerning development projects and their results and have more than 500 project histories in their database. A premise is that the large number of failures of projects of all sizes is not the result of failure of technology, but rather human issues such as project management, communications, high turnover, and lack of motivation contribute to project failure. This second edition provides the text of the first and adds eight new chapters. Readers will discern a host of insights that will contribute to more effective teams and project management. Management's challenge is to create a culture that allows people to work effectively. This book is an important read for any project manager.

Roger Fisher and William Ury. *Getting to Yes.* **New York: Penguin Books, 1991.** Reaching agreement on a specification is a process of negotiating the interests of several parties. This book emphasizes that reaching agreement is more important than risking inflexibility. Negotiation skills to achieve win-win agreements speed up the process and benefit everyone. Fisher and Ury emphasize that it's more important to understand the other party's underlying interests than to focus on a specific position.

Luke Hohmann. *Journey of the Software Professional: A Sociology of Software Development.* **Upper Saddle River, NJ: Prentice Hall PTR, 1997.** This is a book of practical advice for developers and managers who are serious about enhancing their own effectiveness and the effectiveness of their teams. It addresses many of the human or "soft" issues that are so critical in building systems successfully. It provides suggestions for career development, training, development teams, interpersonal relations, communications, and organizational structures, among others.

Watts S. Humphrey. *Introduction to the Team Software Process.* **Reading, MA: Addison-Wesley, 2000.** Humphrey is a superb writer, and this book shares his tremendous insights into what makes software teams work effectively. Although it builds on the personal software process, it's a valuable resource for anyone seeking to improve team effectiveness. Humphrey provides some practical strategies for facilitating teamwork, such as

- Eliminating work that gets in the way of improving the product
- Effectively applying work habits and processes
- Systematically tracking project progress
- Creating an environment that fosters unbridled enthusiasm
- Using *milestone scheduling* to keep schedules aggressive but not unrealistic
- Aligning personal growth goals with the necessary work
- Promoting beneficial attitudes such as a continuous improvement ethic

Humphrey's final chapter, Teamwork, is insightful. This book is a valuable read for any project manager.

Dean Leffingwell. *Calculating Your Return on Investment from More Effective Requirements Management.* (Available at http://www.rational.com/products/ whitepapers/300.jsp.) This reference provides an easy-to-use way to calculate savings from requirements-related efforts. It may be helpful to you if your manager requests data concerning the value of efforts involving the requirements process.

Mark C. Paulk. The "Soft Side" of Software Process Improvement. Pittsburgh, PA: Software Engineering Institute, Carnegie Mellon University, 1999. Paulk is the leading author of the Capability Maturity Model for Software (SW-CMM) and has deep sensitivity to the people-related aspects of the industry. Among many valuable insights addressed in his briefing are (1) the best people outperform the worst by approximately 10:1; (2) the best performer is 2.5 times more productive than the median performer; (3) CMM levels 4 and 5 organizations tend to have required training in team building, negotiation skills, interpersonal skills, domain knowledge, management skills, and technical skills; (4) people tend to be overly optimistic about what they can do; and (5) managers tend to ignore possible events that are very unlikely or very remote, regardless of their consequences. Paulk provides several charts concerning the People CMM. Perhaps most germane to this chapter is that the range in the performance of teams can be 200:1 and that united teams are extraordinarily powerful.

Roger S. Pressman. *Software Engineering: A Practitioner's Approach.* **4th ed. New York: McGraw Hill, 1997.** Pressman is an extremely knowledgeable, internationally known consultant and author who has extensive practical experience as an industry practitioner and manager. He specializes in helping organizations establish effective practices, and he developed an assessment method that helps clients assess their current state of engineering practice. Pressman's Web site provides extensive resources, including 30 templates for engineering documents. See http://www.rspa.com.

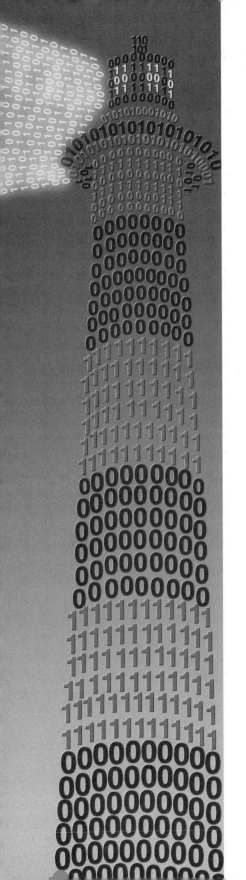

CHAPTER FOUR

Define the *Real* Customer Needs

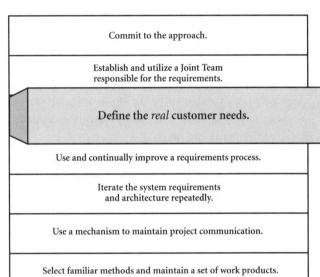

Commit to the approach.
Establish and utilize a Joint Team responsible for the requirements.
Define the *real* customer needs.
Use and continually improve a requirements process.
Iterate the system requirements and architecture repeatedly.
Use a mechanism to maintain project communication.
Select familiar methods and maintain a set of work products.
Perform requirements verification and validation.
Provide an effective mechanism to accommodate requirements changes.
Perform the development effort using known, familiar proven industry, organizational, and project best practices.

T his chapter provides specific recommendations to determine the real requirements for a planned system.

Most any supplier that has designed, developed, and implemented a system for a buyer would assert that it had "performed extensive effort to define the real customer needs." All suppliers go to extensive efforts to meet the needs of buyers of systems. Why, then, this chapter?

As discussed in Chapter 1, industry experience indicates that systems provided by suppliers often do not meet customer needs. In spite of extensive efforts, suppliers fail to measure up to expectations with the delivered systems.

I distinguish between *real* customer requirements and needs and *stated* requirements and needs. There is a huge difference between the two, and this difference accounts for many of our requirements-related problems. Historically, clients have not been able to articulate their real customer requirements and needs. Accordingly, an effective requirements process must provide for the time, resources, mechanisms, methods, techniques, tools, and trained requirements engineers familiar with the application domain to define the real customer requirements and needs.

This problem is not limited to large systems. Small projects[1] also experience the failure to identify the real requirements. My experience is that the practices presented in this book are applicable to projects of all sizes.[2] The differences are in the **tailoring** of the implementation approach. I provide some suggestions in the following chapters.

---

[1]There is no industry agreement on the definition of a "small project." One could consider it a "team." Often it is considered a project involving one to six professionals operating for as long as three to six months, but this definition is arbitrary. Consideration has been given in the industry literature to whether "small projects" are really all that different from "medium-size" or even "large" projects. See Mark Paulk, *Using the Software CMM with Judgment: Small Projects & Small Organizations;* Rita Hadden, *Now What Do We Do?;* and Louise Williams, *SPI Best Practices for Small Projects.* Members of small projects should be encouraged to take what they can from the experiences of larger projects by tailoring the approach, rather than using smallness as an excuse for not taking advantage of industry lessons. For a perspective giving careful attention and focus to "smallness," see Brodman and Johnson, *The LOGOS Tailored CMM for Small Businesses, Small Organizations, and Small Projects.* The changes tailor the Capability Maturity Model for Software (SW-CMM) for a small project environment. Participants in small projects or organizations may find this reference helpful.

[2]Rita Hadden's view based on observations and experience with more than 50 small projects is that professional judgment can be used to scale down and apply key practices appropriately to achieve positive outcomes for small projects. See "How Scalable Are CMM Key Practices?"

Industry consultant Karl Wiegers expresses the problem this way:

Requirements exist in the minds of users, visionaries, and developers, from which they must be gently extracted and massaged into a usable form. They need to be discovered with guidance from a talented requirements engineer who helps users understand what they really need to meet their business needs and helps developers satisfy those needs. Few project roles are more difficult than that of the requirements engineer. Few are more critical.[3]

This chapter provides several recommendations to facilitate getting to the real requirements. Obviously, if we're not using a base of the *real requirements* to perform our system development work, huge amounts of resources are being misspent. These recommendations will help you to redirect these resources in ways that will produce better results.

Recommendations to Facilitate Getting to the *Real* Requirements

The following recommendations help to explain and perform an improved approach and are discussed in turn in the following subsections:

1. Invest 8% to 14% of total program costs on the requirements process. Spend additional time and effort near the beginning of a project to work to identify the real requirements. Ensure joint user and supplier responsibility for requirements. Facilitate clarification of the real requirements. Control changes to requirements.
2. Train program and project managers (PMs) to pay more attention to the requirements process.
3. Identify a **project champion**. A project champion is an *advocate* for the effort, is very familiar with the set of real customer needs for a system, and provides an active role in the development activities, facilitating the tasks of the development team.
4. Develop a definition of the project vision and scope.
5. Identify a requirements engineer and utilize **domain expert**s to perform requirements engineering tasks.
6. Train developers not to make requirements decisions and not to **gold plate**.

---

[3]Karl Wiegers, "Habits of Effective Analysts," p. 65.

7. Utilize a variety of techniques to elicit user requirements and expectations. Use a common set of techniques and tools among all parties involved in a particular project.
8. Train requirements engineers to write good requirements.
9. Document the rationale for each requirement.
10. Utilize methods and automated tools to analyze, prioritize, and track requirements.
11. Utilize peer reviews and inspections.
12. Consider the use of formal methods when appropriate.

The quantity of high-level system requirements for a large system should be on the order of 50 to 200 requirements, not in the thousands (based on Ivy Hooks's experience in supporting requirements efforts at the National Aeronautics and Space Administration for several years). Requirements should be documented graphically and textually and should be made visible to all stakeholders. One way to accomplish this is to invite stakeholders to participate in requirements reviews. A requirements review is a workshop involving the key stakeholders of a project for a short, intensive session that focuses on the definition or review of requirements for the project. Ideally, it is facilitated by an experienced outside facilitator or by a team member who can objectively process inputs and feedback.

Let's review each of these recommendations in turn.

Invest More in the Requirements Process

Many people think of the requirements process as being primarily limited to requirements management, that is, tracking the status and change activity associated with requirements and tracing requirements to the various activities and products of the development effort. Projects expend an estimated 2% to 3% of total project costs on this activity.[4] It is advantageous to define the requirements process more broadly and to expend 8% to 14% of total program costs on it. Special emphasis should be placed on joint user and supplier responsibility for requirements, getting to the real requirements, and controlling changes to requirements.

We know from experience that buyers most often provide suppliers of systems a definition of their requirements ("stated requirements"). This definition

---

[4]Rob Sabourin notes from his extensive consulting work that it is amazing how many organizations and companies do not have *any* requirements process (comment included in Sabourin's review of this manuscript).

may be provided in the form of a statement of work, a Request for Proposal, a **requirements document**, a background description of a problem or need, and in other formats or combinations thereof. Buyers often have strong beliefs about their requirements documents and are strongly committed to their accuracy and validity. The reasons for this are easy to understand: Our customers have a lot of experience in their work and much expertise concerning it. They have spent a lot of time and money developing these **artifacts**. Often, the time spent in internal meetings discussing requirements and working out details about them clarifies, in the minds of the involved individuals, the specific details and characteristics. However, we note that almost always there are differences of opinion *within a customer organization* concerning important aspects of some of these details. It may be that the person writing the requirements in the customer's organization is not the person who is the intended user. Also, experience has shown that people with strong technical skills are not always effective communicators or writers.

Perhaps a valid criticism of work in our industry is that we often accept these artifacts as being complete and accurate and proceed with the task of responding to these requirements—that is, of designing and developing an approach to meet the *stated requirements*.

Experience suggests that we would be well advised to conduct partnering workshops and requirements reviews; to apply other mechanisms, methods, techniques, and tools; and to undertake a concerted effort in partnership with our customers to discover and evolve the *real requirements*.[5] A typical e-commerce application is required to be compatible with things that do not yet exist, implying that developers must be able to **hot swap** software.[6]

---

[5]Goguen regards requirements as "emergent, in the sense that they do not already exist, but rather *emerge* [emphasis added] from interactions between the analyst and the client organization." This is useful because conventional methods of requirements elicitation often assume that users know (1) exactly what they want from a future system and (2) how this system, once implemented, will affect the way they work. Common sense tells us these are not known in the early stages of any effort. See Jirotka and Goguen, *Requirements Engineering: Social and Technical Issues*, p. 194.

[6]*Hot swap* is a term taken from the **hardware** world. It means one can take out a board or component while the system is running and replace it with a new one without shutting down the system. For e-commerce systems we often use multiple servlets/server applications. To "hot swap" is to replace one of them without shutting down the e-commerce site and without losing a transaction. Some software engineering applications should ensure that components are designed to permit "hot swapping." This allows for reaction to new and evolving requirements without shutting down a system.

Some data from industry experience will clarify this point. It's preferable to utilize available data whenever possible to make decisions rather than to rely on intuition, experience, or the suggestions of others. We should "manage by fact." Figure 4-1 shows the effect of investment in a requirements process on total program costs. These data were provided by Werner M. Gruehl, Chief, Cost & Economic Analysis Branch, National Aeronautics and Space Administration headquarters, and were reported by Ivy Hooks.[7] Note that projects that spent less than 5% of total project or program costs on the requirements process experienced an 80% to 200% cost overrun, whereas those that invested 8% to 14% experienced less than a 60% overrun. *These data provide a powerful message to PMs and requirements practitioners: An expenditure of 8% to 14% of total program costs on the requirements process results in the best outcomes as measured by total program costs.*

Train PMs to Pay More Attention to the Requirements Process

Hooks addresses another key issue in her paper "Why Don't Program and Project Managers (PMs) Pay More Attention to the Requirements and the Requirements

Figure 4-1   Effect of Requirements Process Investment on Program Costs

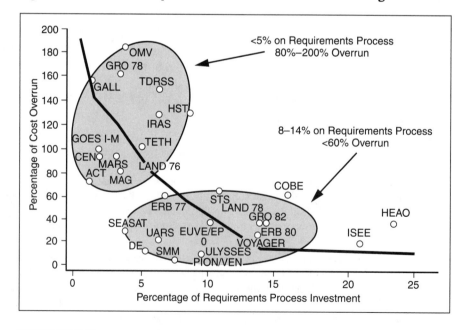

---

[7]Hooks, *Managing Requirements*, pp. 1–2.

Process?" From her 30 years of experience in consulting concerning requirements, she concludes the following:

- PMs assume that everyone knows how to write good requirements, thus the requirements process "will take care of itself."
- PMs tend to come from a technical background and tend to focus on the nontechnical aspects of the program because these are new and alien.
- PMs know they do not fully understand budgets, so more attention goes to budgets.
- The PM's boss is focused on the budget, so the PM places more attention on what interests the boss.

This analysis is consistent with my experience. It is my sincere hope that one use of this book will be to provide practitioners the experience and data to encourage PMs to provide adequate funding for requirements-related activities and to pay close attention to the requirements and the requirements process.[8] This is obviously an issue that needs to be addressed in corporate and organizational training programs for PMs.

Steve McConnell[9] advocates that technical managers should have tools for five kinds of work: estimating, planning, tracking, managing risk, and measuring. He also observes that management skills have at least as much influence on development success as technical skills.

Identify a Project Champion

Among the industry experts in requirements engineering are Dean Leffingwell and Don Widrig of Rational Corporation. Their recent book, *Managing Software Requirements,* is highly recommended. It presents a very useful approach that is focused on utilizing trained teams to perform systems development activities. Chapter 18 of *Managing Software Requirements,* The Champion, provides an excellent discussion of the need for and role of a champion. In their experience

---

[8]SECAT LLC publishes a set of four pocket guides, each designed for a person with specific job responsibilities: the PM, an organizational leader, a system engineer, and one who facilitates performing microassessments (measuring projects against a framework). Each pocket guide provides a series of questions designed to help keep the project on track. A scorecard is provided for each pocket guide to facilitate the tracking progress of improvement activities. The questions in the pocket guides are a distillation of the practices found in the **Systems Engineering** Capability Maturity Model (SE-CMM), an industry framework for systems engineering improvement and measurement. See http://www.secat.com; e-mail, secat@secat.com.

[9]"The Software Manager's Toolkit," *IEEE Software.*

during the past 20 years, a champion was identified in virtually every successful project in which they were involved.[10] Figure 4-2 summarizes this role.

Define the Project Vision and Scope

The project vision and scope document describes the background leading to the decision to develop a new or modified system and provides a description of the system that will be extended by the work of the project. (In Canada, the terms ***manifest*** and ***rules of engagement*** are used. *Manifest* is in used in place of the project charter or the project vision document. The *rules of engagement* are a description of the roles and responsibilities for project decision makers, including

Figure 4-2   The Role of the Champion

- Manage the elicitation process and become comfortable when enough requirements are discovered.
- Manage the conflicting inputs from all stakeholders.
- Make the trade-offs necessary to find the set of features that delivers the highest value to the greatest number of stakeholders.
- Own the product vision.
- Advocate for the product.
- Negotiate with management, users, and developers.
- Defend against feature creep.
- Maintain a "healthy tension" between what the customer desires and what the development team can deliver in the release time frame.
- Be the representative of the official channel between the customer and the development team.
- Manage the expectations of customers, executive management, and the internal marketing and engineering departments.
- Communicate the features of the release to all stakeholders.
- Review the software specifications to ensure that they conform to the true vision represented by the features.
- Manage the changing priorities and the addition and deletion of features.

---

[10]Leffingwell and Widrig, *Managing Software Requirements,* p. 179.

requirement prioritization and escalation procedures.) It is based on the business requirements, and it specifies objectives and priorities. This facilitates a common understanding and communication of the scope of the system that is critical for success. The executive sponsor of the project owns the document.

Figure 4-3 provides a suggested table of contents for an operational concept definition (OCD) document, taken from J-STD-016, the successor standard to DoD-STD-2167A (1988) and MIL-STD-498 (1994). The idea is to create documentation that follows a similar format to facilitate gathering information concerning a planned development effort. Don't feel that you must address every topic in this template. Rather, tailor it for your project environment and needs. Note that the OCD (or whatever you choose to call it) addresses

- The *scope* of the planned effort by providing a system overview
- Documents (references) that provide *background* and related information
- The *current system* or situation; in other words, how the planned need is being met (or not) currently
- The *justification* for the planned development effort. What is it that requires an investment in developing a new system?
- The concept or *vision* for a new or modified system
- *Anticipated impacts* of the new system. How will having a new system affect operations and the organization?
- *Advantages and limitations of the new system* and alternative approaches that were considered

Other excellent references that provide guidance for this work include books by Leffingwell and Widrig[11] and by Wiegers.[12] Figure 4-4 is a template for a vision and scope document provided by Wiegers. This template is simpler than the DoD standard and may be sufficient for your needs.

Identify a Requirements Engineer and Utilize Domain Experts to Perform Requirements Engineering Tasks

My experience is that a project of any size requires an individual assigned as the requirements engineer. Depending on the size of the project, this may be a part-time assignment or may require the full-time effort of several people. *It's valuable*

---

[11]Leffingwell and Widrig, *Managing Software Requirements,* pp. 187–222.

[12]Wiegers, *Software Requirements,* pp. 95–108.

Figure 4-3   Suggested Table of Contents for an OCD

Operational Concept Description (OCD)
Contents
1. Scope
    1.1   Identification
    1.2   System overview
    1.3   Document overview
2. Referenced documents
3. Current system or situation
    3.1   Background, objectives, and scope
    3.2   Operational policies and constraints
    3.3   Description of current system or situation
    3.4   Users or involved personnel
    3.5   Support strategy
4. Justification for and nature of changes
    4.1   Justification for change
    4.2   Description of needed changes
    4.3   Priorities among the changes
    4.4   Changes considered but not included
    4.5   Assumptions and constraints
5. Concept for a new or modified system
    5.1   Background, objectives, and scope
    5.2   Operational policies and constraints
    5.3   Description of the new or modified system
    5.4   Users/affected personnel
    5.5   Support strategy
6. Operational scenarios
7. Summary of impacts
    7.1   Operational impacts
    7.2   Organizational impacts
    7.3   Impacts during development
8. Analysis of the proposed system
    8.1   Summary of advantages
    8.2   Summary of disadvantages/limitations
    8.3   Alternatives and trade-offs considered
9. Notes
A. Annexes

1. **Scope.** This clause should be divided into the following subclauses:
    1.1 **Identification.** This subclause shall contain a full identification of the system to which this document applies, including, as applicable, identification number(s), title(s), abbreviations(s), version number(s), and release number(s).
    1.2 **System overview.** This subclause shall briefly state the purpose of the system to which this document applies. It shall describe the general nature of the system; summarize the history of system development, operation, and maintenance; identify the project sponsor, acquirer, user, developer, and maintenance organizations; identify current and planned operating sites; and list other relevant documents.
    1.3 **Document overview.** This subclause shall summarize the purpose and contents of this document and shall describe any security or privacy protection considerations associated with its use.
2. **Referenced documents.** This clause shall list the number, title, revision, date, and source of all documents referenced in this manual.
3. **Current system or situation.** This clause should be divided into the following subclauses to describe the system or situation as it currently exists.
    3.1 **Background, objectives, and scope.** This subclause shall describe the background, mission or objectives, and scope of the current system or situation.
    3.2 **Operational policies and constraints.** This subclause shall describe any operational policies and constraints that apply to the current system or situation.
    3.3 **Description of current system or situation.** This subclause shall provide a description of the current system or situation, identifying differences associated with different states or modes of operation (for example, regular, maintenance, training, degraded, emergency, alternative-site, wartime, peacetime). The distinction between states and modes is arbitrary. A system may be described in terms of states only, modes only, states within modes, modes within states, or any other scheme that is useful. If the system operates without states or modes, this subclause shall so state,

(continued)

Figure 4-3   Suggested Table of Contents for an OCD (*continued*)

without the need to create artificial distinctions. The description shall include, as applicable:

a. The operational environment and its characteristics

b. Major system components and the interconnections among these components

c. Interfaces to external systems or procedures

d. Capabilities/functions of the current system

e. Charts and accompanying descriptions depicting input, output, data flow, and manual and automated processes sufficient to understand the current system or situation from the user's point of view

f. Performance characteristics, such as speed, throughput, volume, frequency

g. Quality attributes, such as reliability, maintainability, availability, flexibility, portability, usability, efficiency

h. Provisions for safety, security, privacy protection, and continuity of operations in emergencies

3.4 **Users or involved personnel.** This subclause shall describe the types of users of the system, or personnel involved in the current situation, including, as applicable, organizational structures, training/skills, responsibilities, activities, and interactions with one another.

3.5 **Support strategy.** This subclause shall provide an overview of the support strategy for the current system, including, as applicable to this document, maintenance organization(s); facilities; equipment; maintenance software; repair/replacement criteria; maintenance levels and cycles; and storage, distribution, and supply methods.

4. **Justification for and nature of changes.** This clause should be divided into the following subclauses:

4.1 **Justification for change.** This subclause shall

a. Describe new or modified aspects of user needs, threats, missions, objectives, environment, interfaces, personnel, or other factors that require a new or modified system

    b. Summarize deficiencies or limitations in the current system or situation that make it unable to respond to these factors

4.2 **Description of needed changes.** This subclause shall summarize new or modified capabilities/functions, processes, interfaces, or other changes needed to respond to the factors identified in 4.1.

4.3 **Priorities among the changes.** This subclause shall identify priorities among the needed changes. It shall, for example, identify each change as essential, desirable, or optional, and prioritize the desirable and optional changes.

4.4 **Changes considered but not included.** This subclause shall identify changes considered but not included in 4.2, and rationale for not including them.

4.5 **Assumptions and constraints.** This subclause shall identify any assumptions and constraints applicable to the changes identified in this clause.

5. **Concept for a new or modified system.** This clause should be divided into the following subclauses to describe a new or modified system:

5.1 **Background, objectives, and scope.** This subclause shall describe the background, mission or objectives, and scope of the new or modified system.

5.2 **Operational policies and constraints.** This subclause shall describe any operational policies and constraints that apply to the new or modified system.

5.3 **Description of the new or modified system.** This subclause shall provide a description of the new or modified system, identifying differences associated with different states or modes of operation (for example, regular, maintenance, training, degraded, emergency, alternative-site, wartime, peacetime). The distinction between states and modes is arbitrary. A system may be described in terms of states only, modes only, states within modes, modes within states, or any other scheme that is useful. If the system operates without states or modes, this subclause shall so state, without the need to create artificial distinctions. The description shall include, as applicable:

(*continued*)

Figure 4-3   Suggested Table of Contents for an OCD (*continued*)

    a. The operational environment and its characteristics

    b. Major system components and the interconnections among these components

    c. Interfaces to external systems or procedures

    d. Capabilities/functions of the new or modified system

    e. Charts and accompanying descriptions depicting input, output, data flow, and manual and automated processes sufficient to understand the new or modified system or situation from the user's point of view

    f. Performance characteristics, such as speed, throughput, volume, frequency

    g. Quality attributes, such as reliability, maintainability, availability, flexibility, portability, usability, efficiency

    h. Provisions for safety, security, privacy protection, and continuity of operations in emergencies

5.4 **Users/affected personnel.** This subclause shall describe the types of users of the new or modified system, including, as applicable, organizational structures, training/skills, responsibilities, and interactions with one another.

5.5 **Support strategy.** This subclause shall provide an overview of the support strategy for the new or modified system, including, as applicable, maintenance organization(s); facilities; equipment; maintenance software; repair/replacement criteria; maintenance levels and cycles; and storage, distribution, and supply methods.

6. **Operational scenarios.** This clause shall describe one or more operational scenarios that illustrate the role of the new or modified system, its interaction with users, its interface to other systems, and all states or modes identified for the system. The scenarios shall include events, actions, stimuli, information, interactions, etc., as applicable. References may be made to other media, such as videos, to provide part or all of this information.

7. **Summary of impacts.** This clause should be divided into the following subclauses:

7.1 **Operational impacts.** This subclause shall describe anticipated operational impacts on the user, acquirer, developer, and maintenance organizations. These impacts may include changes in interfaces with computer operating centers; change in procedures; use of new data sources; changes in quantity, type, and timing of data to be input to the system; changes in data retention requirements; and new modes of operation based on peacetime, alert, wartime, or emergency conditions.

7.2 **Organizational impacts.** This subclause shall describe anticipated organizational impacts on the user, acquirer, developer, and maintenance organizations. These impacts may include modification of responsibilities; addition or elimination of responsibilities or positions; need for training or retraining; and changes in number, skill levels, position identifiers, or location of personnel in various modes of operation.

7.3 **Impacts during development.** This subclause shall describe anticipated impacts on the user, acquirer, developer, and maintenance organizations during the development effort. These impacts may include meetings/discussions regarding the new system; development or modification of databases; training; parallel operation of the new and existing systems; impacts during testing of the new system; and other activities needed to aid or monitor development.

8. **Analysis of the proposed system.** This clause should be divided into the following subclauses:

8.1 **Summary of advantages.** This subclause shall provide a qualitative and quantitative summary of the advantages to be obtained from the new or modified system. This summary shall include new capabilities, enhanced capabilities, and improved performance, as applicable, and their relationship to deficiencies identified in 4.1.

8.2 **Summary of disadvantages/limitations.** This subclause shall provide a qualitative and quantitative summary of disadvantages or limitations of the new or modified system. These disadvantages and limitations shall include, as applicable, degraded or missing

(continued)

Figure 4-3   Suggested Table of Contents for an OCD (*continued*)

capabilities, degraded or less-than-desired performance, greater-than-desired use of computer hardware resources, undesirable operational impacts, conflicts with user assumptions, and other constraints.

8.3 **Alternatives and trade-offs considered.** This subclause shall identify and describe major alternatives considered to the system or its characteristics, the trade-offs among them, and rationale for the decisions reached.

9. **Notes.** This clause shall contain any general information that aids in understanding this document (e.g., background information, glossary, rationale). This clause shall include an alpabetical listing of all acronyms, abbreviations, and their meanings as used in this document and a list of any terms and definitions needed to understand this document.

A. **Annexes.** Annexes may be used to provide information published separately for convenience in document maintenance (e.g., charts, classified data). As applicable, each annex shall be referenced in the main body of the document where the data would normally have been provided. Annexes may be bound as separate documents for ease in handling. Annexes shall be lettered alphabetically (A, B, etc.).

*for those assigned in this role to have had extensive experience and expertise in the functional area being addressed by the planned system (domain experts or **subject matter experts** [SMEs]).* The reason for utilizing domain experts as requirements engineers is that the requirements need to be understood in the customer's context. This is an extremely important issue. Unfortunately, many projects cripple their requirements efforts by not providing domain experts. This is a false economy. It may be that a project can have the domain expert assume the role of the project champion.

SMEs can be found by recruiting experienced developers from other projects within your organization. Another source is professional staff departing customer organizations for reasons of retirement or a desire for a new opportunity. SMEs function as a critical part of the team by understanding and explaining the

Figure 4-4   Template for a Vision and Scope Document

1. Business Requirements
    1.1   Background
    1.2   Business Opportunity
    1.3   Business Objectives
    1.4   Customer or Market Requirements
    1.5   Value Provided to Customers
    1.6   Business Risks

2. Vision of the Solution
    2.1   Vision Statement
    2.2   Major Features
    2.3   Assumptions and Dependencies

3. Scope and Limitations
    3.1   Scope of Initial Release
    3.2   Scope of Subsequent Releases
    3.3   Limitations and Exclusions

4. Business Context
    4.1   Customer Profiles
    4.2   Project Priorities

5. Product Success Factors

context of the requirements for the planned system.[13] SMEs can determine, based on their experience, whether the requirements are reasonable, how they extend the existing system, how the proposed architecture should be designed, and the impacts on users, among other areas. This approach enables the requirements engineering tasks to be performed more effectively.

A pitfall for which to watch is an SME whose approach is inflexible. An SME who can assist most effectively is one who is open to new ideas, approaches, and technologies.

---

[13]Sabourin notes that it is very difficult in some domains to locate knowledge experts who are able to express requirements clearly. In these situations, a role of the requirements engineer is to map domain expert input to clear requirements. (Comment included in Sabourin's review of this manuscript.)

Train Developers Not to Make Requirements Decisions and Not to Gold Plate

On a small project, the requirements engineer may also be a programmer (developer). On larger projects, we typically have individuals assigned in the developer role. Developers often find themselves in the situation of being required to design and code capabilities for systems when the requirements are not well defined (look ahead to Figure 4-9 for the criteria for a good requirement). Faced with this decision, the easier action is to make some assumptions and keep working, particularly in the face of tight deadlines and unpaid overtime. A better choice would be to interrupt work and get the requirement clarified. Developers need to be trained that this choice is best (and expected). Such "training" needs to be conveyed with good judgment so that technical performers do not feel that they are being overly constrained. Developers who are accustomed to an undisciplined environment may take exception to having to conform to rules. A related problem is a developer who adds features and capabilities that are not required by the specification (gold plating). This may be done because the developer sincerely believes it is appropriate and "best" for all concerned. However, gold plating adds to costs and extends the schedule and may complicate other areas of the system. If a user noticed this feature or capability in one area of the system, he might decide that it should be provided throughout the system! This contributes to requirements creep and results in added costs.

**Utilize a Variety of Techniques to Elicit Customer and
User Requirements and Expectations**

There is extensive information available in the system and software engineering literature concerning requirements elicitation—that is, the effort undertaken by systems and software requirements engineers to understand customer needs and expectations.[14]

Leffingwell and Widrig[15] provide an insightful discussion of useful techniques and tools to elicit user requirements and expectations in their book. These techniques and tools include interviewing, questionnaires, requirements

---

[14]See Sommerville and Sawyer, *Requirements Engineering: A Good Practice Guide.* Another source is Gause and Weinberg's *Exploring Requirements: Quality Before Design,* which provides a thorough discussion of the issues related to elicitation of user needs from customers and users.

[15]See Leffingwell and Widrig, *Managing Software Requirements,* Chapters 7 through 15, which provide guidelines for understanding user needs.

workshops, brainstorming and idea reduction, storyboards, **use cases**, role play-ing, and **prototyping**.[16]

Requirements checklists provide a way to evaluate the content, completeness, and quality of the requirements prior to development. McConnell[17] provides a good checklist in *Code Complete,* and Wiegers[18] provides another for inspection of software requirements specifications at his Web site. If the requirements are explicit, the users can review them and agree to them. If they're not, the develop-ers will end up making requirements decisions during coding, a sure-fire recipe for problems, as discussed earlier. Weinberg, in *The Secrets of Consulting,* provides helpful advice concerning giving and getting advice successfully.

Use Cases

One requirements technique is the use case. Schneider and Winters[19] provide a practical approach. See Figure 4-5 for an example of a use case diagram utilizing the **Unified Modeling Language** (UML) notation. UML is a graphical language for visualizing, specifying, constructing, and documenting the artifacts of a software-intensive system that was adopted by the Object Management Group in late 1997. UML has become a vendor-independent standard for expressing the design of soft-ware systems and is being rapidly adopted throughout industry. UML incorporates use cases as the standard means of capturing and representing requirements.

Many developers believe that use cases and scenarios facilitate team commu-nication. They provide a context for the requirements by expressing sequences of events and a common language for end users and the technical team. They iden-tify system interfaces, enable modeling the system graphically and textually, and are reusable in test and user documentation. Rumbaugh[20] also provides a helpful approach in "Getting Started: Using Use Cases to Capture Requirements."

---

[16]See Connell and Shafer, *Structured Rapid Prototyping,* for a discussion of the benefits of rapid prototyping, tools, and techniques that can be used, and other practical aspects of building prototypes and evolving them into production systems. See also Kaplan et al., *Secrets of Software Quality,* pp. 265–269.

[17]McConnell, *Code Complete,* pp. 32–34.

[18]Available at http://www.processimpact.com/goodies.shtml.

[19]Geri Schneider and Jason P. Winters, *Applying Use Cases: A Practical Guide.*

[20]James Rumbaugh, "Getting Started: Using Use Cases to Capture Requirements." *Journal of Object-Oriented Programming.*

Figure 4-5   Example of a Use Case Diagram

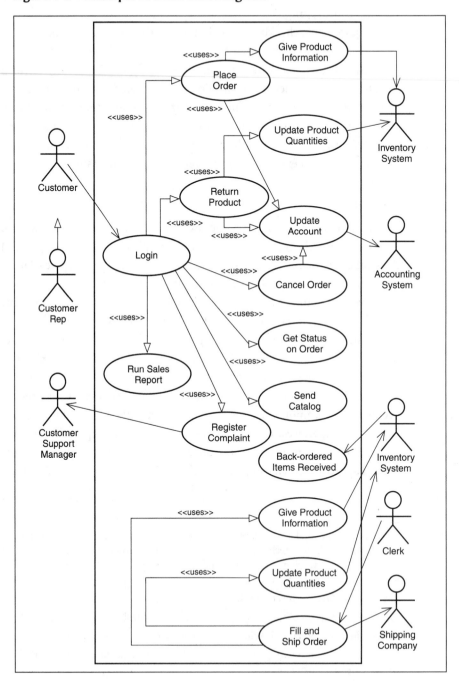

Leffingwell and Widrig[21] provide checklists concerning use cases. Eman Nasr[22] has provided an easy-to-understand basic introduction in his *Use Case Technique for Requirements Engineering*. Wiegers's[23] view is that use cases alone often don't provide enough detail for developers to know just what to build.

Consideration should be given to using use cases to describe the outwardly visible requirements of a system.[24] Use cases allow analysts to identify the required features of a system. They describe the things users of a system want the system to do (sometimes referred to as *scenarios*). Use cases are especially helpful for processes that are iterative and risk driven (which helps identify and address risks early in the program). The high-level use cases should be developed to help determine the scope of the project. What should be included? What can we realistically accomplish given our schedule and budget?[25] The developed use cases can also be utilized as test cases.

As with any method, there are both advantages and disadvantages of using use cases as a method. Among the advantages is that because of the thread of behavior characteristics and the fact that UML includes certain specialized modeling elements and notations (for example, "use case realization"), use cases provide additional value to their role of linking the requirements activities to design and implementation. Among the disadvantages is that use cases are not good

---

[21]*Managing Software Requirements,* pp. 289–292.

[22]Nasr is associated with the Computer Science Department, University of York, in the United Kingdom. E-mail: Eman.Nasr@cs.york.ac.uk.

[23]Karl Wiegers, "10 Requirements Traps to Avoid." *Software Testing and Quality Engineering Magazine.* In addition to describing ten important requirements traps, Wiegers provides keys to excellent requirements, including a collaborative customer-developer partnership for requirements development and management, and prioritizing requirements.

[24]Another good reference is by Daryl Kulak and Eamonn Guiney, *Use Cases: Requirements in Context,* which explains and provides examples of the nine diagrams of the UML (use case diagram, sequence diagram, collaboration diagram, statechart diagram, activity diagram, class diagram, object diagram, component diagram, and deployment diagram). They also provide a comprehensive and thoughtful list of problems related to using use cases (pp. 154–165). See also Korson, *The Misuse of Use Cases.* Korson notes that projects can expend a lot of time and effort on use cases without much benefit when they are not used correctly. Root causes of the misuse of use cases are (1) a requirements process that is neither understood nor properly managed, (2) poor-quality requirements, and (3) poor-quality designs. Analysts sometimes neglect fundamental principles of requirements gathering in the name of use cases.

[25]A reference point based on industry data is that systems and software projects are over-promised by an average of 100% to 200% (The Standish Group, 8,000 projects, 1996).

containers for nonfunctional requirements (such as the-ilities and attributes of the system environment) and design constraints. Dean Leffingwell's book, *Managing Software Requirements,* recommends alternative approaches based on the experience of the project team. In the situation in which the team's experience with the requirements process is limited and the object-oriented (OO) paradigm has not been adopted and used, a conventional software requirements specification approach is recommended.[26] If the team's experience with the requirements process is limited but the team is in the process of adopting the OO paradigm, the recommendation is to work with the use case method but to master it fully before depending on it to represent the requirements.

As noted earlier, the developed use cases can also be utilized as test cases. Bob Poston, Director of Quality Assurance Technology at Aonix, Inc., advocates front-end testing or specification testing to achieve **defect prevention** in a requirements process.[27] Poston asserts that project time and resources allocated to testing (typically 30% or more[28]) can be dramatically reduced, and he recommends adding formality to the requirements phase using a requirements modeling tool and use case notation and scenarios. Provide system-level use cases and then object-level use cases for the design. Add sufficient information to the use case to make it test ready. Poston notes (based on data from Capers Jones) that typically 16% of the test cases are redundant and 10% are irrelevant; therefore, in a typical project, 26% of the test effort is wasted. We need to develop requirements specifications that have in them the data that allow primary specification based test design. Poston cited two examples in his presentation, one in which the defect count dropped 94%[29] and another in which productivity increased 100 fold from 100 test cases in 20 days to 1,000 test cases in 2 days.[30]

---

[26]See the Institute of Electrical and Electronics Engineers' (IEEE) Standard 830, *IEEE Recommended Practice for Requirements Specifications.*

[27]See his presentation from the National SEPG99 Conference, *Generating Test Cases from Use Cases Automatically,* March 1999.

[28]Capers Jones, *Software Quality: Analysis and Guidelines for Success,* p. xxiv. Watts Humphrey's experience is that testing typically removes only 50% of the errors present. You must have quality code going into testing to have quality code coming out (personal e-mail communication with Humphrey, April 17, 2000).

[29]Robert M. Poston. "Counting Down to Zero Software Failures," p. 230.

[30]Richard Adhikari, "Development Process Is a Mixed-Bag Effort."

In summary, my experience is that use of a common set of techniques and tools among all parties involved in a particular project is a much bigger help than one would imagine, because this enables the entire development team to share the same concepts and language. This is more easily recommended than accomplished, however. Each system and software engineer has her/his own experience and familiarity with a set of tools. It's human nature to like to use that with which each of us is most familiar. Getting consensus on the use of a specific set of methods and tools is difficult, and providing the training and the opportunity to use them and become very familiar with their capabilities is expensive and time-consuming. (Also, recall the comments I provided at the end of Chapter 1 concerning systems and software engineers and the recommended context for readers of this book.)

Train Requirements Engineers to Write Good Requirements

There is strong evidence of the value of utilizing trained requirements engineers. Trained requirements engineers correlate with

- Well-written, unambiguous requirements statements
- The ability to utilize an effective automated requirements tool
- More effective use of project resources because of reduced rework

The Impact of Requirements Errors

Industry research shows that requirements errors are both the most common and also the most expensive defects in the technical work. Figure 4-6 quantifies the typical types of requirements errors.

Hooks and Farry[31] report that more than 80% of all product defects are inserted in the requirements definition stage of product development. This means that we can save money! If we provide good requirements, we can eliminate 80% of the rework problems. Rework costs are estimated at 45% of total project costs.[32] *Thus, by taking 80% of 45%, we learn that 36% (more than one third) of total project costs (based on industry data) potentially can be avoided by driving requirements errors out of the work products.* I'll acknowledge that it would

---

[31]*Customer-Centered Products,* p. 3.

[32]Leffingwell, "Calculating Your Return Investment from More Effective Requirements Management," p. 3. Available at http://www.rational.com/products/whitepapers/300.jsp. Rational Corporation. Available at http://www.rational.com/index.jtmpl.

Figure 4-6   Types of Nonclerical Requirements Errors

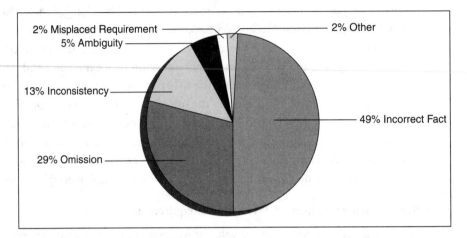

be difficult to achieve this amount of savings. However, *clearly a significant portion of this waste should be redirected by any and every development effort* through use of the practices recommended in this book and other process improvements. *From the perspective of the PM, the savings achieved by employing effective requirements practices should be redirected to pay for the needed effort and any associated training, methods, techniques, and tools required.*

The Importance of Requirements to Program Costs

Managers would be well advised to take careful note of the relative cost to fix an error. Barry Boehm[33] analyzed 63 software development projects in corporations such as IBM, GTE, and TRW and determined the ranges in cost for the error types described earlier that were created by false assumptions in the requirements phase but not detected until later phases (Figure 4-7).

Figure 4-8 shows the value of investing in an effective requirements process in which the real requirements are identified and in which requirements errors are driven out of the requirements work products during the earliest possible phase of system development. The cost to repair a requirements defect costs

---

[33]See Barry W. Boehm, *Software Engineering Economics.* These figures actually may be conservative because Boehm studied only those projects that were completed. See Gause and Weinberg, *Exploring Requirements: Quality Before Design,* for a discussion of the cost of ambiguity and how to remove it (pp. 17–21).

Figure 4-7   Relative Cost to Fix an Error

Phase in Which the Error Is Found	Cost Ratio
Requirements	1
Design	3–6
Coding	10
Development Testing	15–40
Acceptance Testing	30–70
Operation	40–1,000

Figure 4-8   Relative Cost to Fix Requirements Defects When Discovered in Later Stages

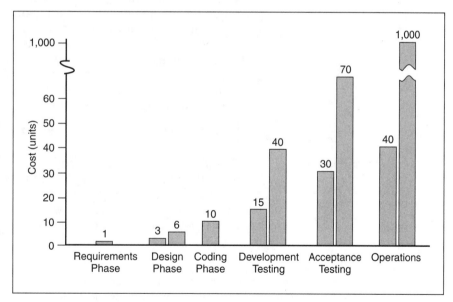

more the later in the project life cycle the error is discovered. For example, it costs 15 to 40 times as much to correct a requirements error during development testing than if we resolve the error earlier. This is a very strong argument for investing more in the requirements process.

What Is a Good Requirement?

There are several good articles and white papers on what is considered a good requirement.[34] Figure 4-9 presents a summary checklist of the criteria for a good requirement, providing criteria and a description of each.

Figure 4-9   Criteria of a Good Requirement

Criterion	Description
Necessary	Can the system meet prioritized, real needs without it? If yes, the requirement isn't necessary.
Verifiable	Can one ensure that the requirement is met in the system? If not, the requirement should be removed or revised. Note: The verification method and level at which the requirement can be verified should be determined explicitly as part of the development for each of the requirements. (The verification level is the location in the system where the requirement is met (for example, the "system level," the "segment level," and the "subsystem level).[35]
Attainable	Can the requirement be met in the system under development?
Unambiguous	Can the requirement be interpreted in more than one way? If yes, the requirement should be clarified or removed. Ambiguous or poorly worded writing can lead to serious misunderstandings and

---

[34]See the Compliance Automation Web site at http://www.complianceautomation.com/ to access excellent papers concerning requirements. Several are required reading for anyone seriously involved with requirements: *Guide for Managing and Writing Requirements,* which is a thorough treatment; *Writing Good Requirements,* which provides helpful hints to avoid many of the most common requirements writing problems; *Characteristics of Good Requirements,* which describes major characteristics of well-defined requirements, and *Managing Requirements,* which provides important insights into the requirements process. The greeting at this Web site reflects the wisdom of extensive experience: "People who write bad requirements should not be surprised when they get bad products, but they always are!"

[35]See Grady, *System Validation and Verification,* pp. 101–102, for a discussion of verification levels.

Criterion	Description
	needless rework. Note: Specifications should include a list of acronyms and a glossary of terms to improve clarity.
Complete	Are all conditions under which the requirement applies stated? Also, does the specification document all known requirements? (Requirements are typically classified as functional, performance, interface, constraints, and environment.)
Consistent	Can the requirement be met without conflicting with all other requirements? If not, the requirement should be revised or removed.
Traceable	Is the origin (source) of the requirement known, and can the requirement be referenced (located) throughout the system? The automated requirements tool should enable finding the location in the system where each requirement is met.
Allocated	Can the requirement be allocated to an element of the system design where it can be implemented? If not, the requirement needs to be revised or eliminated.[36]
Concise	Is the requirement stated simply and clearly?
Implementation free	The requirement should state what must be done without indicating how. The treatment of interface requirements is generally an exception.
Standard constructs	Requirements are stated as imperative needs using "shall." Statements indicating "goals" or using the word "will" are not imperatives.
Unique identifier	Each requirement should have a unique identifying number that assists in identification, maintaining change history, and providing traceability.

---

[36]The alternative is to risk a major costly change in the system or software architecture.

A "good" requirement is not necessarily a "real" requirement. The requirement may meet our criteria for a good requirement, but the requirement may not meet a real need of the users of the planned system. We discover the real requirements by following the recommendations provided in this chapter.

Oliver and colleagues[37] provide a good requirements taxonomy and believe that the engineering effort and costs associated with assessing requirements can be reduced substantially with modeling.

Document the Rationale for Each Requirement

Industry sources indicate that by taking the effort to document why each requirement is needed, as many as half of the "requirements" can be eliminated. The documentation step reduces the life cycle cost of system development significantly by obviating the need for follow-on work for unnecessary requirements. The rationale describes some or all of the following related information:[38]

- Assumptions
- Why it is needed
- How it is related to expected operations
- Design decisions

An example of documenting the rationale for a requirement is the following: Requirement 101 is needed in the system to enable the users of the system to receive feedback that their request was transmitted. In documenting the rationale for requirements, the requirements engineer may

- Gather data to enable a projection of how the activity involved may vary depending on different circumstances and uses of the system
- Perform a **trade study** to determine alternative ways to address the requirement
- Consider alternatives and provide the basis for the selected alternative

The easiest way to capture rationale is as each requirement is written. No requirement should be put into the specification until its rationale is well understood.

---

[37]Oliver et al., *Engineering Complex Systems with Models and Objects,* pp. 104–115. VITECH's automated tool, CORE, has behavioral modeling capabilities. See http://www.vtcorp.com.

[38]Ivy Hooks, *Guide for Managing and Writing Requirements,* p. 5–4. See pp. 5–4 through 5–6 for a more extensive discussion of why the documentation step is critical and how to do it.

Utilize Methods and Automated Tools to Analyze, Prioritize, and Track Requirements

As suggested previously, the broader term *requirements process* involves many aspects of the project throughout its entire life cycle, not just "requirements management." However, the automated tools available today are often described as requirements management tools. See Figure 4-10 for a list of several of the available tools and their related Web sites. Note that the International Council on Systems Engineering's Tools Working Group provides information concerning a large set of tools at its Web site, http://www.incose.org/tools/tooltax.html. Many projects have been supported by office automation tools such as Microsoft Word or Microsoft Excel and database applications such as Informix to manage requirements, but these tools are relatively limited in their capabilities (although they can provide some of the capabilities needed for a particular project). Many organizations have developed their own requirements tools (some have developed several), but this approach is not cost-effective, given the tools available on the market today.

A sophisticated requirements tool is able to do much more than requirements management. It should be able to facilitate requirements elicitation, help with prioritization of requirements, provide traceability[39] of requirements throughout the development effort (to design, implementation, and test verification, for example) and allow for assignment of requirements to subsequent releases of system products. It should allow assignment of an unlimited number of attributes (characteristics of requirements) to any and all requirements. See Figure 4-11 for a sample requirements matrix that shows attributes. Attributes allow users to associate data with objects, table markers, table cells, modules, and projects. For example, there are two kinds of attributes in DOORS, user-defined attributes and system-defined attributes. User-defined attributes may be built from specific attribute types such as text, integer, date, and so forth and are instantiated by users for their own needs. System-defined attributes, however, are predefined by DOORS and automatically record essential and highly useful information in the background. Attributes allow you to associate information with individual or related groups of requirements and often facilitate analysis of requirements data

---

[39]Traceability gives essential assistance in understanding the relationships that exist within and across software requirements, design, and implementation, and it is critical to the development process. See James D. Palmer, "Traceability." See also the definition and guidelines for requirements traceability in Figure 9-5.

Figure 4-10   Commercial Requirements Tools, Vendors, and Web Sites

Tool	Vendor	Web Site
Caliber RM	Technology Builders, Inc., Atlanta, Georgia	http://www.tbi.com
C.A.R.E. 2.0	SOPHIST Group, Nuremberg, Germany	http://www.sophist.de
CORE	VITECH Corporation, Vienna, Virginia	http://www.vtcorp.com
DOORS	Telelogic, Malmo, Sweden	http://www.telelogic.com/doors
RDD ISEE	Holagent Corporation, Gilroy, California	http://www.holagent.com
Requisite Pro (ReqPro)	Rational Software Corporation, Lexington, Massachusetts	http://www.rational.com
RTM Workshop	Integrated Chipware, Inc., Reston, Virginia	http://www.chipware.com
SLATE	TD Technologies, Richardson, Texas	http://www.tdtech.com
SynergyRM	CMD Corporation, Dallas, Texas	http://www.cmdcorp.com
Vital Link	Compliance Automation, Inc., Boerne, Texas	http://www.complianceautomation.com
Xtie-RT Requirements Tracer	Teledyne Brown Engineering, Los Angeles, California	http://www.tbe.com

via filtering and sorting based on attribute values. System-defined attributes may also be used for filtering and sorting. Although they are, for the most part, read-only and are not user modifiable, they perform essential and automatic information gathering.

Figure 4-11   Sample Requirements Attribute Matrix

NFAK0 Tag	Requirement text	Priority	Status	Cost	Difficulty	Stability	Assigned to	Unique ID	Location	Author	Revision	Date	Reason	Traced-from	Traced-to	RootTag#
NFAK0208	The time required for the equipment to warm up prior to operation shall not exceed one (1) minute from a cold start at −20 degrees C.	Medium	Approved		Medium	Medium		510	NFA Annex K section C	Chardon	1.0001	9/16/99 18:25	Marked trace to NFASSS289.	NFASSS289		208

Approaches, Tools, and Methods for Prioritizing Requirements

It's important to be able to prioritize the system and software requirements. An excellent discussion of this topic is provided by Karl Wiegers.[40] He suggests two scales, each with three-levels: (1) high/medium/low and (2) essential/conditional/ optional. One can visualize how utilizing these scales at an appropriate level of abstraction (for example, the use case level, the feature level, or the functional requirement level) will facilitate dealing with the common problem of having a limited development budget for release 1.0! Wiegers discusses his semiquantitative analytical approach and provides an example for a sample project: "Any actions we take to move requirements prioritization from the political arena into an objective and analytical one will improve the project's ability to deliver the most important functionality in the most appropriate order" (p. 30). This is recommended reading for managers and requirements practitioners. Wiegers provides a set of useful tools at his Web site, including a Microsoft Excel requirements prioritization spreadsheet.[41]

Another method for prioritizing requirements was developed by Karlsson and Ryan.[42] Their concern was that there are usually more requirements than can

---

[40]Karl Wiegers, "First Things First: Prioritizing Requirements," pp. 24–30.

[41]Available at http://www.processimpact.com/goodies.shtml.

[42]Joachim Karlsson and Kevin Ryan, "A Cost-Value Approach for Prioritizing Requirements," pp. 67–74.

be implemented given stakeholders' time and resource constraints (sound familiar?). They sought a way to select a subset of the customers' requirements and still produce a system that met their needs. The process they developed is described well in the referenced article. It has been applied successfully to two commercial projects, and these are also described. The Analytic Hierarchy Process (AHP) is used to compare requirements pairwise according to their relative value and cost. The approach is considered simple, fast, and accurate and yields accurate results and holds stakeholder satisfaction as both the ultimate goal and the guiding theme. Stakeholder satisfaction addresses maximum quality, minimum costs, and short time-to-market. Karlsson and Ryan believe that this cost-value approach is a useful first step in addressing a criticism of software engineering for lacking the trade-off analysis that is a component of multidisciplinary systems engineering. They feel that this approach is similar to that of the Quality Attribute Requirements and Conflict Consultant tool within Barry Boehm's WinWin system.[43]

Boehm has continued to evolve the WinWin Spiral Model to develop system and software requirements and architectural solutions based on winning conditions negotiated among a project's stakeholders.[44] The WinWin negotiation tool is a UNIX workstation-based groupware support system that allows stakeholders to enter winning conditions, explore their interactions, and negotiate mutual agreements on the specifics of the project. The model and support system feature a central role for quantitative trade-off analysis tools such as COCOMO. This method is obviously more complex than the other two, but the research is a promising effort. Many publications are available at the Web site concerning the win-win approach.

These methods for prioritizing requirements offer a significant opportunity to strengthen and improve your requirements process further. See the discussion of the rationale for prioritizing requirements in Chapter 8. All requirements are not equal—some are more important to customers and users than others. It is the job of the system developers (the requirements engineers, specifically) in concert with the customer to figure out how to prioritize the requirements and how to size the development effort to meet the project budget and schedule. The good news is that proven methods are available to help. The challenge is to use them.

[43]See Boehm and H. In, "Identifying Quality-Requirements Conflicts," pp. 25–35.
[44]Available at http://sunset.usc.edu/research/WINWIN/index.html.

Collect Requirements from Multiple Viewpoints

From our experience, we know that information about the requirements for the planned system needs to be elicited from a variety of stakeholder perspectives. Sommerville and Sawyer[45] have provided a good discussion of this topic in their book *Requirements Engineering: A Good Practice Guide*. In Chapter 13 they describe the basic principle underlying various viewpoints. They recommend a systematic approach called PREview (which stands for process and requirements engineering viewpoints), developed from experience with large systems engineering projects. Figure 4-12 provides an overview of how PREview checklists

Figure 4-12   The PREview Process

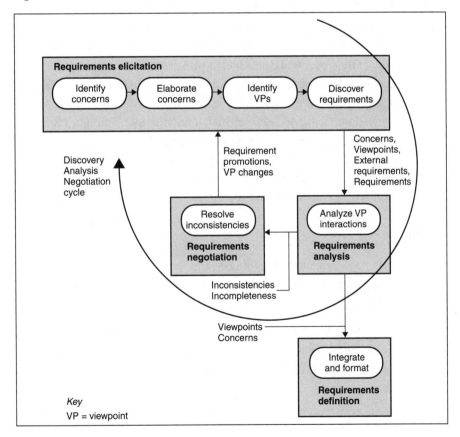

[45]See pp. 90–93 and 359–388. See also the Web site for this book, http://www.comp.lancs.ac.uk/computing/resources/re-gpg/.

and tables are used when iterating requirements elicitation/discovery, requirements analysis, and requirements negotiation.

Viewpoint-oriented analysis is obviously more expensive than an unstructured, informal approach to requirements elicitation. However, it may prove to be a good investment. As with any process improvement, an organization may want to "pilot" it, using a relatively small project. As noted in a recent article by Sommerville and colleagues,[46] they believe PREview helps improve the quality of requirements specification by providing a framework for analysis based on the key business concerns that define the success or failure of a project. PREview does not define how priorities, inconsistencies, and redundancies are resolved. This is the task of the joint team.

Consider the Use of Formal Methods When Appropriate

A formal method in software development is a method that provides a formal language for describing a software artifact such as a specification, design, or source code. Formal proofs are possible, in principle, about properties of the artifact so expressed. Vienneau[47] recommends using formal methods to help adequately capture requirements and cautions that many software engineers have adopted new methodologies without understanding the root concepts. He believes formal methods promise to yield benefits in quality and productivity. He notes that formal methods are typically used in organizations at SW-CMM level 3 and above and asserts that an organization that can figure out how to integrate formal methods effectively into their current process will be able to gain a competitive advantage.

Pitfalls

We've captured a lot of experience and lessons learned in this chapter. Here are some stumbling blocks you may run into and suggestions for how to deal with them:

1. It's very difficult to find one person who has the qualities of a domain or an SME *and* is a trained requirements engineer. Often it's easier to place someone with *one* of these credentials in the role of the requirements engineer.

---

[46]Sommerville et al., "Viewpoints for Requirements Elicitation: A Practical Approach."

[47]Vienneau, "A Review of Formal Methods." The discipline of a formal specification can result in fewer specification errors. Using specifications written in a formal language to complement natural language descriptions can make the contract between a user and a developer more precise.

My experience is that it's worth the extra effort and cost to find that one person who has both qualities. The reason is that the domain expert who is also a trained requirements engineer will provide the project invaluable advice concerning the real requirements. If you can't find one person with both skills, my suggestion is to train someone who is a domain expert in requirements engineering. This training will help a domain expert balance her preconceived ideas concerning the solutions with the concept of eliciting the real requirements and being sensitive to implementation issues.

2. Customers will try to put much of the burden for defining requirements on developers. "You tell me; you're the expert," they'll say! Not really. Developers may be trained and proficient in developing systems, but they are not the ones who should decide on real customer needs and expectations. As I've emphasized, *it requires a joint effort to define the real requirements*. As noted earlier, *it is important to train requirements engineers and developers not to make assumptions, not to make requirements decisions, and not to gold plate.* You'll find that this investment in training and discipline is valuable.

3. Project start-up situations are often hectic. It's difficult to pay attention to all of the tasks that need to be addressed. This is certainly true with respect to initiating and installing effective requirements practices. Consider utilizing an internal or external expert to assist with needed activities.

4. Don't use "smallness" as an excuse for not taking advantage of the practices, recommendations, and suggestions provided in this book. These are proven practices—on small projects and on larger ones. Tailor your approach based on common sense. Make good use of the underlying ideas and concepts.

Summary

This chapter highlights that the customer's stated needs require careful scrutiny to determine the real needs. Several specific recommendations and suggestions are advocated to help you determine the real customer needs and requirements. You will find that you can save effort and money, as well as do a better job (improve customer satisfaction), by addressing these recommendations. Please don't ignore them because they are presented concisely. I've emphasized that a huge amount of waste (almost half the costs on a typical project) is caused by using the normal approach—relying on the customer's *stated* requirements. Informed PMs and requirements engineers can redirect resources that are typically wasted to the implementation of these recommendations and suggestions. Enlist the support of your PM, and utilize a requirements specialist to implement these proven ideas. An organization should undertake implementation of these recommendations gradually and seek to evolve an approach that is continuously improved, based on your own experience and what works in your environment.

Key References and Suggested Readings

Barry Boehm. WinWin Spiral Model & Groupware Support System. 1998 Available at http://sunset.usc.edu/research/WINWIN/index.html. Dr. Boehm is Director of the University of Southern California Center for Software Engineering. The Center is under contract to the Defense Advanced Research Projects Agency via the Air Force Research Laboratory (formerly known as Rome Laboratories). It plans to develop (in collaboration with The Aerospace Corporation) a robust version of the WinWin System and to apply it to the domain of satellite ground stations.

Barry Boehm, Alexander Egyed, Julie Kwan, Dan Port, Archita Shah, and Ray Madachy. "Using the WinWin Spiral Model: A Case Study." *IEEE Computer* 1998:31 33–44. This University of Southern California Center for Software Engineering research project has three primary elements: (1) Theory W, a management theory and approach that says making winners of the system's key stakeholders is a necessary and sufficient condition for project success; (2) the WinWin Spiral Model, which extends the spiral software development model by adding Theory W activities to the front of each cycle; and (3) WinWin, a groupware tool that makes it easier for distributed stakeholders to negotiate mutually satisfactory system specifications. The authors found in this work that the most important outcome of product definition is not a rigorous specification but a team of stakeholders with enough trust and shared vision to adapt effectively to unexpected changes. The researchers believe that the approach will transition well to industry use.

Daniel P. Freedman and Gerald M. Weinberg. *Handbook of Walkthroughs, Inspections, and Technical Reviews*. 3rd ed. Chicago: Scott, Foresman and Co., 1990. This book provides a variety of examples of peer reviews and is a good source for organizations that want to consider alternative approaches.

Donald C. Gause and Gerald M. Weinberg. *Are Your Lights On? How to Know What the Problem REALLY Is*. 2nd ed. New York: Dorset House Publishing, 1989. As the title suggests, this book is interesting and light reading but offers valuable insights concerning real needs. The authors' perspective is that customers need assistance in defining their real requirements. A good requirements process will (1) identify the real problem, (2) determine the problem's "owner," (3) identify its root cause, and (4) determine whether to solve it. This is recommended reading for requirements engineers and their customers.

Tom Gilb and Dorothy Graham. *Software Inspection.* Reading, MA: Addison-Wesley, 1993. This book is about inspections of any work product, not just software. The authors' approach is very rigorous and therefore requires more training and is more expensive than normal peer reviews. However, it results in more defects being removed earlier, thus saving costs later in the development cycle. This book is invaluable for an organization that is committed to using inspections of work products—a proven method with good payback. Note that Rob Sabourin offers an economical inspections training and implementation approach. Contact him at rsabourin@amibug.com.

Rita Hadden. "How Scalable Are CMM Key Practices?" *CROSSTALK* 1998: vol. 11(4) 18–23. Hadden provides process improvement consulting services for organizations of all sizes. She notes that many practitioners are convinced that models such as the SW-CMM are not practical for small organizations because the cost of applying the recommended practices outweighs benefits. Her experience with more than 50 small projects does not support this view. The article describes using a disciplined, repeatable approach for projects of short duration. She concludes that CMM key practices are scalable.

Ivy Hooks. *Guide for Managing and Writing Requirements.* 1994. Available at ivyh@complianceautomation.com. This is a concise, well-written guidebook based on extensive experience by a practicing requirements engineer and consultant. It addresses scoping a project, managing requirements, how systems are organized, and levels of requirements, writing good requirements, requirements attributes, and specifications.

Ivy Hooks. *Managing Requirements.* 1994. This white paper is available at the Compliance Automation Web site http://www.complianceautomation.com/. It provides a good analysis of how failure to invest in the requirements process affects projects, and it describes major problems based on Hooks's experience. Also, it describes some of the characteristics of good requirements.

Ivy Hooks. *Writing Good Requirements: A One-Day Tutorial.* McLean, VA, 1997 Compliance Automation, Inc. Sponsored by the Washington metropolitan area chapter of the International Council on Systems Engineering, June 1997. This is an example of the types of briefings and courses that can be provided to facilitate a project or an organization in dealing with the requirements process. The pearl here is to ensure that you *have* a requirements process and that you take advantage of industry best practices in executing it. Don't find your own way and learn the errors of your ways at considerable financial, personal, project, and organizational costs.

Pradip Kar and Michelle Bailey. *Characteristics of Good Requirements.* 1996. Available at http://www.complianceautomation.com/. This document provides a valuable, readily available discussion of the characteristics of individual and aggregate requirements (note that characteristics of individual requirements are applicable to aggregates too). Kar and Bailey emphasize that writing good requirements is difficult, requires careful thinking and analysis, but is not magical. Time spent up front, carefully defining and articulating the requirements, is essential to ensuring a high-quality product. This is recommended reading for requirements engineers.

Joachim Karlsson and Kevin Ryan. "A Cost-Value Approach for Prioritizing Requirements." *IEEE Software* 14(5) 1997: 67–74. This is an excellent article that explains a method for prioritizing requirements (see the summary of their method provided in this chapter). Karlsson and Ryan provide a process for using the cost-value approach, utilizing the Analytic Hierarchy Process (AHP), which is also explained in their article.

Geri Schneider and Jason P. Winters. *Applying Use Cases: A Practical Guide.* Reading, MA: Addison-Wesley, 1998. This is a practical guide to developing and using use cases. Schneider and Winters provide examples from their experience and provide a case study that offers insight into common errors. An illustration of the UML notation for diagramming use cases is provided. Of particular use to requirements engineers is a "how-to" discussion on applying use cases to identify requirements.

I. Sommerville, P. Sawyer, and S. Viller. "Viewpoints for Requirements Elicitation: A Practical Approach." In: *Proceedings of the 1998 International Conference on Requirements Engineering* (ICRE'98), April 6–10, 1998, Colorado Springs, CO. New York: IEEE Computer Society, 1998: 74–81. Sommerville and colleagues introduce an approach called PREview to organize requirements derived from radically different sources. They show how concerns that are key business drivers of the requirements elicitation process may be used to elicit and validate system requirements. They note that PREview has been designed to allow incremental requirements elicitation (see Figure 4-12 for a high-level view of the PREview process).

Gerald M. Weinberg. *The Secrets of Consulting.* **New York: Dorset House Publishing, 1986.** Weinberg defines consulting as the art of influencing people at their request. As noted by Virginia Satir in the foreword, this book actually advises people on how they can take charge of their own growth. The author provides a light-hearted view of the role of a consultant, sharing valuable insights about people. A fundamental tenet is that we all need to follow a personal learning program. Several sources for readings and other experiences are provided.

Karl Wiegers. "First Things First: Prioritizing Requirements." *Software Development Magazine* **1999: 7(10):24–30.** This is a good explanation of why requirements need to be prioritized and a helpful description of how to do it. Wiegers provides a Microsoft Excel requirements prioritization spreadsheet and other requirements tools that can be downloaded from his Web site, http://www.processimpact.com.

Karl Wiegers. "Habits of Effective Analysts." *Software Development Magazine* **2000: 8(10):62–65.** See also http://www.swd.mgazine.com. Wiegers provides thoughtful and provocative insights concerning the role of the requirements engineer (also called the requirements analyst, business analyst, systems analyst, or requirements manager), patterned after Steven Covey's acclaimed book *The Seven Habits of Highly Effective People* (Fireside, 1989). He emphasizes that requirements engineering has its own skill set and body of knowledge, which is given scant attention in most computer science educational curricula and even by most systems and software engineering organizations. Many organizations expect developers or project managers to handle this vital function on their own. A competent requirements engineer must combine communication, facilitation, and interpersonal skills with technical and business domain knowledge. Even a dynamite developer or a systems-savvy user needs suitable preparation before acting in this role. Wiegers recommends that every organization should develop an experienced cadre of requirements analysts, even though requirements engineering may not be a full-time function on every project. This article is recommended reading for all PMs and task leaders.

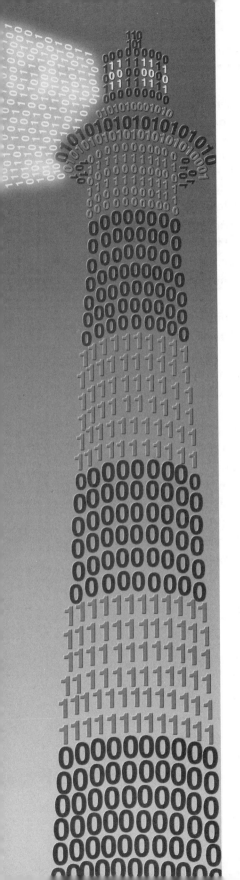

CHAPTER FIVE

Use and Continually Improve a Requirements Process

Commit to the approach.
Establish and utilize a Joint Team responsible for the requirements.
Define the *real* customer needs.
Use and continually improve a requirements process.
Iterate the system requirements and architecture repeatedly.
Use a mechanism to maintain project communication.
Select familiar methods and maintain a set of work products.
Perform requirements verification and validation.
Provide an effective mechanism to accommodate requirements changes.
Perform the development effort using known, familiar proven industry, organizational, and project best practices.

This chapter explains the value of using a requirements process as an integral component of any system or software development effort and indicates what should be included in the process.

The purpose of this chapter is to convince you to use a requirements process or, if you already have one, to consider making some improvements to it. In this chapter, I define a process and describe how a **process flowchart** is constructed. I describe why a requirements process is needed and present goals of requirements engineers. I provide a sample requirements process that has been used by dozens of projects and has been refined over several years. I describe how the process can be modified or tailored for use by other organizations and projects. The value of a Web-based library is also described.

The specific details of the process used are less important than *having* a process. The mechanisms, methods, techniques, and tools that work in your environment should be incorporated into the process. Note that *anyone* at any level in an organization can recommend that a requirements process be used—you need not be a manager, technical director, senior architect, system engineer, or lead developer. If you have read this far, it's apparent that your perception is that your organization can benefit (that is, be more effective) by designing, implementing, training, deploying, and using a (better) requirements process. I put "better" in parentheses because if your organization is developing systems and/or software, you no doubt already *have* a process. It may not be documented, trained, or widely deployed and used, but it's likely that you *do* have a process. So, the challenge is to perform *process improvement* (PI). It's also likely that coworkers in your organization will be receptive to this effort, because they too recognize that the weaknesses in the current requirements process is one reason that your organization is experiencing some problems.

What Is a Process?

Recall from Chapter 1 that a process is a set of activities that results in accomplishment of a task and achievement of an outcome. A process typically has a high-level or "macro" flowchart that provides a summary. A process usually has several customers, each of whom has specific, valid requirements it expects to be met from the performance or completion of the process. A process typically involves several different groups, departments, or organizations. A process consists of defined steps, some of which may require a defined subprocess or "micro" process. A process is normally initiated by a customer need and is typically completed by the satisfaction of that need.

One way of describing a process is to draw a flowchart depicting the steps and actions involved and to write a narrative providing the information needed to explain the process. The process description provides information such as the process identification, process purpose, related standards, related processes, version number, customer description, customer requirements, entrance criteria, inputs, outputs, exit criteria, responsibilities, tasks, tools, resources, quality indicators, and process indicators.

How Is a Process Designed?

Various templates are available for use in drawing process flowcharts. Figure 5-1 is the template most frequently used at Litton PRC. This template is explained and trained in a three-day quality improvement (QI) course called *Quality in Daily Work*.[1]

Prior to drawing the process flowchart, it's important to give careful attention to the areas shown at the top of the template:

- **Process Description**—This consists of the process identification (an abbreviation and a number are assigned) and the name of the process is provided.
- **Process Customer**—The individuals or organizations that receive products or services as a result of using the process are listed. It's important to consider carefully who the customers are. Almost always, there is more than one customer; often there are several customers. By carefully defining all of the customers of a process, we increase the likelihood that the process will be effective in satisfying customer requirements.
- **Customer Valid Requirements**—This relates to the fact that each individual or organization determined to be a customer of the process has expectations of it. Those expectations that are considered to be reasonable by the designers of the process are termed *customer valid requirements*. These are the requirements of the process that must be met by the successful performance or execution of the process. Note that some expectations may be beyond the capability of the process or may not be appropriate for it.

---

[1]This course is part of a series of QI courses developed by Qualtec Quality Services, Inc., formerly a part of Florida Power and Light Company.

Figure 5-1   Process Flowchart Template

Process Title		
Process Description: Process ID Process Name	**Process Customer:**	**Customer Valid Requirements:**
Process Flowchart		

Dept./ Person	
Step/ Time	

Process Title   Process ID Vx.xx

The next section on the template is the Process Flowchart section. The departments or persons involved in the process are identified at the top of the template. The steps in the process are listed down the left side of the template. A standard set of flowcharting symbols is adopted by the organization and is used to describe the process flow. For example, the customer need to be met by the process may be identified in a circle at the beginning of the process flow, with rectangles used to identify the next-level process steps. The symbol is placed under the area at the top of the template that reflects the individual or organization responsible for performing that step. Arrows show the sequence of the process steps.

The process flowchart is accompanied by a narrative process description (PD) that provides the information shown in Figure 5-2.

Figure 5-2   Process Description Template

Process	**Title** (Unique name of the process)
XX000	XX is the two-letter process area identifier. 000 reflects the number of the top-level macro process (the overview). Subprocesses are numbered 100, 200, 300, and so forth.
Objective:	The objective of the procedure is stated.
Responsible Group:	The group or groups responsible for the procedure.
Entrance Criteria:	Criteria that must be satisfied before the activity can be initiated.
Inputs:	Work products (internal and external) that are used during the activity.
Procedural Steps:	Individual tasks to be accomplished during the activity. Tasks are atomic. In other words, they are not further decomposed into separate process definitions. If a procedure is described, the tasks are listed in sequential order.
Review:	The reviewers of the activity's work products.
Approval:	Individuals and positions that give approval to the activity's work products.
Output:	Work products (both internal and external) that are produced during the activity.
Output Recipients:	Client and project staff to whom the activity's output work products are delivered.
Exit Criteria:	Criteria that must be satisfied before the activity can be completed. In other words, exit criteria tell how to know when a process can end.

(continued)

Figure 5-2   Process Description Template (*continued*)

Process Indicator:	Derived from the procedure tasks. It is used to indicate how successful the procedure is proceeding on task.
Quality Indicator:	Derived from the procedure objective. It is used to indicate whether the procedure is meeting its objective and to quantify the "goodness" of its products.
Comments:	Guidance given for the tailoring of this particular activity.
Source of Activity:	Reference to the requirement that warrants this activity. For example, it might refer to the CMM (CM Plan 8.4.2.d or CMM goal, activity).
Author:	The name of the person writing this procedure.
Revision:	Current revision of the activity. Revision 0.1 indicates the first draft. Revision 1.1 indicates a draft of Revision 1. (Remember that revision 1 is assigned only after approval.) The revision date and time appear in the page footer. This is the date and time that the file was last saved.

Notice that a process-oriented approach

- Defines the processes
- Specifies the customers of the process
- Defines the requirements considered appropriate or valid for all process customers
- Specifies the steps involved in getting something accomplished
- Indicates the sequence of steps

Having a documented process enables its reuse by other departments, projects, or organizations. Thus the effort required for other organizations to develop the same process can be avoided, providing that there is a mechanism to share information and artifacts. The approach used to perform a process is repeatable. By having the process documented, other organizations can make suggestions concerning how to improve it. These improvement suggestions can be shared and used by all of the organizations using the process. In executing the process, we strive for customer satisfaction. Aspects of customer satisfaction include quality, cost, schedule, safety, and corporate responsibility.

Why Is a Requirements Process Needed?

The many aspects of a requirements process were described in Chapter 1. It's generally acknowledged by system and software engineering practitioners (and even accepted by most managers) that having a documented process provides a standard way of accomplishing a set of actions in support of a needed business activity or **function**, and this is a good thing. Having a documented process permits performance of the process in a repeatable manner throughout an organization. Performing a process in a repeatable manner permits reuse, which saves time and money, because

- Performers have a better understanding of what to do and how to do it
- Performers can move from one organization or project to another and already be familiar with what to do
- Potential improvements to the process can be identified, suggested, implemented, and deployed
- Training can be provided to describe improvements that are applicable to all

In short, by having a documented process,[2] the work force is empowered to achieve the benefits described earlier.

Figure 5-3 indicates the rationale for requirements engineering (RE) based on industry data. These data are from the well-known and often quoted Standish Group *The CHAOS Report*.[3] Among the major contributing factors for poor results in our industry are a lack of user input, incomplete requirements, and changing requirements. A requirements process that incorporates effective requirements practices addresses these deficiencies by including steps and methods to address weaknesses. Moreover, there is leverage in making improvements to the

---

[2]In an information hyperflow environment in which the cycle time from initiation to fulfillment is very fast, there is zero latency entropy (no time lag between information introduction and utilization when supported by the appropriate information technology). Web-based intranet technologies require that we keep our documented processes current. This facilitates a focus on continuous improvement of the process rather than suggesting limitations of the people involved in the process.

[3]The Standish Group. *The CHAOS Report*. Dennis, MA: The Standish Group International, 1995.

Figure 5-3   The Rationale for Requirements Engineering

- Fifty-three percent of industry's investment on application develop-ment projects is a casualty of cost overruns and failed projects.
- Major contributing factors include lack of user input (13%), incomplete requirements (12%), and changing requirements (12%).
- Reducing requirements errors is the single most effective action devel-opers can take to improve project outcomes.
- There is as much as a 200:1 cost savings from finding errors in the re-quirements stage versus during the maintenance stage of the life cycle.
- Requirement errors are the largest class of errors typically found in a project (41–56% of errors discovered).
- The cost of rework is typically 45% of project costs.

requirements process because the requirements provide the basis for all of the follow-on activities in the project. The fact that requirements errors are the largest class of errors typically found in a project lends support for expending more time and effort on the requirements process. And the situation that the cost of rework is typically 45% of project costs suggests that reducing rework can pay for needed process improvements. Figure 5-4 provides some industry experience.

Among the reasons for utilizing an automated requirements tool is that it facilitates working with customers and improving the understanding of their real needs. The insight from *Testing Techniques Newsletter* that 80% of all defects are inserted in the requirements phase supports *The CHAOS Report* finding that re-ducing requirements errors is the single most effective action developers can take to improve project outcomes. The data indicating the types of nonclerical require-ments errors suggest that with improved requirements analysis, these can be avoided. Ivy Hooks[4] advises that a 30% change in the requirements during the development process will double the cost of the program. And we wonder why projects wind up exceeding their budgets by factors of two to ten. It's trouble-some that managers are not committed to the organization's developed and

---

[4]Ivy Hooks's experience as reported at the Writing Good Requirements Tutorial, McLean, Virginia, June 1997. Based on the cost analysis data of the National Aeronautics and Space Administration.

Figure 5-4   Industry Experience

- The primary reason for having an automated requirements tool is to improve with our customer the understanding of customer needs.
- Eighty percent of all defects of systems are inserted during the requirements phase.
- A 30% change in requirements during the system life cycle will double the cost of the program.
- The impact of finding and fixing a problem in various phases:

Cost	Phase
x	Requirements
3–6x	Design
10x	Coding
15–40x	Development Testing
30–70x	Acceptance Testing
40–1,000x	Operations

- Therefore, the costs of errors in our assumptions about requirements escalate the later in the life cycle the error is found.
- Types of nonclerical requirements errors

Incorrect fact	49%
Omission	29%
Inconsistency	13%
Ambiguity	5%
Misplaced requirement (wrong section)	2%
Other	2%
Total	100%

- Managers are not committed to the processes they develop and document. They change them as they please.

documented processes. This suggests that the exigencies and pressures of the moment are more important to them than the benefits of having a process and being committed to process improvement. Sadly, this seems to be true in many situations.

Figure 5-5 offers some "lessons learned" for system success from industry experience.[5] You'll note that several themes of this book are reflected in these lessons. These "lessons learned" need to be incorporated into the requirements process using effective requirements practices.

Figure 5-5   Lessons Learned for Systems Success from Industry Experience

1.   In today's business environment, a partnership relationship between customers and contractor throughout the systems life cycle is prerequisite to success.

2.   Approximately 8% to 12% of the total program/project costs should be spent defining and clarifying requirements (jointly working to discuss, define, and prioritize requirements issues).

3.   Document the rationale (why the requirement is needed). By performing this step, you may be able to eliminate as much as 50% of the stated requirements.

- Also, later you may be able to change things for the better if you understand the rationale for previous decisions.
- Consider your situation if those who defined the requirements are no longer available.
- Document dependencies between requirements.

4.   At the system level, 50 to 200 requirements are workable.

5.   Alternatives to asking, "What are your requirements?":

- What do you need?
- Why do you need it?
- How are you going to use it?
- What problems are you having with the existing system?
- What needs to be changed?

6.   Watch for specification of an *implementation*. For example, the airplane shall have three engines versus the airplane shall be able to fly with one engine out.

---

[5]I often wonder if *lessons learned* refers to a phenomenon concerning things *observed* rather than a lesson truly learned and then applied in future work. See Petroski, *To Engineer Is Human*, for some interesting insights.

7. Controlling requirements changes during the system life cycle is critical to controlling the program cost. Use the Joint Team to understand the impact and to work implied contract changes.

8. The types of requirements errors noted earlier *can be* addressed by challenging requirements and their assumptions.

- We have to ask.
- We have to find out.

9. A rigorous peer review process (preferably, a formal inspection) of requirements documents (once they are in good shape) is valuable.

10. Those working and reviewing requirements must understand the context. A critical mass of the development team should experience and understand (go to, be in, get background about, become familiar with) the environment of the current (and desired) system.

11. Write "lessons-learned" frequently to gain and share information/ preferences concerning customers' needs and expectations.

12. Build mechanisms into project activities to require all development groups to share information about their activities with the other engineering groups. *Proactively share information.* Establish an ethic of supporting one another as a project value.

13. Use the right people and good methods. Take the time to do it right.

14. Acknowledge good work.

Note: The term *requirements document* is frequently used to refer to a repository of the attributes in a system.

Goals of Requirements Engineers

Figure 5-6 suggests some goals for good requirements engineers. Note how these goals relate to the industry data provided earlier. By identifying incorrect assumptions, ensuring consistency, and increasing compliance, requirements engineers are improving the basis for the work required to design and develop a system. Requirements engineers can provide major benefits by reducing misunderstandings (improving communication) between organizations and individuals involved in the project. By being focused on continuous improvement, they can improve the responsiveness of suppliers and the satisfaction of all customers, both external and internal. The last goal, write good requirements, was addressed in Chapter 4.

Figure 5-6   Goals of Good Requirements Engineers

- Identify incorrect assumptions.
- Ensure consistency.
- Increase compliance.
- Reduce misunderstandings between organizations and individuals.
- Improve the responsiveness of suppliers.
- Improve the satisfaction of all customers.
- Write good requirements.
- Emerge the *real* requirements.

Figure 5-7 indicates some activities requirements engineers should undertake before requirements are written. The up-front process refers to the need for requirements engineers to gain the perspective of the users and the customers of a system as they perform the initial work during the development effort. The idea of assembling and educating the team seems obvious, but it's amazing how we ignore this simple practice. It's essential to form a team of capable, committed people. A conscious effort needs to be made to provide them the background of the project and to get them on the same "wavelength." An element of this effort is establishing a quality culture. An apt description of a quality culture is the presence of an attitude of continuous improvement and customer satisfaction throughout an organization. A characteristic of a quality culture is the availability of training concerning the mechanisms, methods, techniques, and tools to be employed on a particular project. In defining documents, explore with your customers the potential savings and value in using electronic versions rather than hard copy and the savings that can be achieved from timely reviews and approvals. Develop a checklist outline of the essential documentation. Plan for change. We know from our experience that change will happen. To the extent that we provide for change, we will be able to accommodate it better.

Figure 5-7   Before You Write Requirements

- Perform the "up-front" process (gain the perspective of the users and customers of the system).
- Assemble and educate the team.
- Define documents.
- Define outline (checklist).
- Plan for change.

Figure 5-8 describes the "up-front" process—that is, factors that impact the determination of the real requirements. The up-front process refers to the need for requirements engineers to walk in the shoes of the users and customers. We need to determine and understand the drivers for the project. We should spend time in the customer's locations to gain an understanding of their needs and their environment. We must understand and document the scope of the project, defining external interfaces and system components, and developing an outline for the system or project specifications. The best results are achieved when the requirements engineers on a project are domain or subject matter experts, because they have extensive experience in the area being addressed by the project.

Figure 5-9 describes what drives requirements. Requirements engineers need to be familiar with these drivers. The more familiar they are, the better the

Figure 5-8   The Up-front Process

- Determine drivers.
- Understand customer needs and environment.
- Understand and document the scope of your project.
- Define external interfaces.
- Define system components.
- Define specifications outline.

Figure 5-9   What Drives Requirements?

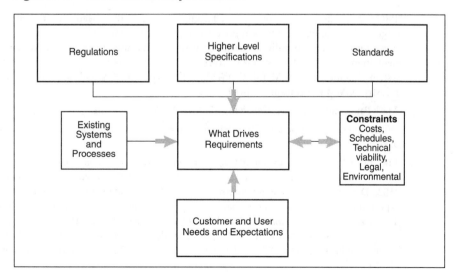

probability of being able to write good requirements. There are always constraints on any system or effort, and these need to be understood.

A Sample Requirements Process

Litton PRC[6] has had a corporate requirements process defined and deployed since 1994. Of course, many projects utilized a process prior to the genesis of a corporate process. Initially, a corporate Requirements Management (RM) process was designed, compliant with the Capability Maturity Model for Software (SW-CMM), developed by the Software Engineering Institute (SEI).[7] This process addressed the software life cycle only. In 1995, a full system life cycle RM process was developed to support the needs of a project that included system engineering activities.[8] In 1997, the Enterprise Process Improvement Collaboration (EPIC) developed the SE-CMM.[9] See Figure 5-10 for the list of process areas (PAs) addressed in this model.

A PRC requirements working group (RWG) that consisted of 18 requirements engineers from a set of projects, led by one of PRC's full-time process engineers (me) was formed. Based on their experience, professional reading, and participation in industry conferences such as the Institute of Electrical and Electronic Engineers International Conference on Requirements Engineering, the members of the RWG created a new PRC requirements process compliant with both the

---

[6]PRC is a wholly owned subsidiary of Litton Industries. PRC's headquarters is in McLean, Virginia. The company employs approximately 5,500 people in 200 locations and is a system integrator for a large and diverse customer base. PRC has used the SW-CMM as its development framework for the last dozen years. PRC has also used other CMMs, including the Systems Engineering CMM (SE-CMM) and the People CMM and is actively involved in industry's CMM Integration (CMMI) effort.

[7]Mark Paulk and colleagues, *Capability Maturity Model for Software*.

[8]With thanks to developers at PRC's Bellevue, Nebraska, site, particularly Karl Allen and Sheila Jackson.

[9]Enterprise Process Improvement Collaboration (EPIC). *A Systems Engineering Capability Maturity Model*. The process areas (PAs) in the SE-CMM that pertain to requirements are PA02, Derive and Allocate Requirements, and PA06, Understand Customer Needs and Expectations. Note that this model has been superceded by Electronics Industries Association (EIA) 731–1, *Systems Engineering Capability*. EIA 731–1 also replaces the *Systems Engineering Capability Assessment Model* (SECAM), which was developed by the International Council on Systems Engineering (INCOSE). A companion document is EIA 632, *Processes for Engineering a System*.

Figure 5-10   SE-CMM PAs

Engineering	Project	Organizational
Analyze candidate solutions	Ensure quality	Define organization's SE process
Derive and allocate requirements	Manage configurations	Improve organization's SE process
Evolve system architecture	Manage risk	Manage product line evolution
Integrate disciplines	Monitor and control technical effort	
Integrate system	Plan technical effort	Manage SE support environment
Understand customer needs and expectations		Manage SE training
Verify and validate system		Coordinate with suppliers

SW-CMM and the SE-CMM.[10] It consists of the four flowcharts provided in Figures 5-11 through 5-14—a macro (or high-level) flowchart and three micro (or lower level) processes. The mechanisms, methods, techniques, and tools that were effective and useful on the projects were incorporated into accompanying narrative process descriptions (PDs) of each of the four flowcharts.

This summary of the requirements process is named RE Macro/RE000, PRC Requirements Process. The process customer is not limited to just PRC's customer; it also includes the project staff (system developers). The customer requirements that are considered valid include the following:

- An effective system
- Completed within budget
- On-time delivery
- Win-win partnership relationship throughout the system life cycle

---

[10]Note that the process models continue to evolve. Department of Defense (DoD) industry and the SEI have collaborated to develop the CMMI. This model is a major step forward for system engineering. The basic requirements practices remain intact.

Figure 5-11 Requirements Process Macro (high level)

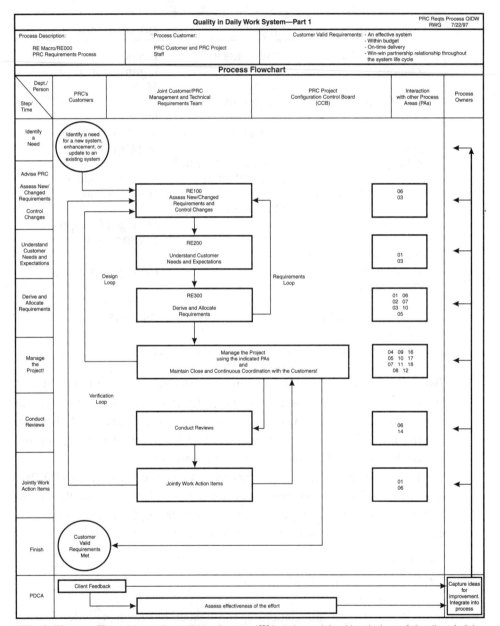

NOTES: 1. The PRC requirements (RE) process is characterized by partnership between the customer and PRC, by extensive communication and close and continous coordination; and by use of methods and tools to gain an increasingly more robust understanding of customer needs and expectations throughout the system life cycle.
2. The project CCB consists of the project manager and the leads from all involved engineering groups. This is a mechanism to manage the project in a coordinated, effective manner. It could include a customer representative; be the "Joint Team," and on a small project even be one or two people.
3. There are two entrance points to RE200: one from the initial assessment and another representing changes requested by the customer after the initial assessment.
4. The composition of the members of the Joint Team may change over the course of the system development effort as different levels are defined and addressed.
5. The requirements produced by the RE process will be impacted and changed by activities in the system architecture process.

The last customer valid requirement noted here makes this process unique. To execute the process effectively, the participants in the process must agree at the beginning of the contract performance that they will perform as partners, committed to project success. The partnering workshop described in Chapter 2 provides the foundation to achieve this customer valid requirement.

This macro flowchart lists three subprocesses that are called out by the high-level process:

RE100: Assess New/Changed Requirements and Control Changes

RE200: Understand Customer Needs and Expectations

RE300: Derive and Allocate Requirements

Note the very significant role of the joint team in all three subprocesses. A flowchart for each of the three subprocesses is provided in Figures 5-12 through 5-14.

In RE100, the joint team is formed. The rationale for having a joint team and a discussion of how to form it were provided in Chapter 3. Note that typical products of this subprocess include

- Minutes of meetings
- An initial operational concept definition (OCD)
- Selection of an automated requirements tool
- An updated OCD
- Updated data for controlling changes in the requirements traceability matrix (RTM)
- Analyses
- An initial assessment
- An updated RTM
- Ideas for improvements to integrate into the process

RE200, Understand Customer Needs and Expectations, is the most critical subprocess. This micro or subprocess name is the same as PA 06 of the SE-CMM. The rationale for why this microprocess is so critical and the activities performed was described in Chapter 4. Typical work products of RE200 include

- A requirements document (also known as a **functional document**); a repository of the attributes in the system
- Minutes of meetings
- Validated requirements

Figure 5-12   Requirements Process Micro: Assess New/Changed Requirements and Control Changes

Quality in Daily Work System—Part 1		PRC Reqts Process QIDWRWG 7/22/97
Process Description: RE100 Assess New/Changed Requirements and Control Changes	Process Customer: PRC Customer and PRC Project Staff	Customer Valid Requirements: - Develop and agree upon definition of project scope

Process Flowchart

Dept./Person / Step/Time	Joint Customer/PRC Management and Technical Requirements Team	Products	Process Owners
Identification of Need	Need to Agree Upon Project Scope and Approach → Form Joint Team	-Minutes of Meetings	←
Perform Initial Assessment	Available Project Information, Descriptions, and Requirements → Utilizing available information and descriptions, develop: -Est. Project scope -OCD Concept Also, review: -Candidate tools to track requirements	-Initial Operational Concept Definition (OCD) -Selection of a Requirements Tool -Minutes of Meetings	←
Assess New/Changed Requirements	Customer Provides New Changed Requirements → Analyze new requirements and changes to existing requirements using -Joint work groups -Automated RTM -QFD -Impact Analysis -RTM Reports Determine the effect of new/changed requirements on: -OCD -RTM Data -Project Scope -Recommended Project Changes; Feedback from RE300 (Reqts. Loop) Related Processes (Design Loop) V&V Process (Ver. Loop)	-Updated OCD -Update Data for controlling changes in RTM -Analyses -Minutes of Meetings -Initial Assessment	←
Control Changes	Control Changes in RTM by updating: -Change history -Links to lower level requirements -Links to Design Elements -Links to Verification Data	-Updated RTM	←
PDCA	Client Feedback → Assess effectiveness of the effort	Ideas for Improvements to Integrate into process	

NOTES: 1. This is the first subprocess of the PRC requirements process. The objective is to perform an initial assessment of the project to establish its scope, to form an integrated "Joint Team," to analyze all new and changed requirements, and to control the changes.
2. The inputs to this effort include any available information provided by the customer plus feedback from all successor design, management, and verification processes. The outputs are an Operating Concept Definition (OCD), the selection of an automated tool to manage all other requirement processes, and the data needed to track, manage, and verify the system requirements.
3. The project scope sets customer expectations and includes needs, goals and objectives, mission definition, operational concept, customer requirements, constraints, schedules, budgets, and authority and responsibility.
4. The OCD describes why the capability or system is needed, how it fits into what is being done, and known information and requirements.
5. The concept of having a Joint Customer/PRC Team reflects that there is joint responsibility throughout the system life cycle for definition of requirements and for agreement on any changes to requirements.
6. For brevity, the selected requirements tool is referred to as the *requirements traceability matrix* (RTM). All outputs of the activities in the processes are input into the RTM, so that it continuously reflects the current status of the developing system.

Figure 5-13 Requirements Process Micro: Understand Customer Needs and Expectations

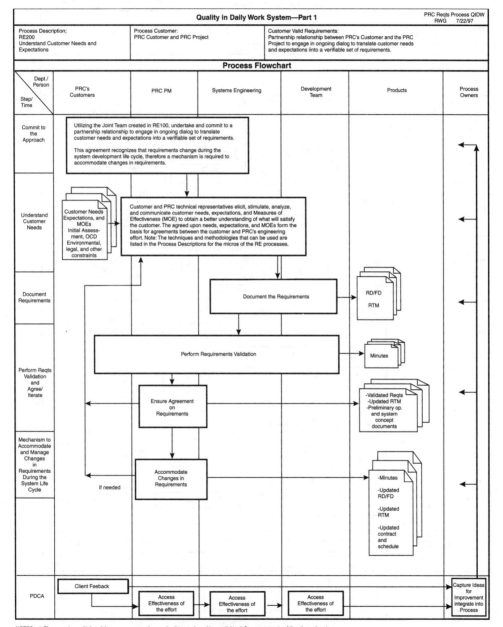

Quality in Daily Work System—Part 1

PRC Reqts Process QIDW
RWG 7/22/97

Process Description;
RE200
Understand Customer Needs and Expectations

Process Customer:
PRC Customer and PRC Project

Customer Valid Requirements:
Partnership relationship between PRC's Customer and the PRC Project to engage in ongoing dialog to translate customer needs and expectations iinto a verifiable set of requirements.

Process Flowchart

NOTES: 1. There can be multiples of these processes going on simultaneously and in parallel to define components of the planned system.
2. Applicable metrics to measure this process include time to complete RE200 and number of defects in requirements.
3. The RE200 process is characterized by partnership, extensive communication, and by use of methods and tools to gain an increasingly more robust understanding of customer needs.

Figure 5-14   Requirements Process Micro: Define and Allocate Requirements

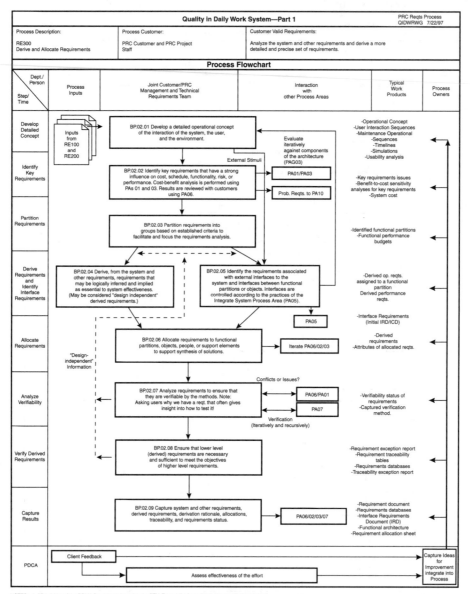

NOTES: 1. All activities of the RE300 Process are input into the RTM. Traceability from all activities must be maintained.
2. Applicable metrics to measure this process include time to complete RE300 and number of defects in requirements.
3. The RE300 Process is also characterized by partnership, extensive communication, and by use of methods and tools to gain an increasingly more robust understanding of customer needs.
4. Joint Application Design is a recommended method because the iterative joint effort often produces better results and understanding. Operational concepts, simulations, and prototypes are key to user-centered development and maintenance processes.
5. There can be multiples of these processes going on simultaneously and in parallel to define components of the planned system.
6. Recommend formal CCB approval of requirements outputs.
7. With regard to the "Allocate Requirements" step, note that we can't really allocate requirements until we know the pieces (components) of the system. This step requires iteration with the system architecture process.

- An updated RTM
- Preliminary operational and system concept documents
- Updated contract
- Updated schedule
- Ideas for improvement to integrate into the process

RE300, Derive and Allocate Requirements, incorporates the steps of PA 02 of the SE-CMM, which has the same name. The typical work products produced in RE300 include the following:

- Operational concept
- User interaction sequences
- Maintenance operational sequences
- Time lines
- Simulations
- Usability analyses
- Key requirements issues
- Benefit-to-cost sensitivity analyses for key requirements
- System cost estimates
- Identified functional partitions
- Functional performance budgets
- Derived operational requirements assigned to a functional partition
- Derived performance requirements
- Interface requirements
- Derived requirements
- Attributes of allocated requirements
- Verifiability status of requirements
- Captured **verification method**
- Requirements exception report
- **Requirements traceability** tables
- Requirements databases
- Traceability exception report
- Requirements document
- Interface requirements document
- **Functional architecture**
- Requirements allocation sheet
- Ideas for improvement to integrate into the process

We have found from our experience that projects that effectively utilize a few specific requirements practices achieve better results than those that don't. Some of these practices are the following:

1. Expend proportionately more effort on understanding customers' needs and expectations (8% to 14% of total project costs[11]) and involve customers and users throughout the RE process.
2. Create a mechanism for joint customer/contractor responsibility for the requirements. Today, users and developers should *collaborate* to build applications.
3. Utilize both an *organization* requirements policy and a *project* requirements policy to encourage and enforce good practices. A template for a project requirements policy is provided in Figure 5-15.
4. Recognize that requirements definition and the development of the architecture for the system are iterative—that is, each impacts the other, so the requirements process and the system architecture process must be performed iteratively and in close coordination with one another.[12]
5. Prioritize the requirements, focus the initial effort on high-priority requirements, allow for discovery of new requirements during the development process, and don't pretend that all requirements can be addressed in the first release.
6. Utilize an automated requirements tool to maintain lists of requirements and to tag each requirement with *attributes* to facilitate tracking and to change history, sorting, filtering, and cross-referencing. Also, each requirement should be tagged with its priority, difficulty, risk, and stability. Analysis of the various combinations facilitates decisions regarding which requirements to address in initial and subsequent releases. Sabourin[13] advocates use of the attributes' "importance" (relative severity of the requirement relative to other needs), "source," "weighting" (how important the requirement is to the source), and "reason" (for the requirement as stated by the source).

---

[11]Steve McConnell recommends that well-run projects should devote 20% to 30% of schedule and effort to planning, requirements, and architecture. See *Code Complete,* pp. 50–51, for suggestions concerning different situations (formal/informal project, stable/unstable requirements).

[12]Len Bass et al., *Software Architecture in Practice.* PRC recommends stronger integration of requirements process activities into the system architecture process. See Chapter 6 in this book.

[13]Robert Sabourin, review comments regarding this manuscript.

Figure 5-15   Template for a Project Requirements Policy

1.0 **PURPOSE.** The purpose of this document is to provide a project policy concerning the requirements for a system. For purposes of performing system development or enhancement effort on this project, the following are included within the scope of the Requirements (RE) Process:

1.1   To define the functional/high level requirements for a new system or capability; or for enhancements or updates to a system or capability (Requirements Definition). This includes compliance with Process Area (PA) 06, Understand Customer Needs and Expectations, of the System Capability Maturity Model (SE-CMM).

1.2   To perform analysis of requirements and requirements elicitation (the use of a variety of techniques to achieve a more rigorous and agreed upon [with the customer] description of system requirements); to resolve issues concerning requirements; to provide peer review of the requirements document; and to provide for review and approval by appropriate project managers (Requirements Analysis, Software Product Engineering [PE] KPA).

1.3   To evaluate requirements on the basis of a set of criteria deemed appropriate by the Project (such as feasible, appropriate to implement in software, clearly stated, consistent with each other, testable, and complete (when considered as a set). Note: the group responsible for system and acceptance testing of the software should verify that each software requirement can be tested (Requirements Analysis).

1.4   To put the requirements document under configuration management.

1.5   To provide a basis for estimating, planning, performing, and tracking the software project's activities throughout the software development life cycle.

1.6   To allocate requirements to software, hardware, training, documentation, installation, communications, database, and other system components (Requirements Allocation). This includes compliance with Process Area (PA) 02, Derive and Allocate

(continued)

Figure 5-15 Template for a Project Requirements Policy (*continued*)

Requirements, of the System Engineering Capability Maturity Model (SE-CMM).

1.7 To document the functional/high-level requirements, create a documented requirements document, and put the requirements into an automated requirements traceability matrix or tool of some type which has the capability to track additional, lower-level requirements throughout the system life cycle and to verify that all valid requirements are met and where in the system they are satisfied. (Requirements Management, SE KPA CMM).

1.8 To provide the ability to adjust the affected software plans, work products, and activities to remain consistent with the updated requirements whenever system requrements are changed during the system life cycle (Requirements Management, SE KPA).

1.9 To provide a draft Functional Description (FD)/functional baseline for the system or capability.

1.10 To ensure that appropriate support tools, methods, disciplines, and training are selected, utilized, and integrated in support of this process.

1.11 To provide for review of requirements by the QA group to ensure they are complete, correct, consistent, feasible, and testable, and that the products comply with the standards and requirements specified for them.

2.0 **BACKGROUND.** Experience has shown that a formal process resulting in an agreed-upon definition of requirements for new systems, new capabilities, updates, or enhancements to systems is a prerequisite to proceeding to system/capability design; and also that failure to do this results in rework and unnecessary costs and delays in schedule. Accordingly the XYZ Project has adopted this policy for managing system requirements.

3.0 **ASSUMPTIONS.**

3.1 For purposes of systems and software development, Customer requirements are not limited to software but may also include hardware, training, documentation, installation, communications, database, and other system components.

3.2 The XYZ Project's RE Process will be compliant with the Requirements Management (RM) Key Process Area (KPA), in the Capability Maturity Model for Software (SW-CMM) as well as the requirements-related aspects of the Software Product Engineering (SE) KPA; and the Systems Engineering Capability Maturity Model (SE-CMM), specifically, PA01, Analyze Candidate Solutions; PA06, Understand Customer Needs and Expectations; PA02, Derive and Allocate Requirements; and PA03 Evolve System Architecture.

4.0 **POLICY.** The following organizational policy will be utilized for all systems and software efforts for managing the requirements:

4.1 Project requirements activities and processes will comply with the PRC Requirements Policy.

4.2 Requirements for systems/capabilities will be documented.

4.3 Requirements will be reviewed via a joint process of the Customer's management and technical representatives and PRC developers/other engineering groups (OEGs) including test, QA, CM, and documentation support.

4.3.1 The purpose of this process wll be to document agreed upon descriptions of the requirements, to communicate a thorough understanding of the requirements, and to prioritize requirements.

4.3.2 Each requirement will be evaluated on the basis of the following criteria:

- Clearly stated
- Understandable
- Testable (in the new/updated system)
- Complete (when considered as a set)
- Feasible
- Consistent
- Documented
- Agreed-upon (between the Customer and PRC)

(continued)

Figure 5-15   Template for a Project Requirements Policy (*continued*)

> 4.3.3 Requirements for each new/updated system/capability will be documented in a Requirements Definition (RD), including the rationale for the selected alternative.
>
> 4.3.4 Changes to requirements will be provided by the Customer in writing so that PRC can evaluate them and provide appropriate feedback and resolution. Note that industry experience is that a 30% change in requirements results in 100% increase in the cost of the project. Therefore, changes in requirements should also include changes in the project's cost, schedule, and contract.
>
> 5.0   **REFERENCES.**
>
> 5.1 Requirements Processes and Process Descriptions
>
> 5.2 Requirements Management Tools
>
> 5.3 Requirements Process Training Course and Training Materials
>
> 5.4 Related artifacts in the project Process Asset Library (PAL)

7. Build prototype systems before initial major development activities.
8. Strive to find ways of reducing complexity and computer jargon in requirements.
9. Avoid approaches, methods, techniques, and tools that claim to be panaceas.

How Can Organizations Create or Tailor a Requirements Process?

Some believe that developing or having flowcharts for a process such as those provided earlier reflects the majority of the effort. I don't subscribe to this view. It's the knowledge, commitment, and awareness of the *people* who are performing any process that makes the difference. Here are some recommendations:

1. Gain organizational commitment to the decision to improve the requirements process (see Chapter 2 for suggestions concerning how to gain commitment).
2. Form a working group of people who are interested in improving the requirements process. See Figure 5-16 for a description of some of the benefits of using an organizational working group.

Figure 5-16   The Value of an Organizational Working Group

- Allows the organization to benefit from the experience of its projects and the expertise of key staff members.
- Seeds the organization with persons who share a common body of knowledge and who have come into consensus on key topics.
- Is a resource to the remainder of the organization.
- Facilitates use of the developed knowledge and artifacts for use in winning new business (proposals, lead marketing briefings, and so on).
- Encourages a common way of doing things; supports repeatability and reuse.
- Encourages and facilitates selection of appropriate methods and tools as well as their deployment and implementation.
- Encourages us to measure the effectiveness of the process and the benefits of institutionalization.
- Allows participation in industry leading-edge efforts (such as transition packages, or "jump-start kits").

3. Document the requirements process currently in use.
4. Evolve a "to-be" requirements process. This is a requirements process considered to be more effective, based on reading and any experience or advice that can be garnered.
5. "Pilot" the "to-be" process and refine it. Incorporate the mechanisms, methods, techniques, and tools that have been used successfully in your organization.
6. Consider potential Process Improvements (PIs).

Tailoring of Processes

One hears a lot in our system and software engineering community about tailoring. Exactly what is tailoring, and how does one "tailor"?

Tailoring is modifying a standard or "corporate" process or product to meet the needs of a particular project or program. The rationale for this approach is that by reusing a corporate or standard process or product, we can save time and continuously improve the process or product. Over time, this saves money and will result in a standard way of doing business that will reap great benefits in terms of business practices and profitability. If this approach is *not* followed, each project is basically doing its own thing, precluding having a standard way of doing business, and shutting off the opportunity for continuous improvement.

One performs tailoring by modifying the process flowchart and its accompanying PD (or any document) to meet the needs of the particular project. In my experience, much more is made of the effort required to tailor than needs to be. It's simply an effort to reuse a process or an artifact. One might need to modify the flowchart to reflect the experience of a particular customer. For example, the customer might have an approach it uses to accomplish certain activities. Great! Incorporate that, involving your customer, and then gain the customer's buy-in to the use of the process. Contribute your tailored artifacts to your organization's process asset library so that they are available and the ideas can be reused. By taking advantage of ideas from several projects, the corporate process may improve and a new version may be made available, allowing the entire organization to take advantage of PIs.[14]

Consider selecting separate projects for piloting a new PI initiative or experiment. Compare results with projects not utilizing new initiatives. Consider the use of peer pressure to challenge managers and others to "move forward."

Web Support: An Organizational Process Asset Library

Many organizations are developing and using internal Web-based process asset libraries. These electronic libraries facilitate the access and use of policies, process flowcharts, PDs, training materials, methods, techniques, tools, suggested metrics, templates, references, plans, and so forth. An example of the effective use of an organizational Web-based library is presented in Figure 5-17—in a summary of the contents of PRC's requirements transition package/jump-start kit. The idea is to provide a project a set of artifacts to facilitate the start of a process or to strengthen an existing practice, providing it the benefits of the lessons experienced and learned. The approach of using jump-start kits has been utilized extensively at PRC, saving projects time, effort, and money.

---

[14]See Royce, *Software Project Management*, pp. 209–220, for an excellent discussion concerning tailoring of processes. Royce emphasizes that the process framework must be configured to the specific characteristics of the project and that the scale of the project (particularly the team size) drives the process configuration more than any other factor. Other key factors include stakeholder relationships, process flexibility, process maturity, architectural risk, and domain experience.

Figure 5-17   Sample Requirements Jump-start Kit

- The organizational policy for requirements
- Updated requirements process and process descriptions
- Recommended methods for each part of the process
- Suggested tools
- Tailoring guidance
- Examples of processes from projects using the process
- Suggested metrics
- Training materials
- Template for a project requirements policy
- Link to a working group roster (to facilitate easy coordination with persons willing to help)
- References

Summary

A documented, reusable requirements process that incorporates the mechanisms, methods, techniques, and tools that work in your environment and that is continuously improved will save your project time and money. Having a documented process provides a standard way to perform requirements activities. A sample template for designing a process in your organization is valuable for reuse. Requirements engineering can provide value based on industry experience. A set of goals of requirements engineers can focus the requirements engineering activities. A requirements process that has been used successfully provides a basis for tailoring. Process tailoring involves modifying existing artifacts such as those provided in this book for use in your environment. An organizational process asset library is valuable because it facilitates sharing reusable artifacts. Continuous improvement of all process-related activities enables an organization to achieve world-class status in approximately five years.[15]

Key References and Suggested Readings

The CMMI project is a collaborative effort sponsored by the U.S. DoD Office of the Secretary of Defense/Acquisition, Technology, and Logistics and the National

---

[15]Based on the experience of industry consultant Richard Zultner.

Defense Industrial Association (NDIA), with participation by government, industry, and the SEI. The project's objective is to develop a product suite that provides industry and government with a set of integrated products to support process and product improvement. The intent is to preserve government and industry investment in PI and to enhance the use of multiple models. The project's outputs will be integrated models, assessment methods, and training materials. The DoD's concerns were to stop proliferation of CMMs and to standardize one model. Work continues at a frantic pace on this project. However, because industry has a lot of effort and money invested in the SW-CMM (and to a lesser extent, the SE-CMM), implementation may not proceed as quickly as some anticipate. See http://www.sei.cmu.edu/cmm/cmms/cmms.integration.html.

Peter DeGrace and Leslie Hulet Stahl. *Wicked Problems, Righteous Solutions.* Englewood Cliffs, NJ: Yourdon Press, 1990. The authors look at the assumptions and expectations associated with life cycle models such as waterfall, incremental, spiral, and "all at once." They analyze the pros and cons of prototyping. They enable one to look at "wicked" software problems with a different perspective. Their view is that we are lucky as developers to get 90% of the most important requirements at the outset of a project (p. 69).

EIA. *ANSI/EIA 632, Processes for Engineering a System.* Arlington, VA: EIA, 1998. EIA 632 came about because the U.S. DoD determined in 1994 that MIL-STD-499B would not be released as a military standard. EIA's Committee on Systems Engineering (the EIA G-47 Committee) agreed to undertake the task of "demilitarizing" 499B and releasing it as an industry standard. The intent was to revise the military version in accordance with commercial practices to broaden the suitability of the standard for other government agencies and commercial industry. EIA 632 provides a comprehensive, structured, disciplined approach for all life cycle phases. The systems engineering process is applied iteratively throughout the system life cycle. Key aspects of industry's initiatives are captured to identify and integrate requirements better and to implement multidisciplinary teamwork, including potential suppliers, early in establishing the requirements. Other key aspects include establishing clear measurements of system responsiveness, encouraging innovation in products and practices, and focusing on process control rather than inspection. Also, risk management is encouraged.

EIA. *EIA/IS 731, Systems Engineering Capability.* Arlington, VA: EIA, 1998. The EIA G-47 Committee initiated an effort to merge the INCOSE SECAM and the

EPIC SE-CMM in 1996. EIA interim standard (IS) 731, Version 1.0, was released on January 20, 1998. It contained two parts: Part 1 was the Systems Engineering Capability Model (SECM), and Part 2 was the SECM Appraisal Method. The purpose of this standard is to support the development and improvement of system engineering. Attention to this standard has become overcome by events because of the CMMI initiative, being driven by the U.S. DoD and being worked by the NDIA by representatives of EIA and the SEI.

Enterprise Process Improvement Collaboration (EPIC). *A Systems Engineering Capability Maturity Model.* **Version 1.1. Pittsburgh, PA: SEI, Carnegie-Mellon University, 1995.** To download a copy, visit http://www.sei.cmu.edu/ publications/documents/95.reports/95.mm.003.html. Following the development of the SW-CMM, some systems engineers determined that they would create a similar model for systems engineering. Version 1.0 of the SE-CMM was piloted in 1994, and Version 1.1 was released on November 1, 1995. This model is extremely useful. It contains 18 PAs, each with base practices. An SE-CMM Appraisal Method (SAM) was also developed. SAM Version 1.1 is dated March 1996. It too was developed by the SE-CMM collaboration members, primarily systems engineers from major companies. See http://www.sei.cmu.edu/publications/ documents/94.reports/94.hb.005.html.

J. Davidson Frame. *Managing Projects in Organizations.* **Rev. ed. San Francisco, CA: Jossey-Bass Publishers, 1995.** Frame provides a practical, hands-on approach with attention to behavioral aspects. He emphasizes the importance of ensuring that the project is based on a clear need and specifying what the project should accomplish. He addresses the importance of requirements in the context of real needs.

Litton PRC. *Phoenix Software Process Improvement Reference Guide.* **3rd ed. McLean, Virginia: Litton PRC, April 1996.** This is a desk guide for developers that summarizes the corporate PI program. Such a book facilitates PI by providing a readily available source of policies, processes, resources available, schedule of PI activities, training courses, metrics, acronyms, work breakdown structure for the PI program, and examples of formats to be used (for example, for a project PI plan). It begins with a discussion of senior management sponsorship and oversight of the PI efforts and addresses many mechanisms that have been put in place to maintain the momentum of the PI program. It's recommended that organizations consider providing a similar volume, whether in hard copy, on-line, or both.

Steve McConnell. *Code Complete.* **Redmond, WA: Microsoft Press, 1993.** This is a practical handbook for software construction. McConnell's focus in this book is to advance the common practice of software development to the leading edge. He provides research and programming experience to facilitate development of high-quality software. McConnell provides a chapter entitled Where to Go for More Information, with descriptions of some of the industry's best books, articles, and organizations. This is recommended reading for any software developer. Although the book predates the Web and client-server technology, most developers I know continue to value the practical and useful advice provided here.

Steve McConnell. "The Power of Process." *IEEE Computer* **1998 31(3) pp. 100–102.** Also available at http://www.construx.com/stevemcc/articles/art09.htm. This is a concise, straightforward, clear discussion of the value of using a process. Examples of cutting time-to-market and reducing costs and defects by factors of three to ten are provided from actual organizations. McConnell challenges the view that process is rigid, restrictive, and inefficient. This article is valuable reading for managers of systems and software projects.

Suzanne Robertson and James Robertson. *Mastering the Requirements Process.* **Harlow, UK: Addison-Wesley, 1999.** The heart of this book is the Volere Requirements Process Model, a detailed guide. An excellent requirements specification template is available on-line at http://www.atlsysguild.com/GuildSite/Robs/Template.html. Several examples of requirements are provided.

U.S. DoD, Fort Belvior, VA: Defense Standardization Program Office. *Communicating Requirements.* **SD-16. 1998.** Available at http://www.dsp.dla.mil. This handbook provides a comprehensive discussion of the requirements process within the DoD, with emphasis on clear, performance-based statements of requirements. The handbook recognizes that a single approach cannot accommodate the varying array of materiel acquisitions. It provides a requirements process, describes the evolution of requirements, provides descriptions of the requirements documents (such as the mission needs statement, operational requirements document, functional description, statement of work [SOW], and system specification), explains the requirements generation flow, describes the analysis supporting requirements determination, provides examples of statements of objectives, presents an acquisition case study, and provides a sample SOW.

Gerald Weinberg. *Becoming a Technical Leader: An Organic Problem-Solving Approach.* **New York: Dorset House, 1986.** This is a very readable book that provides good advice based on experience. Weinberg addresses different leadership styles and focuses on the problem-solving style as the one generally utilized by successful technical leaders. This is a recommended desk guide for technical leaders. See also http://www.geraldmweinberg.com/.

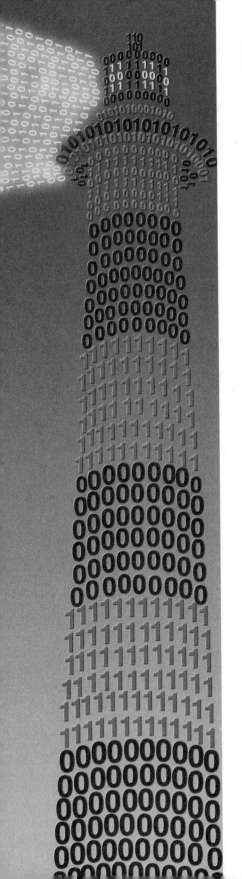

CHAPTER SIX

Iterate the System Requirements and Architecture Repeatedly

Commit to the approach.
Establish and utilize a Joint Team responsible for the requirements.
Define the *real* customer needs.
Use and continually improve a requirements process.
Iterate the system requirements and architecture repeatedly.
Use a mechanism to maintain project communication.
Select familiar methods and maintain a set of work products.
Perform requirements verification and validation.
Provide an effective mechanism to accommodate requirements changes.
Perform the development effort using known, familiar proven industry, organizational, and project best practices.

This chapter stresses the impact of the system requirements and the system architecture on each other. An iterative approach, in which each is considered in the context of the other, repeatedly, will result in better requirements[1] and a more **robust architecture**.[2] Also, a small team of system designers should review the requirements for implementation impacts, particularly cost, schedule, and risk.

Systems professionals often address the system architecture (SA) *after* the requirements are "finished" or "finalized." However, we know from our experience that the system requirements are *never* finished or finalized. Typically, there are extensive refinements and changes to the requirements as system development proceeds. Also, we've learned that the physical architecture of a system influences and changes the requirements. Accordingly, an effective requirements practice is to iterate the system requirements and the SA repeatedly until we are satisfied with both. The iteration should be completed in a finite period of time. Either we arrive at something workable or we recognize that we don't have a project yet.

In this chapter I describe the system engineering process (SEP) and provide recommendations concerning the interaction of the requirements and architecture processes. A system architecture process is presented in flowchart form. Reference is made to important industry documentation available concerning **architectural frameworks**.

The System Engineering Process

Many organizations employ the SEP, which consists of requirements analysis, functional analysis/allocation, synthesis, and systems analysis and control progressively throughout the system life cycle for all programs. The SEP uses customer needs, stated requirements, technology base information, prior output data, and tailored standards and specifications as inputs to create a balanced system solution. The SEP provides three overall feedback loops used iteratively until

---

[1]"Better requirements" refers to the real requirements that meet our criteria for good requirements as discussed in Chapter 4. Chapter 6 suggests that by iterating the requirements with the planned architecture, additional improvements can be achieved in the quality of both the requirements and the architecture.

[2]A "robust" architecture is an underlying structure of a system that can readily meet and adapt to real requirements.

the final system solution is obtained. The three feedback loops (shown in Figure 6-1) are the following:

1. **The requirements loop** iterates between the requirements analysis process and the functional analysis/specification process until the lowest practical levels of system functions, performance requirements, and design constraints are achieved.
2. **The design loop** iterates between the functional analysis/specification process and the synthesis process until the best product concept and SA that satisfy the system functions and performance requirements are achieved.
3. **The verification loop** iterates among the requirements analysis, functional analysis/specification, and synthesis processes to show that all requirements are satisfied by the system. Verification is the process of checking designs, code, test plans, and final products to ensure that they satisfy the requirements. Often, missing or incomplete requirements are discovered during the verification loop.

Systems analysis and control measure progress, evaluate alternatives, select preferred alternatives, and document data and decisions used and generated for all three loops. A top-level diagrammatic view of the SEP is shown in Figure 6-1.

Figure 6-1   The System Engineering Process

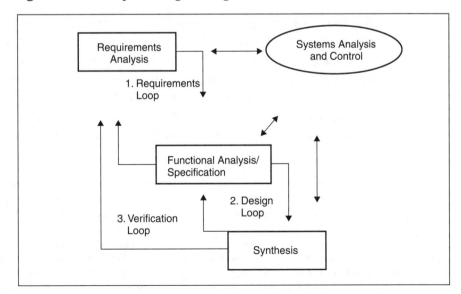

In the sample requirements process provided in the previous chapter, both RE200 (Understand Customer Needs and Expectations) and RE300 (Derive and Allocate Requirements) interact with the process of evolving the SA. We've advocated the approach of identifying a workable number (say, on the order of 50 to 200) of system-level requirements for a large system.[3] Some of these high-level requirements influence the architecture for the system. Cost-benefit analysis may be performed on these key requirements to analyze and determine the most cost-effective solution. Key requirements that show a relatively low benefit-to-cost ratio, high risk, or long development schedule are candidates for negotiation with the customer or buyer.

Recommendations

The following recommendations concerning the interaction of the requirements and architecture processes facilitate the implementation and use of this effective requirements practice.

Consider the "Designability" of the System When Addressing the Requirements

John M. (Mike) Reaves, system architect with Litton Data Systems in Agoura Hills, California, believes that design should play a key role in requirements development:

> While that may seem to place the cart in front of the horse, as engineers, we are constantly judged by our ability to deliver actual working systems on time and on budget. Therefore, no matter how well the system satisfies the customer's needs, we run the risk that the customer will never see the system, unless we can build it within the cost and schedule that we promise. Few would argue with the notion that the first order determinant of development costs/time will be the product specification. Once requirements are solidified,

---

[3]In general, the determination of the appropriate number of system-level requirements should be based on the complexity of the system under construction. A guideline is to identify a sufficient number of system-level requirements to describe the system expected to be built. In Mike Reaves's experience (System Architect, Litton Data Systems Division), a requirement density of one requirement per thousand source lines of code of a planned system is the approximate order of magnitude to capture the vision of the customer and to estimate the cost and schedule required to build the system. In his view, the requirements specification should contain every performance requirement that the customer will use to determine whether the job was done correctly.

the die is cast in terms of establishing the lower bound on cost and delivery schedule. I recommend that concurrent with requirements elaboration, we involve a small team of designers to review requirements for the implementation impacts—to cost, schedule, and risk at the minimum (although there are a lot of other attributes that need to be taken into consideration). They would be responsible for red-flagging requirements that will be found to be troublesome. Sometimes these may be resolved by a simple tailoring that doesn't adversely affect operational utility. When that is not possible, a subteam should be assigned to investigate trade-offs (resulting in the incorporation of new technologies or tools, or just safer ways to amortize risks via process steps—say, through early prototyping) that will make it possible to meet them. In the case that no thoroughly effective means can be found to meet a requirement, then it needs to be reviewed again with the customer. He must be thoroughly apprised of the issue and be encouraged to do a cost versus benefit trade study from the user perspective. The CAIV [Cost as an Independent Variable] process, which is mandated by acquisition "law" in the United States, is a process that is closely aligned with this approach.[4] By doing design trades concurrently with requirements development, we can largely avoid the catastrophic effects of having to cull the bad requirements from the "real" ones late in the development program.[5]

The Software Engineering Institute (SEI) has recently issued a technical report that presents the architecture based design (ABD) method for designing high-level software architecture for a product line or long-lived system.[6]

---

[4]CAIV is the U.S. Department of Defense's (DoD's) acquisition methodology of making technical and schedule performance a function of available (budgeted) resources.

[5]Feedback from Mike Reaves's review of this manuscript.

[6]Felix Bachmann and colleagues, *The Architecture Based Design Method*. Designing an architecture for a product line or long-lived system is difficult because detailed requirements are not known in advance. The ABD method fulfills functional, quality, and business requirements at a level of abstraction that allows for the necessary variation when producing specific products. Its application relies on an understanding of the architectural mechanisms used to achieve this fulfillment. The method provides a series of steps for designing the conceptual software architecture. The conceptual software architecture provides organization of function, identification of synchronization points for independent threads of control, and allocation of function to processors. The method ends when commitments to classes, processes, and operating system threads begin to be made. In addition, one output of the method is a collection of software templates that constrain the implementation of components of different types. The software templates include a description of how components interact with shared services and also include "citizenship" responsibilities for components.

Allocate Requirements to Functional Partitions, Objects, People, or Support Elements to Support Synthesis of Solutions

The purpose of this task is to facilitate development of the functional architecture at successively lower partitions. Wiley[7] emphasizes that the initial partitioning of a system is both challenging and important. Some partitioning schemes decompose from the **top down**. However, because humans typically don't categorize and classify from the top down, a system can be partitioned beginning somewhere in the middle of the hierarchy with familiar user activities. This approach is referred to as **middle out**, and it partitions the system in a more intuitive, natural way. Wiley believes this partitioning approach is beneficial to project management, system development, and verification. In addition, the approach fosters communication with the users throughout the development effort.

Requirements are initially allocated to functional partitions (which may include functions, or objects, and subfunctions) and ultimately to system elements and components. The allocations are performed so that the derived requirements can be implemented to satisfy the higher level requirements. When it appears that a requirement is to be satisfied jointly by several system elements, it is necessary to derive separate requirements for each system element.

Alternatives should be considered regarding the allocation of requirements to people versus the system.[8] The support element (including processes, production, maintenance, and environmental constraints) should be evaluated for allocation of derived requirements.

Utilize a System Architecture Process

The following pages provide flowcharts (Figure 6-2) as an example of an SA process.

The diagram syntax and semantics utilized in these figures were explained in the previous chapter. SA000 refers to the SA summary or macroprocess, the SA equivalent of the requirements (RE) 000 macro (Figure 5-11). The Program Architecture Team is the group of technical experts assigned to design the program-level

---

[7]Wiley, *Essential System Requirements*, pp. 22–24, 38.

[8]This is often overlooked as a means for reducing the complexity of the SA. For instance, the degree of automation that a system is required to provide will often place severe constraints on the SA that will show up in cost, schedule, and risk. Relying on the cognition of a system's operators, rather than complex decision-making hardware or software can sometimes soften a requirement. Therefore, consideration should be given to making careful trade-offs in this area.

Figure 6-2   SA Process Flow

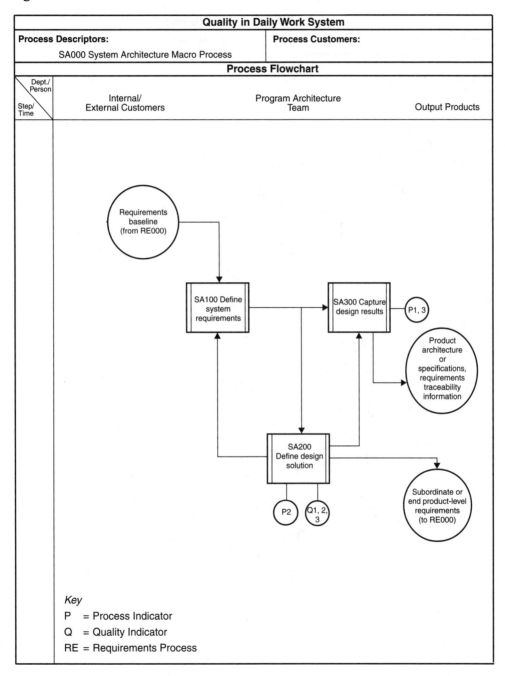

Figure 6-2   SA Process Flow (*continued*)

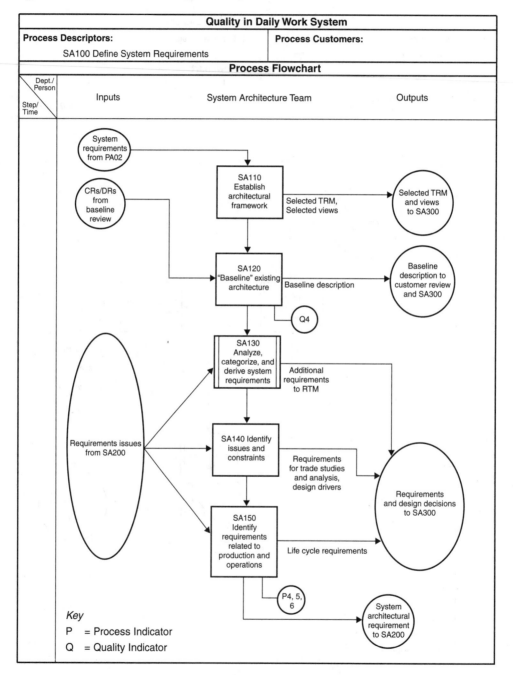

Figure 6-2   SA Process Flow (*continued*)

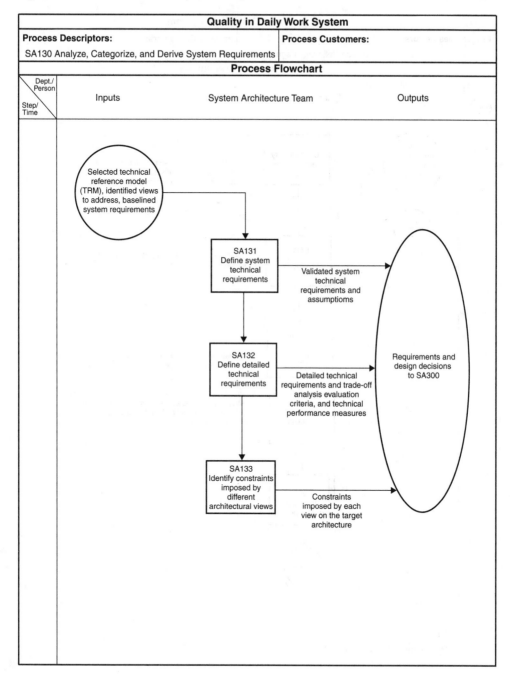

Quality in Daily Work System	
Process Descriptors:	**Process Customers:**
SA130 Analyze, Categorize, and Derive System Requirements	

Process Flowchart

Dept./Person / Step/Time	Inputs	System Architecture Team	Outputs

Selected technical reference model (TRM), identified views to address, baselined system requirements

SA131
Define system technical requirements

Validated system technical requirements and assumptioms

SA132
Define detailed technical requirements

Detailed technical requirements and trade-off analysis evaluation criteria, and technical performance measures

Requirements and design decisions to SA300

SA133
Identify constraints imposed by different architectural views

Constraints imposed by each view on the target architecture

Figure 6-2   SA Process Flow (*continued*)

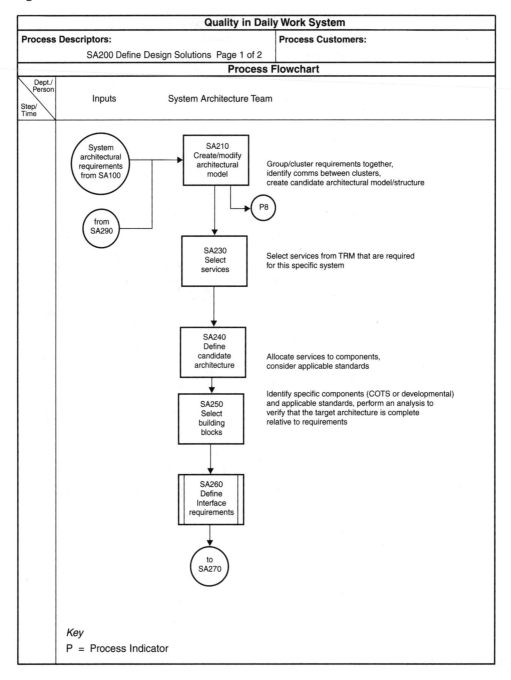

Quality in Daily Work System	
Process Descriptors:	**Process Customers:**
SA200 Define Design Solutions Page 1 of 2	

Process Flowchart

Dept./Person

Step/Time

Inputs   System Architecture Team

System architectural requirements from SA100

SA210 Create/modify architectural model

Group/cluster requirements together, identify comms between clusters, create candidate architectural model/structure

P8

from SA290

SA230 Select services

Select services from TRM that are required for this specific system

SA240 Define candidate architecture

Allocate services to components, consider applicable standards

SA250 Select building blocks

Identify specific components (COTS or developmental) and applicable standards, perform an analysis to verify that the target architecture is complete relative to requirements

SA260 Define Interface requirements

to SA270

Key
P = Process Indicator

Figure 6-2   SA Process Flow (*continued*)

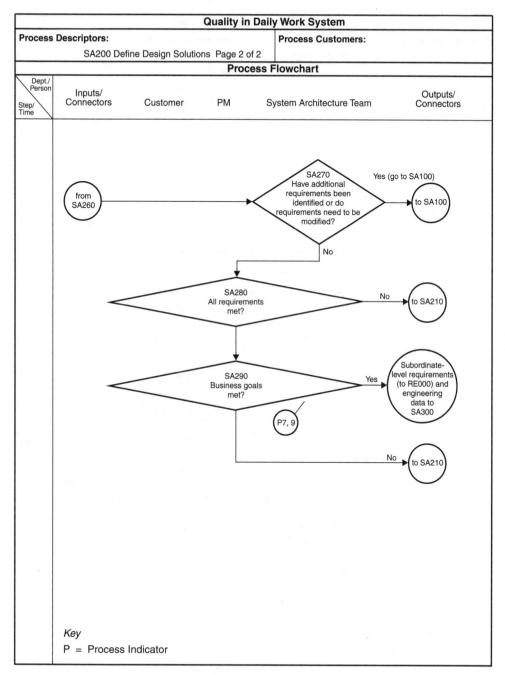

Quality in Daily Work System	
Process Descriptors:	**Process Customers:**

SA200 Define Design Solutions Page 2 of 2

Process Flowchart

Dept./Person — Step/Time

Inputs/Connectors | Customer | PM | System Architecture Team | Outputs/Connectors

from SA260

SA270
Have additional requirements been identified or do requirements need to be modified?

Yes (go to SA100) → to SA100

No

SA280
All requirements met?

No → to SA210

SA290
Business goals met?

Yes → Subordinate-level requirements (to RE000) and engineering data to SA300

P7, 9

No → to SA210

Key
P = Process Indicator

Figure 6-2   SA Process Flow (*continued*)

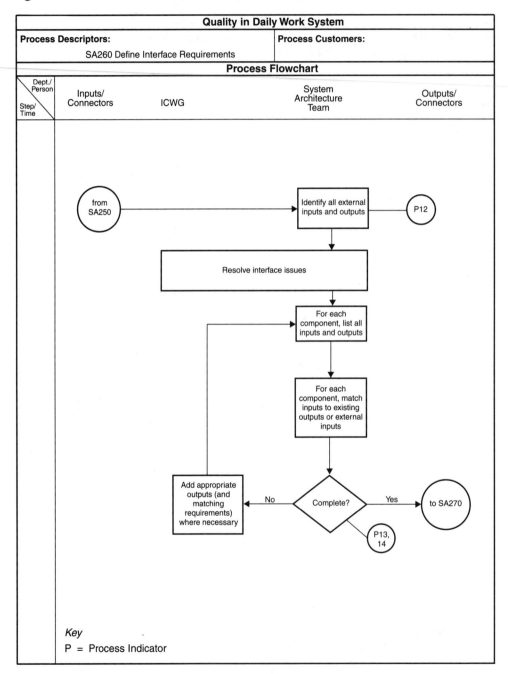

Quality in Daily Work System		
Process Descriptors:		**Process Customers:**
SA260 Define Interface Requirements		
Process Flowchart		

Dept./Person

Step/Time

Inputs/Connectors   ICWG   System Architecture Team   Outputs/Connectors

from SA250

Identify all external inputs and outputs

P12

Resolve interface issues

For each component, list all inputs and outputs

For each component, match inputs to existing outputs or external inputs

Add appropriate outputs (and matching requirements) where necessary

No ← Complete? → Yes

P13, 14

to SA270

Key

P = Process Indicator

Figure 6-2   SA Process Flow (*continued*)

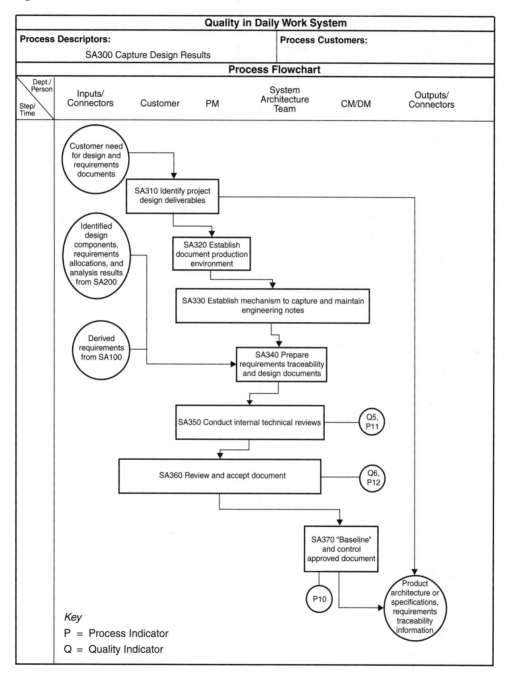

Quality in Daily Work System		
Process Descriptors:		**Process Customers:**
SA300 Capture Design Results		

Process Flowchart

Key
P = Process Indicator
Q = Quality Indicator

architecture for the planned system. This team will include the requirements engineer and, therefore, involves at least one member of the joint team. PA02 refers to process area 02 of the Systems Engineering Capability Maturity Model (SE-CMM), Derive and Allocate Requirements. SA100, 200, and 300 are the next-level subprocesses of the SA process. Each of these subprocesses has lower level processes. For example, the lower level processes of SA100 are SA110, 120, 130, 140, and 150. Process (P) and quality (Q) metrics that measure the effectiveness of the process and the quality of the products respectively are defined. TRM refers to the **technical reference model**, and RTM refers to the requirements traceability matrix discussed previously. The TRM is a structure that allows the components of an information system to be described in a consistent manner.

The purpose of the SA process is to establish and evolve a system design. The SA also provides a reference model and common terminology for all system components. As noted earlier in the discussion of the requirements process, the specific steps of the process are less important than *having* a process and, over time, incorporating the mechanisms, methods, techniques, and tools that work in your organization.

The SA describes the components (building blocks) that make up the system, the interrelationships (connections) between the components, and the constraints of the system. Users of an SA process will want to familiarize themselves with principles of The Open Group's Architectural Framework (TOGAF).[9] The TOGAF is an example of an architecture framework specific to **information technology** (IT) systems and therefore may not be applicable to all SA tasks.[10] An **"open" architecture** exists when the underlying structure of the system (the hardware and software) is defined in such a way that allows additional capabilities to be added with little or no adjustment.

At the macro level, note that the **requirements baseline**[11] from the requirements process is the input that enables determination of the system requirements,

---

[9]TOGAF is a tool for defining an IT architecture. It is described in a document that is published by The Open Group on its public Web server. See http://www.opengroup.org/public/arch/. The TOGAF may be reproduced freely by any organization wishing to use it to develop an information SA for use within that organization.

[10]A technique that should be encouraged is to maintain a catalog of architecture frameworks that can be reused intact or tailored as needed for each future system implementation.

[11]A requirements baseline is the set of requirements associated with a particular release of a product or system.

which in turn enables definition of the design solution. In SA100, the first micro-process, the architectural framework is established and a **baseline** architecture is developed. The next three microprocesses all reflect the interaction between requirements and architecture development, and evolution activities. Additional detail is provided in the next flowchart. SA200 describes the steps involved in defining the design solution. The SA100 and SA200 subprocesses form a loop but in reality are interactive processes. During the interaction of SA100 and SA200, different sets of system components are evaluated, requirements are allocated to these components, and requirements are derived as necessary to support inter-action among the elements in each set. This looping continues until a set of sys-tem components and their derived and allocated requirements that meets the system's technical requirements and the program's business goals are identified.

Interface requirements are defined in SA260.[12] The purpose of the SA300 microprocess is to capture design results. Capturing design results is an ongoing effort that continues in parallel with both SA100 and SA200. This is a good opportunity to note that, too often, we provide the rationale for why we *do* things, but hardly ever do we document why we've decided *not* to do some-thing.[13] In performing design activities (as in other areas of technical work), it's important to capture and document this information as decisions are made, for the benefit of those who at some later date may be considering related decisions. If we don't, people will not have the benefit of our work and analysis. For example, documented rationale concerning why a specific design was rejected could pre-vent having to redo the analysis at a later date.

The SA process moves from the system level to successive subordinate struc-tures at lower levels, as shown in Figure 6-3.

Derived requirements are requirements that are further refined from a primary source requirement or from a higher level requirement. A derived requirement can also be a requirement that results from choosing a specific implementation or

---

[12]See Hooks and Farry, *Customer-Centered Products,* Chapter 6, for a good discussion concern-ing identifying and managing interfaces. They point out that many projects neglect to detail and control interfaces until testing or operation, and they recommend that interfaces be iden-tified early. The reason for this is that missing or incorrect interfaces are a major cause of cost overruns and product failures. This effort should be documented comprehensively to avoid rework and unpleasant surprises late in development.

[13]There is some research being sponsored by the Defense Advanced Research Projects Agency (under the Evolutionary Design of Computer Systems Program) that is funding the development of tools for design rationale capture. See http://www.darpa.mil/ito/research/edcs/index.html.

Figure 6-3   Iterative System Decomposition

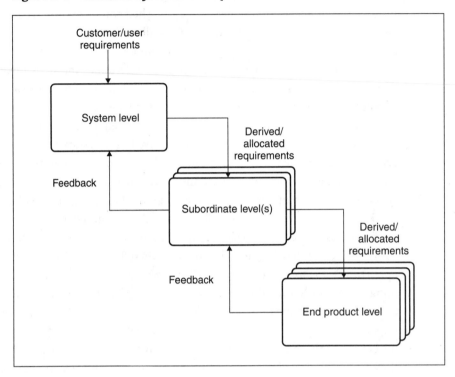

system element. Allocated requirements are requirements that have been assigned to architectural components of the system such as a hardware or software configuration item. Figure 6-3 describes how the highest (system) level requirements are assigned to subordinate levels and finally to the end product level. Feedback is provided and changes are made until the SA best addresses the requirements.

Consider Open Systems Standards

An open architecture implies lower risk that the evolution of the system will result in major revisions of the product architecture. (One might observe that open architectures may invite prolonged minor revisions that in turn impact the stability of the requirements.) Also, a purpose in seeking compliance with **open systems** standards is to achieve independence from proprietary standards of vendors—to be able to include open systems-compliant components in our systems. The standard interfaces make it possible to buy components from any supplier with standard products, making the system easier to buy, easier to maintain, and more flexible and scalable. The term *branding* refers to products and vendors that have passed an open systems compliance requirement. Another important aspect is that technology reuse encompasses a determination of which standards will be incorporated by the system implementation as well as commercial off-the-shelf (COTS)/government off-the-shelf (GOTS) and legacy components (particularly software) that can help defray costs and shorten schedules. This is becoming a very serious issue in being competitive.

Specific SAs have to be defined by the details of their implementation. However, a *framework* such as TOGAF (noted earlier) can be defined in a standards-based way. An architectural framework describes a whole family of related architectures, allowing an individual architecture to be created by selection from and modification of the framework components. It describes an information system in terms of a model, made up of a set of conceptual building blocks, and shows how the building blocks fit together. Figure 6-4 is an overview of the process of architecture development. Information about the benefits and constraints of the existing implementation, together with requirements for change are combined using an architectural framework, resulting in an architecture or set of architecture alternatives.

A TRM (Figure 6-5) allows the components of an existing or planned information system and the relationships between the components to be recorded in a mutually consistent manner. Specification of a TRM is important because it provides a mechanism for defining what is to be included in the resulting system. It defines the *services* that are needed.

Figure 6-4   Architecture Development Process Overview

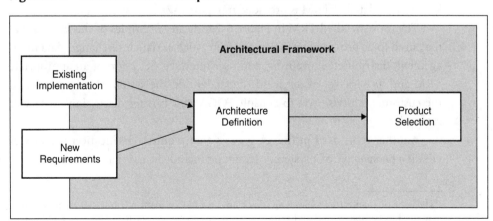

Figure 6-5   TRM High-Level View

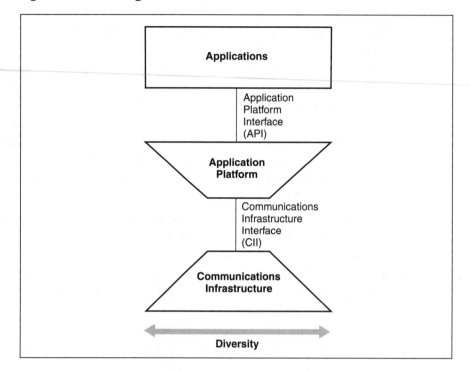

The basic TRM in Figure 6-5 applies equally to local and distributed scenarios. Specific architectures derived from the TRM may show separate application platforms (Figure 6-6).

A more detailed TRM is provided in Figure 6-7.

The more detailed TRM in Figure 6-7 indicates examples of the *services* that may need to be provided by the architecture, such as data interchange, data management, distributed computing, and user interface. Selection of an appropriate TRM and its basic set of services is dependent on the system requirements and the customer. I advise you to consult TOGAF for further discussion on service categories.

Another term used in the SA process that requires clarification is ***views***. A view is a perspective of a system.[14] Examples include functional, implementation,

---

[14]The issue of architecture views is an important one, in that many attributes of an architecture may need to be understood and trade-offs made among them. Each view would highlight an attribute such as reliability, availability, maintainability, performance, security, and so forth, but

Figure 6-6   Distributed Computing Architecture Diagram

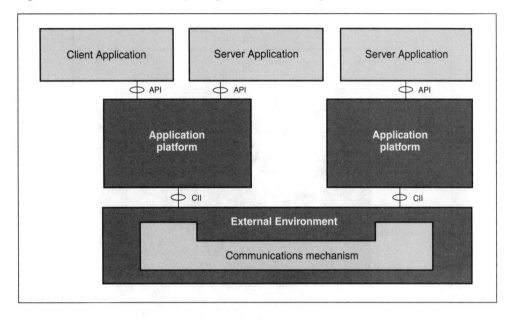

and physical views. The purpose of taking many views into consideration during the SA process is to ensure that all relevant aspects of the final target architecture have been considered, so that the target system will meet all of the requirements put on it. The *functional view* considers the operational aspects of the system— what it is intended to do. The *implementation views* look at constraints on the system, which arise because of the components from which it is built. Examples of implementation views include the management view, the security view, the builder's view, the data management view, and the user view. *Physical views* consider the system's physical components, where they are located, and what physical constraints apply to the system as a result. Physical views include the computing view and the communications view. More information about these views may be found in Part IV of *TOGAF* (The Open Systems Group, 1999).

The architecture development process envisioned by The Open Systems Group is described in Figure 6-8.

---

it must be recognized that almost all views are coupled (in other words, modifications that affect one beneficially will affect others deleteriously). The topic of making architecture trades (and tools for assisting them) is important. This provides a context for a discussion of prototypes and simulations. The SEI *Architecture Tradeoff Analysis Method* is a good primer on the topic.

Figure 6-7   Detailed TRM

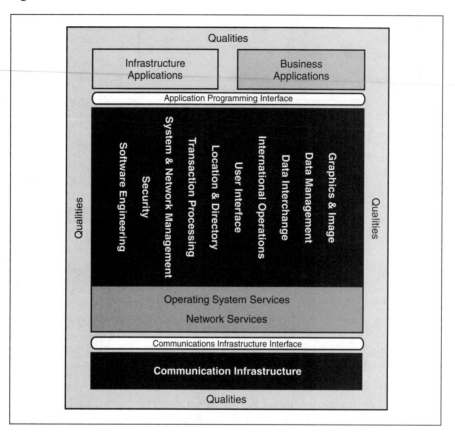

The PRC SA process addresses the part of the cycle in the B and C bubbles. In developing the PRC SA process, the architecture team incorporated the more detailed architecture development process recommended in the TOGAF. This process was designed to be compliant with PA03, Evolve System Architecture, of the SE-CMM.[15]

---

[15]As noted previously, *A Systems Engineering Capability Maturity Model* was written by a group of systems engineers representing U.S. companies that collaborated as the Enterprise Process Improvement Collaboration. The structure of the SE-CMM is somewhat similar to the software CMM. It provides 18 PAs, each with a list of base practices, which in turn have a description, typical work products, and notes. The document is extremely useful and may be downloaded from http://www.sei.cmu.edu/publications/documents/95.reports/95.mm.003.html

Figure 6-8   Architecture Development Cycle

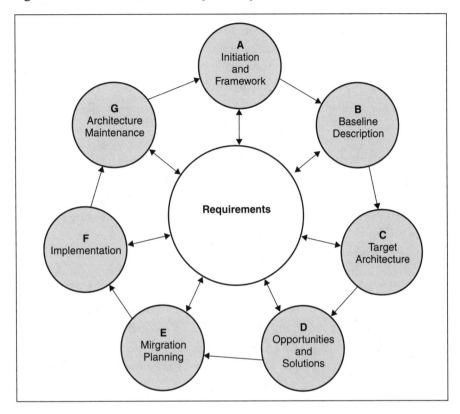

Guidelines for "Architecting"

The following are guidelines that apply to the architecting process:

1. System architecting is a top-down evolutionary process starting with requirements and working down to implementable or procurable building blocks that meet the requirements. Often it is also necessary to go from the **bottom up** as well in deriving an architecture. Any place where a technical risk exists is a candidate for this approach.

2. There usually is not a single right answer. There are often many good answers, and the trade-offs between them are not necessarily obvious without an iterative evaluation process.

3. An iterative process is needed because additional information impacts the known requirements, the architecture, and the design.

4. The SA process should start during the bid/proposal phase of projects if one exists.

5. Be aware that any time we utilize a tool, such as the CS/10,000[16] architecture development tool, we create expectations on the part of our customers. The tendency observed in our customers when provided early architecture pictures or descriptions is to jump to the conclusion that the system is understood and therefore that we should proceed to the next step in the development of the system. We need to work with customers to caution that we may need a more complete understanding of the target system based on a thorough SA process, rather than proceed prematurely. Proceeding with development in the absence of a thorough understanding only results in later and expensive rework, in my experience. The exit criteria from subprocesses and loops may be judgmental. They may meet our needs now, but new information may change the architecture significantly.

6. Services are partitioned in our design choices and in the selection of COTS products.

7. Examine all assumptions to determine whether they need to be allocated to lower levels of the architecture, and allocate downward if appropriate.

8. Use a common taxonomy for components of the system.

9. There are constraints that must be considered. For example, the customer may specify that NT will be used as the operating system. If the customer is committed to such assumptions or constraints, this may have a significant impact on the architecture.

---

[16]The CS/10,000 is an automated expert assistant software engine (EASE) developed and marketed by Client/Server Connection, Ltd. See http://www.cscl.com/. The CS/10,000 EASE assists in the design, planning, management, and documentation of plans, projects, and programs. A primary function of the CS/10,000 is to assist IT organizations in standardizing their IT processes as well as to document and manage projects and methodologies from conception to full life cycle completion. The product is useful in analyzing requirements for a system and in developing the client-server configuration, the networking configuration, the project plan, and the documentation. It facilitates managing the project plan and tracking resources. One module, the Product Selector, facilitates selecting hardware and software products that meet requirements. Users can easily add vendors and products to the database to address their unique requirements. Detailed information on these products can then be located easily using a graphical look-up interface. The Estimator Advisor module uses a neural network and learns how long the organization takes to complete actual tasks and projects based on past project data. The product is built on an object-oriented knowledge base that includes its methodologies, architectures, documentation templates, and estimation factors. This architecture facilitates creating new knowledge bases. The company has new knowledge base content development on the drawing board in the market areas where demand has been identified, such as CMM, data analysis, information security for e-commerce, and others.

10. There is great variability in how critical design requirements are defined.

11. Architects must understand services and views as defined and have experience in developing architectures. It is this experience that enables a more effective performance of the SA process.

12. Use care when suggesting a solution if you suspect that all of the requirements are not known. Apply risk management techniques.

13. There is no such thing as completeness with respect to a target SA, because as soon as additional information becomes known, the target architecture is impacted.

Another View

It is always insightful to me when I have an experience that provides a totally different perspective. This happened when I was privileged to hear Eberhardt Rechtin's presentation, *Systems Architecting of Software Structures, or Why Eagles Can't Swim* at Litton Industries' Software Technology Management Conference. A lesson he offered was the following: "Never assume that the original statement of the problem is the best or even correct." A premise from his experience is that achievements of unprecedented solutions determine whether any enterprise will be successful in the long run. These were statements I could support from my own experience. However, Eberhardt went on with some other statements that provided a different view:

1. Reuse is a terrible thing. There are tremendous risks because the reuses have no understanding of the assumptions that were made in the original product.

2. COTS is a terrible thing. Who knows what's in the software that could hurt the objectives and intent of the current effort?

3. Structure precludes the ability to have a revolutionary idea.

4. One must "do architecting" together with the customer because it is the customer who decides what can be funded.

5. Companies often make unstated assumptions that are built into their proposals. It's no wonder they lose!

Rechtin advocates having one architect for every 100 engineers.[17]

---

[17]Statements are summarized from Rechtin's presentation. For more insights along these lines, see Rechtin, *Systems Architecting of Organizations: Why Eagles Can't Swim.*

Summary

Iterating the system requirements and the SA repeatedly is an effective requirements practice. The SEP provides three feedback loops (requirements, design, and verification) that facilitate creating a balanced system solution. Recommendations that support the implementation and use of this effective requirements practice include (1) consider the designability of the system when addressing the requirements; (2) allocate requirements to functional partitions, objects, people, or support elements to support the synthesis of solutions; (3) use an SA process such as that described in the flowcharts in Figure 6-2, ensuring that results of the analysis are captured for use by others at a later date; and (4) consider open systems standards such as the TOGAF. Use of a TRM facilitates recording the components of an existing or planned information system consistently. I encourage you to consider several guidelines for developing architectures that are based on practical experience.

Key References and Suggested Readings

James L. Adams. *Conceptual Blockbusting: A Guide to Better Ideas.* 3rd ed. Reading, MA: Perseus Books, 1986. A stimulus to creative thinking and flexibility, this book is filled with exercises and thoughtful problems that stretch one's mind. It is a great supplement to software design books, aiding algorithm development and the process of partitioning a system into pieces.

Felix Bachmann, Len Bass, Gary Chastek, Patrick Donohoe, and Fabio Peruzzi. *The Architecture Based Design Method.* Technical report CMU/SEI-2000-TR-001, ESC-TR-2000-001. Pittsburg, PA: SEI, 2000. The ABD method fulfills functional, quality, and business requirements at a level of abstraction that allows for variation in producing products. The method provides a series of steps to organize functions, to identify synchronization points for independent threads of control, and to allocate functions to processors. See http://www.sei.cmu.edu/publications/documents/00.reports/00tr001.html.

Len Bass, Paul Clements, and Rick Kazman. *Software Architecture in Practice.* Reading, MA: Addison-Wesley, 1998. Drawing on their experience building and evaluating architectures, Bass and colleagues introduce the concepts and practices concerning how a system is designed and how the system's components interact with each other. Several case studies undertaken with the SEI are provided to illustrate real-world constraints and opportunities. The authors discuss methods for analyzing architectures for quality attributes and provide a good discussion of architecture reviews.

Derek Hatley, Peter Hruschka, and Imtiaz Pirbhai. *Process for System Architecture and Requirements Engineering.* **New York: Dorset House, 2000.** This book is really about concepts and systems development, especially those involving multiple disciplines. It provides a framework for modeling systems, an architectural model, and a requirements model. The requirements model consists of three submodels (the entity model, process model, and control model) and their supporting specifications. There is a good explanation of the role of the system architect/system engineer (pp. 200–201). The authors use case studies of a hospital's patient-monitoring system and of a multidisciplinary groundwater analysis system to illustrate their principles. An appendix describes misconceptions of the Hatley/Pirbhai methods.

Christine Hofmeister, Robert Nord, and Dilip Soni. *Applied Software Architecture.* **Reading, MA: Addison-Wesley, 2000.** This book is another in Addison-Wesley's Object Technology Series. It provides practical guidelines and techniques for producing quality designs, focusing on four views—conceptual, module, execution, and code. Part III presents four architectures developed by the authors at Siemens Corporate Research in Princeton, New Jersey. Hofmeister and colleagues provide examples of what goes into the architecture, the engineering concerns addressed, and how notation is used to describe it. Design trade-offs made by the different architects to solve architectural issues are presented.

W. H. Inmon, John A. Zachman, and Jonathan G. Geiger. *Data Stores, Data Warehousing, and the Zachman Framework: Managing Enterprise Knowledge.* **New York: McGraw Hill, 1997.** One of the keys to success for modern corporations is access to the right information at the right time at the right place in the right form. The Zachman Framework was formally published in 1987 to describe an architecture for capturing the aspects of an information system. The Zachman Framework is a model that major organizations can use to view and communicate their enterprise information infrastructure. One of the major applications of the Zachman Framework is to help companies to migrate from legacy systems. It helps companies attain knowledge so that they can be more responsive to change and better poised to compete.

Ivar Jacobson, Martin Griss, and Patrick Jonsson. *Software Reuse: Architecture Process and Organization for Business Success.* **New York: ACM Press, 1997.** The authors' vision is that this book will facilitate the practice of object-oriented component-based software engineering. Their belief is that systematic, large-scale reuse, coupled with object technology, is the only way to improve radically the process of software development. Substantial degrees of reuse can be achieved only by radically changing traditional software architectures and development processes. Jacobson and colleagues emphasize that object technology does not yield reuse automatically. An explicit reuse agenda and a systematic approach to design and process are required to achieve a high level of reuse. They provide a framework called the Reuse-Driven Software Engineering Business (RSEB). The work is based on Jacobson's **use case-driven** architecture and process modeling. An appendix addresses the use of the Unified Modeling Language in the RSEB.

Paul Kaminski. *Reducing Life Cycle Costs for New and Fielded Systems.* **Office of the Deputy Undersecretary of Defense for Aquisition Reform. December 4, 1995.** This is a memorandum for the secretaries of the military department and others that describes the DoD policy and strategy to develop and field affordable weapons systems. It includes the CAIV Working Group paper that describes the CAIV approach. See also http://www.acq.osd.mil/ar/.

Rick Kazman and S. Jeromy Carriere. "Playing Detective: Reconstructing Software Architecture from Available Evidence." *Automated Software Engineering,* **1999;6:107–138.** New systems development efforts are often constrained by existing legacy applications. Analysts need to be able to extract information from existing systems to use to develop architectures. This paper presents Dali—an open, lightweight **workbench**[18]—that aids an analyst in extracting, manipulating,

---

[18]A workbench is a suite of development tools. Doug Smith has provided some examples of a workbench: http://www.spr.com/Products/FP_Workbench/fp_workbench.htm: Function Point Workbench is a Windows-based tool that expedites function point analysis by providing facilities to store, update, and analyze individual counts. http://www.hallogram.com/devworkbench/: Actuate Developer Workbench is an integrated e.Report development environment that enables developers to create quickly e.Report designs that access any data source and present information in any conceivable layout. Developer Workbench offers a productive, visual development environment but also offers developers the added flexibility and power of a programming language to create complex designs. http://www.atg.com/products/das/ddw.html: The Dynamo Developer Workbench is a visual developer tool with built-in wizards that allows application developers to assemble and configure prebuilt components rapidly into full-blown, deployable, scalable applications. (See http://www.pqsystems.com/qwpover.htm) Quality Workbench Professional helps you keep day-to-day control over your quality system. It features document control, audit tracking, nonconformity and corrective action records, and document management via the Internet.

and interpreting architectural information. Kazman and Carriere emphasize that no tool is right for all jobs and that no extraction technique is useful without user interaction.

Henry Petroski. *To Engineer Is Human.* **New York: St. Martin's Press, 1992.** Petroski provides insights into engineering failures. He believes that understanding failure is central to understanding engineering, because engineering design has as its objective the obviation of failure. This is an interesting and important construct in the context of systems and software engineering.

Eberhardt Rechtin and Mark W. Maier. *The Art of System Architecting.* **New York: CRC Press, 1997.** Rechtin and Maier provide a table with almost 200 **heuristics** for systems-level architecting, providing access to the underpinnings of principal design guidelines. For example, "a system will develop and evolve much more rapidly if there are stable intermediate forms than if there are not." They note that software is rapidly becoming the centerpiece of complex system design, in the sense that an increasing fraction of system performance and complexity is captured in software. Rechtin and Maier discuss both the architecting of software and the impact of software on system architecting.

Eberhardt Rechtin. *Systems Architecting of Organizations: Why Eagles Can't Swim.* **New York: CRC Press, 1999.** Rechtin addresses this book to the challenge of maintaining organizational survival and excellence while adjusting to the new world of global communications, transportation, economics, and multinational security. He identifies factors that can lead to excellence in one field or period of time, but to potential weaknesses in another, and offers insights to address these factors.

Software Engineering Institute. *The Architecture Tradeoff Analysis Method.* **1999.** Available at http://www.sei.cmu.edu/activities/ata/ATAM/tsld004.htm. The purpose of the Architecture Tradeoff Analysis Method is to assess the consequences of architectural decision alternatives in light of quality attribute requirements.

The Chief Information Officers (CIO) Council. *Federal Enterprise Architectural Framework.* **Version 1.1. September 1999.** Available at http://www.itpolicy.gsa.gov/mke/archplus/archhome.htm. This framework was developed beginning in April 1998 to promote shared development for common U.S. government processes, **interoperability** and sharing of information among government agencies and other entities. The Clinger-Cohen Act of 1996 assigned CIOs with the responsibility to develop IT architectures. The framework consists of approaches, models, and definitions for communicating the overall organization and relationships of architecture components required for developing and maintaining a Federal Enterprise Architecture. It utilizes the National Institute of Standards and Technology Enterprise Architecture Model.

The Open Group. *The Open Group's Architectural Framework (TOGAF).* Available at http://www.opengroup.org/public/arch/. TOGAF is a tool for defining an IT architecture. TOGAF was developed by The Open Group's own members, working within the TOGAF Program. The original development of TOGAF in 1995 was based on the Technical Architecture Framework for Information Management (TAFIM), developed by the U.S. DoD. The DoD gave The Open Group explicit permission and encouragement to create TOGAF by building on the TAFIM, which itself was the result of many years of development effort and many millions of dollars of U.S. government investment. Starting from this foundation, the members of The Open Group's TOGAF Program developed successive versions of TOGAF in subsequent years and published each version on The Open Group's public Web site. If you are new to the field of IT architecture and/or TOGAF, you may find it worthwhile to read the set of frequently asked questions at this Web site. Here you will find answers to questions such as what is an architectural framework and what are the benefits to an organization by using TOGAF.

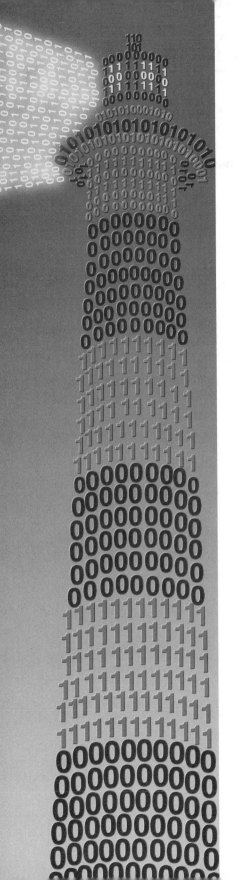

CHAPTER SEVEN

Use a Mechanism to Maintain Project Communication

Commit to the approach.
Establish and utilize a joint team responsible for the requirements.
Define the *real* customer needs.
Use and continually improve a requirements process.
Iterate the system requirements and architecture repeatedly.
Use a mechanism to maintain project communication.
Select familiar methods and maintain a set of work products.
Perform requirements verification and validation.
Provide an effective mechanism to accommodate requirements changes.
Perform the development effort using known, familiar proven industry, organizational, and project best practices.

This chapter stresses the critical importance of having effective communications and coordination with your customers, between and among all project groups and subcontractors, and between all performers on a project. Suggestions for how to achieve effective communications are provided.

Setting the Stage

Have you ever worked on a project in which the people were competent and committed but progress was hindered because of a lack of communication and coordination? I have! *It turns out that effective communication is a key ingredient in achieving project success.* This is hardly surprising. What is surprising is that program and project managers (PMs) often don't take proactive steps to ensure or at least foster effective communication.

In my own experience, one of the most difficult challenges in a system or software development project is to keep members of the technical teams aware of what the other is doing and to ensure that these efforts are mutually supportive and coordinated.[1]

Natural Human Tendency

The natural human tendency is for individuals to focus on their own work activities and do their best to get the needed work done. There are some problems with this approach though:

- *My* understanding of what I need to do to support the team best may not be accurate or consistent with the perception of other members of the team or my manager.
- Requirements, plans, processes, mechanisms, methods, techniques, and tools change. How am I to stay up to date?
- My work may dovetail closely with someone else's. How do I relate what I'm doing in a way that best supports the people working in related areas of the project and vice versa?

---

[1]Note that intergroup coordination is a key process area for level 3 of the Capability Maturity Model for Software. See Paulk and colleagues, *Key Practices of the Capability Maturity Model*, pp. L3-83 to L3-93 for several suggestions and ideas concerning how to provide effective coordination. Intergroup coordination is typically a weak area on projects.

These concerns and issues suggest the need for a mechanism to manage the project in a coordinated, effective manner.

A Proactive Approach to Achieve Effective Communication

What would be a proactive step to achieve project communication and coordination? The necessary goal is to ensure effective communication and coordination with the customer and between the leads of each of the groups on the project throughout the development effort:

- Project management
- Systems engineering
- Requirements engineering
- Software development
- Configuration management
- Quality assurance
- Integration and test
- Documentation
- All subcontractors
- Other groups specific to the project not listed here, such as project control/ budget or planning/tracking

Providing information to the *lead* for a group does not necessarily mean that the information gets to the *members* of that group. Accordingly, it's important for the PM and the chairs of project teams to emphasize an attitude and expectation of open and full communication and coordination. Successful projects are characterized by documentation of their work activities and work products. For example, it's important that meeting minutes are taken and made available in a timely manner. These and other documentation artifacts should be readily accessible by all project performers in the project's electronic library.

A related issue is that effective communication is difficult. The same words can mean different things to different people because of a host of factors. The topic of effective communication is beyond the scope of this book. However, the expectation by organizations and project leaders in conveying that it is each person's responsibility to communicate effectively can go a long way to minimizing the impact of communication issues.

The goal of effective communication can be facilitated by utilizing a project subteam consisting of the PM, the leads for each of the groups, the leads for each subcontractor, and possibly a customer representative. It's less important what you call it than that this mechanism is provided. One approach that has been used successfully is to call this subteam the project configuration control board (CCB).

An Example Mechanism

Recall the inclusion of the project CCB mechanism in the sample requirements process presented in Chapter 5. Figure 7-1 is the requirements macro (high-level) process.

Note that the process flowchart in Figure 7-1 indicates that the project is managed by the project CCB, which provides a mechanism for close and continuous communication and coordination of all of the groups supporting the project.

Other CCBs may be utilized on a project, such as a CCB to control hardware or software baselines. The project CCB (or whatever you choose to call it) is responsible for ensuring that decisions are made with the participation and involvement of all groups affected, that information concerning all decisions reaches all project team members, and that everybody knows what's going on. No doubt you can understand and appreciate the value of this mechanism based on your own experience in trying to get things done in organizations and on projects.

Some challenge the approach of involving a customer representative on the project CCB. After all, how can we possibly talk candidly and air our dirty laundry with our customers right there in the room? The truth is, if there are any issues or problems (and there always are), the customer probably senses them and, in any case, will learn about them eventually. *Why not utilize the experience, perspective, and resources from the customer to help address the issues and problems?* Involving the customer along the way enables the customer to understand how the issues and problems developed. Most likely, the problems have a customer aspect to them. Often, the customer representative can take actions to mitigate problems and risks through initiatives and efforts by customer folks. If we are blessed with a customer representative who has decision-making authority, this can be a tremendous help in having actions taken that further strengthen and improve our joint team effort. Recall the "partnership agreement" in which both parties agreed to be committed jointly to project success. This partnering can be effective not only for a custom development environment but also for a product development environment.

Utilizing the joint team itself as the project CCB is workable, providing that all groups and subcontractors are represented. On a small project the joint team and/or project CCB can be as small as two people. *The use of a mechanism for project coordination will reduce the risks of information not being known to project participants.*

Figure 7-1 The Requirements Macroprocess

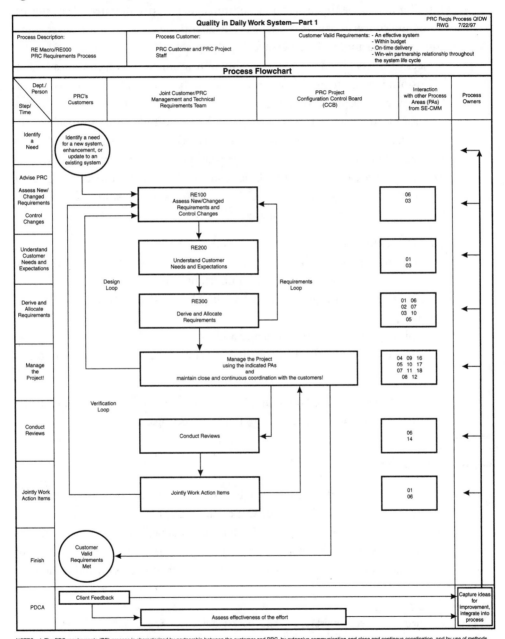

NOTES: 1. The PRC requirements (RE) process is characterized by partnership between the customer and PRC, by extensive communication and close and continous coordination, and by use of methods and tools to gain an increasingly more robust understanding of customer needs and expectations throughout the system life cycle.
2. The project CCB consists of the project manager and the leads from all involved engineering groups. This is a mechanism to manage the project in a coordinated, effective manner. It could include a customer representative; be the "Joint Team," and on a small project even be one or two people.
3. There are two entrance points to RE200: one from the initial assessment and another representing changes requested by the customer after the initial assessment.
4. The composition of the members of the Joint Team may change over the course of the system development effort as different levels are defined and addressed.
5. The requirements produced by the RE process will be impacted and changed by activities in the system architecture process.

Regular meetings (most often, weekly) of the project CCB provide a mechanism for managing the project in a coordinated, effective manner. Ideas, suggestions, and concerns can be brought to the attention of the project leaders, and a commonsense approach can evolve. It helps greatly if all of the members of the project CCB have been trained in quality improvement (QI) techniques such as brainstorming, multivoting, root cause analysis, barriers-and-aids analysis, countermeasures, and process management.[2] Another key contributor to the effectiveness of any team is the knowledge, training, attitude, and approach of the *team leader,* who does not necessarily have to be the PM. Because the PM is often saddled with a variety of additional organizational duties and responsibilities, as well as being responsible for the project, she may designate someone else as the project CCB chairperson or team leader. In my experience, some of the characteristics of an effective CCB chair are

- Good planning and organizational skills
- A good sense of what's important so that an inordinate amount of time and attention isn't focused on the less important aspects
- Able to look at the big picture (what's best for the overall team)
- Tact
- Able to gain everyone's confidence and support
- Able to negotiate effectively off-line to bring about consensus and to facilitate team progress

The ideal situation is when the PM is actively involved with project management responsibilities and participates in these meetings.

When Negativism Shows Up

How does one deal with the project CCB member who is always being negative? We often run into this situation in our work efforts, don't we? There's always at least one individual who says things can't be done; that management hasn't done this or that; that others can't be depended on; that the customer has caused all manner of dysfunction by doing (or not doing) x, y, and z, and the list goes on and on and on.

---

[2]Six Sigma Qualtec publishes a useful pocket guide, *QI Story: Tools and Techniques, A Guidebook to Problem Solving,* that provides a concise description of these tools. To order copies, contact Six Sigma Qualtec at 480-586-2600. Another useful pocket guide of tools for continuous improvement is *The Memory Jogger,* written by Brassard and Ritter, and published by GOAL/QPC.

Here is an opportunity to exercise some leadership and foster team synergy! I may respond to negativism by observing that it's my responsibility to affect the actions that I can influence, to put forward my best efforts, and to take the attitude that the glass is half full rather than half empty. By following through on this theme tactfully but firmly and persistently, one can usually turn someone around or, at the very least, keep him from perturbing teamwork. It is extremely helpful if many or most members of the team have been trained in interpersonal skills, team leader or team building, building relationships as the foundation for all successful endeavors, and similar training experiences.[3] This is another example of the value of providing training.

Another Valuable Mechanism—Brown Bags

Another mechanism that is very effective in maintaining intergroup coordination is to provide a series of informal lunchtime "brown bag" presentations at which each engineering group briefs the others concerning current efforts and activities. The typical result is that a few lightbulbs will go off in each session: "I didn't realize your group was doing that. We need to get together and talk!" Other effective mechanisms to facilitate communication include the joint team, the partnering workshop, requirements workshops, and the project CCB.

Guidelines for Effective Meetings

We know from our experience that we must manage meetings carefully. We spend a lot of time preparing for, leading, and attending meetings. Many practitioners believe that there is a huge waste of resources consumed in meetings.[4] Consider the following guidelines for effective meetings:

---

[3]One training experience that has made a big difference in my life is a one-day seminar provided by Steven Gaffney titled *The Fish Isn't Sick . . . The Water Is Dirty*. Gaffney challenges each participant to select for the coursework during a one-day workshop the worst relationship each participant has at that moment. He then proceeds to provide a process to allow you to turn it around. I picked two—both worked!

[4]Ivy Hooks noted in her review of this manuscript that she reduced attendance at meetings by more than half when she was a manager. This allowed people to maintain focus on their work activities, rather than be required to attend meetings. Also, during meetings, she committed to providing needed information to participants within 24 hours of the meeting to be responsive to the needs to maintain momentum of project efforts. Finally, she instituted an appeal process to enable differences of opinion to be addressed and resolved.

1. Prior to organizing a meeting, consider whether the meeting is really needed. For example, can the needed coordination be accomplished by calling one or a few people, by sending an e-mail message, or through personal informal contact?

2. Limit participants to those required to accomplish the purpose of the meeting.

3. The individual requesting the meeting ("meeting host") should prepare a brief statement in advance of the meeting indicating: (1) the *purpose* and location of the meeting; (2) the *agenda* for the meeting, indicating who is responsible for each topic; and (3) the *time limit* of the meeting or "PAL" (purpose, agenda, and limit). Creating the PAL necessitates thinking through what needs to be addressed and accomplished before and during the meeting. Distributing the PAL prior to the meeting facilitates preparation by other participants, ensures everyone knows where the meeting will be held, and helps ensure that the time in the meeting is utilized well (a "quality meeting").

4. The agenda should reflect the planned time and the time limit for specific topics. This approach enables participants who don't need to be present for the entire meeting to attend the meeting for a more limited amount of time when their presence is needed.

5. The time and time limits of agenda items need to be controlled by the meeting leader.

6. The organization or project should establish expectations that all meetings will begin and end on time. **Institutionalization** of this value not only saves time but also demonstrates respect for other people.

7. Meeting leaders should start the meeting at the scheduled time. This habit results in people showing up a minute or two early.

8. At the beginning of the meeting, a "recorder" should be designated to take minutes of the meeting. The PAL document can reflect the individuals who have acted in this role at previous meetings by indicating the dates each person has served as recorder at the top of the PAL. This approach facilitates sharing this responsibility so that one individual is not saddled with this task continuously.

9. During any meeting, tasks that require action and follow-up will be identified. These should be added to the project's or team's *Action Item (AI) List* that is included in the meeting minutes. For each AI, identify what needs to be done, who will do it, and the planned completion date. The AI list should

have a fourth column labeled Date Completed. The meeting host should maintain status information on AIs by checking on this at each meeting.

10. At the end of the meeting, the meeting host should ask the recorder to review the AIs that were created during the meeting. It may be necessary to clarify some AIs. The person to whom the AI is assigned should concur with the assignment and the scheduled completion date. Also, consider spending a few minutes to discuss how the meeting went. What can be done to make things better? This procedure enacts Deming's Plan-Do-Check-Act (PDCA) cycle and gives each person participating in the meeting an opportunity to reflect on the meeting and comment in a spirit of continuous improvement. The meeting host can simply indicate, "Let's do PDCA," approximately 10 to 15 minutes prior to the scheduled meeting ending time. In my experience, many excellent ideas have resulted from performing PDCA.

It's likely that your organization or project can become more efficient and effective by applying these meeting guidelines, tailored as appropriate for your environment. You will observe that use of these guidelines contributes to better morale. People appreciate being respected and valued, and implementation and application of meeting guidelines communicates that people are being appreciated and valued. This contributes to a positive work environment and also facilitates work force retention.

Guidelines for Effective E-mail Communication[5]

Reading and writing e-mail has become a major time eater. Here are some guidelines for effective e-mail communication[6]:

1. Try not to let reading and writing e-mail become your top-priority task. Use the automatic preview feature to scan for critical or urgent e-mail messages twice or more daily, and then tackle your priority tasks for the day before

---

[5]With thanks to Craig Hollenbach, Doug Smith, Earl Hoovler, Penny Waugh, Barb Dreon, and Bette Rutherford (all of Litton PRC) for their inputs and suggestions.

[6]Visit the following Web sites for more information: *Writing Effective E-mail,* available at http://www.delta.edu/~anburke/emtips.html; Netiquette home page, http://www.albion.com/netiquette/index.html. Lists/reviews of Netiquette sites: http://www.go.com/WebDir/Technology/E_mail/E_mail_etiquette, http://email.about.com/internet/email/cs/netiquette/index.htm.

becoming consumed by reading and writing e-mail messages. Don't allow any e-mail (or telephone call) to preempt your priority tasks automatically.

2. Don't compose an e-mail message unless it is needed.

3. Be as concise as possible.

4. Send your e-mail only to those who need to take action on it. By limiting the distribution to those with a "need to know," we support everyone's need to keep up with e-mail flow. This also supports overall productivity.

5. Copy only those who really need to know. An exception is e-mail messages that are intended to share information requiring broad distribution in support of effective communication and teamwork. We don't want to create an impression inadvertently that we are withholding information or limiting sharing of general information to a few key people.

6. Respond promptly to e-mail appropriate to your activities.

7. Before sending "All project" e-mail, consider whether it is really necessary for everyone to be provided the information.

8. Try to capture the essence of your e-mail message in the subject line. For example, if the e-mail is a reminder for people to attend an important meeting, put the meeting name, date, time, and location in the subject line. Reminders are good because people need them. You may not need to say anything in the body of the message! Another approach is to send a meeting reminder with AIs and assignments early enough so that the procrastinators can get them done before the meeting, but not so early that they continue to procrastinate. Make announcements "just in time." Sending things too early means people just forget about them.

9. Try to summarize in the first few lines of the message the purpose of the e-mail (beyond that captured in the subject), the requested action to be taken, and its urgency or deadline. Then provide details. This allows readers who preview e-mail to understand better if they need to respond, the urgency and nature of the response needed, or if the communication is primarily for information purposes.

10. Be wary of writing e-mail that you would not be willing to have distributed as a memo on the company letterhead. For example, jokes without your facial gestures can be misinterpreted even when :-) gets added, and irate comments once committed to text can take on a life of their own. Be professional in writing e-mail even when being informal. If e-mail received seems inflammatory in nature, consider communicating by phone or in person to diffuse potential tension, and do this always after you have had a chance to

calm down. It is much easier to press the Send button for an ill-considered e-mail message than it is to take it back.

11. Consider putting the most important information in the first paragraph. This is good for several reasons:

    - People tire of reading long messages.
    - Verbiage in the front is read first and probably more than any other text.
    - Some e-mail clients preview only the first 50 words, so if it doesn't say it in 50 words or less, it won't be read.
    - It demonstrates respect for people to be terse and to the point because everyone's time is valuable.

12. Review the sender and subject matter before opening e-mail. If the e-mail message appears to be a mass mailing or the subject matter is not relevant to your job, delete the message without opening it.

13. Some meetings that are meant just to disburse information are better handled via e-mail.

14. Use the "out-of-office" feature to advise others when you are not going to be in the office. This alerts senders that they may need to contact someone else or make a note to contact you when you return. Also, suggest an alternative point of contact who may be able to address time-sensitive or critical topics.

15. If you are going to be out of the office for several days, consider taking your computer and dealing with e-mail daily. This helps reduce the impact of returning to the office to face hundreds of e-mail messages.

16. Consider including content in the body of the e-mail message, rather than as an attachment.

17. After opening an e-mail message, deal with it then. Don't put it in a folder "to be worked on later." This tactic makes the best use of your time in the long run because you don't have to deal with the same event twice or more. Also, it relieves some stress concerning all of those "to do's" that "need to be done."

18. Use the importance option tag appropriately to help others determine their need to read an e-mail message.

19. Use the meeting scheduler feature. Keep your electronic calendar current to allow others to know your availability.

20. In a lengthy e-mail message, summarize the rest of the message in the opening paragraph so that people can jump to the part that is important to them.

- Underline or use a bold font to highlight tasks you are asking people to perform. If you don't make it obvious, they won't see it.
- Regularly ask people if they prefer to be dropped from your e-mail list.
- Use tracking options judiciously.

21. Use the "Reply to All" even more judiciously. How many e-mail messages have we seen in which people just say "me too" or inadvertently send a personal response to a blanket request?

22. Don't use e-mail for sensitive or emotional topics, and consider using emoticons ("smileys") when you say something you intend to be humorous.

23. If your recipients don't all use a common suite of e-mail and office applications, conform to the lowest common denominator, which may include

- Formatting (may not have support for bold, underline, tabs, fixed versus proportional font, HTML)
- Special characters (bullets, curly quotation marks, fractions, line feeds)
- Application file formats (for example, documents in PDF, RTF, or text; using "Save As" for earlier versions of the software)
- Line lengths of 65, 72, or 80 characters with hard carriage returns
- Support for only a single attached file

24. Identify yourself with a *short* (four lines or less) signature file that includes your e-mail address.

25. Adopt and institutionalize organizational e-mail guidelines:

- Use graphics, clip art, or rich text formatting (different fonts, large type sizes, and so on) judiciously. See Figure 7-2 for some guidelines on the use of graphics in e-mail messages.

Figure 7-2   Guidelines for Use of Graphics in E-mail Messages

Messages are often sent out over e-mail services that contain graphics or clip art or use rich text formatting (different fonts, large type sizes, etc.). The use of graphics in many cases does enhance the overall look of a message and may also improve readership. However, there is a definite downside to using graphics that everyone should be sensitive to: the negative impact of the size of a graphic-laden message on the speed of opening these messages and the space taken up in an individual's mailbox.

Most people have limited mailbox storage, and when they receive a message containing graphics (e.g., organizational logos, clip art, etc.), their storage limit may be exceeded, thus preventing further use of the service without first deleting messages to get back under the storage threshold. Opening a large e-mail message can be a time-consuming process for employees connected remotely. Here are some basic guidelines for the use of graphics in e-mail messages:

- Check the file size of any graphic you wish to embed or attach to a message. If it's larger than 100Kb, it will take time.
- Consider who your audience is. Is your message going to a large distribution? If your image(s) are large, you may need to forgo embedded graphics or compress them first before including or attaching them.
- HTML messages are good for broadcast e-mails because they are typically smaller (less than 20K) and can have several embedded graphics and backgrounds. Once you open an HTML message, all the graphics are linked to a shared location (typically a Web server). For a slower connect modem user, this is good news, because you can open the text portion of the message quickly and then you link to a Web server for the graphics. Note that there is added effort and preparation time to create HTML messages.

MS Office 2000 has HTML as a "Save as . . ." option, which provides senders with familiar applications and the ability to design new or transform existing templates. The only added step would be to place the linking graphics in a shared folder or Web server. Microsoft has more details on this at

<http://officeupdate.microsoft.com/2000/articles/oldecorativeHTMLemail.htm>
<http://officeupdate.microsoft.com/2000/articles/olhtmlpictures.htm>

HTML messages can be read with Outlook 97 and Express 4.0. HTML messages are also ideal for "Outlook for the Web" users because you are already in an HTML-savvy browser.

The use of graphics, clip art, and rich text format in e-mail messages is part of today's business culture. Given the potential negative impact to your fellow coworkers, they should be used wisely and judiciously.

- Don't send large enclosures. Rather, advise of the availability of large documents so that only those individuals who really need them can request them. Utilize the Internet and intranets to provide links to large documents.

26. Minimize the use of e-mail for announcing standard meetings and whether a particular system is off-line or on-line (schedule regular downtime when the system is minimally needed).
27. Discourage use of e-mail for personal uses ("Your lights are on," "Farewell," tickets for games and shows, chain letters, and fundraisers).
28. Consider customizing your options by selecting automatic spellcheck before sending e-mail messages.
29. Discourage forwarding of general information that may result in people receiving duplicates of announcements and so forth.
30. Don't try to settle conflicts through e-mail. Rather, work in person with the individual involved.
31. If you are addressing a problem through e-mail, always ensure it is addressed at the lowest level before escalating to the next level.
32. Don't assume that an e-mail message has been received. Technical problems may prevent receipt.
33. Use mixed case and fonts that are sized to make it easy to read (10 to 12 points, depending on the font). Oversized fonts and ALL CAPS can often give the impression you are SHOUTING. ☺[7]

The Value of a Common Vocabulary

It's valuable for the participants in a project to agree on a set of common vocabulary. This helps ensure that everyone on the project is using words in the same way. One way to accomplish this is for all participants to contribute to a draft project glossary. A QI team can be tasked with the responsibility to reach consensus on all terms. A peer review of their work product will help resolve contested definitions. The peer review moderator can decide on a definition when the group can't or won't reach consensus. The final work product can be released for project use, recognizing that nothing is ever perfect.

---

[7]A table displaying a set of emoticons is available at http://www.albion.com/netiquette/book/0963702513p59.html.

The Use of Vertical Experts

Rob Sabourin (President, AmiBug.com, Inc.) provided an example of this technique. When defining product requirements, Purkinje, Inc. (a Montreal-based medical software company) relies on the inputs of medical professionals including doctors, nurses, and other clinicians. A pool of several hundred vertical market experts is used to elaborate and quantify these needs depending on the medical specialty, venue, geography, and other attributes. What may appear to a software engineer as a nuance can mean life or death to a patient. How can one describe an attribute such as color, texture, flexibility, or sound in such a way that it has precise medical meaning? What is recorded at the point of care must be clear and semantically correct.

Very often needs are difficult to quantify or to state objectively because they relate to the manner in which medical knowledge is represented, to be used at the point of care by physicians writing a clinical note. Medical knowledge-driven requirements are elaborated in a structure that ensures that business needs are met, the knowledge base evolves, and representation may be used in the general market.

Product management defines business needs as stated by the customer and tries to get as much context data as possible to support the need. For example if a new area of knowledge representation is needed, will it be used for inpatient or ambulatory care?

A team of knowledge engineers works with product management to identify which specific medical expertise may be required. Doctors from the knowledge engineering team consult with doctors at the customer site—to review as peers— what is required. Is the scope consistent? Is the business need a real requirement as stated? What is discovered is the real medical need. Knowledge engineers, with the support of specialty experts, develop a detailed proposal of the knowledge representation, which then must be validated by external experts to ensure no conflicts or omissions are found. It is only at this time that the knowledge will be "developed" or "implemented" in the clinical note writer.

In Sabourin's experience, there were no clear answers to disagreements among vertical experts. There was widespread disagreement concerning what was required. It is therefore very important that the requirements engineer be very objective and attempt to separate and iterate among vertical professionals to achieve good requirements.

Avoid Multiple Locations

A factor that complicates development efforts is not having all members of the development team at one physical location. One can argue that in today's environment, technology and communications capabilities overcome this potential problem. However, in my experience, not having all members of the technical team at the same physical location is a significant risk that complicates communication and coordination extraordinarily. In one situation, having engineering efforts at two different physical locations was a major contributing factor to a failed project. Consider this risk seriously and mitigate it extensively.

A Final Recommendation

As I have emphasized, system requirements are critical because they provide the basis for all of the follow-on development effort. Accordingly, I recommend that all requirements outputs and products

- Pass through the project CCB
- Are accorded full-up (formal) configuration management

These mechanisms ensure that added attention is given to requirements outputs and products and that the strongest control of them is provided. This will help keep the requirements in control and will facilitate maintaining control of the project.

Summary

Effective communications and coordination are prerequisites to project success. Proactive steps should be taken to foster effective communication. The natural human tendency is to work hard but somewhat in isolation from related activities. A project CCB can provide a mechanism for close and continuous communication and coordination of all of the groups supporting a project. The use of a mechanism for project coordination will reduce the risks of information not being known to project participants. Regular meetings (most often weekly) of the project CCB provide a way to manage the project in a coordinated, effective manner. Another mechanism that is very effective in maintaining intergroup coordination is to provide a series of lunchtime "brown bag" presentations, at which each engineering group briefs the others concerning current efforts and activities. Other techniques include newsletters and off-site workshops or retreats. Organizations and projects can increase efficiency and effectiveness by institutionalizing the suggested guidelines for effective meetings. Individuals can improve their productivity and effectiveness by applying the guidelines for effective e-mail use. Institutionalization of both sets of guidelines not only saves time and money but also contributes to creating a positive work environment, high morale, and retention. Any project is well advised to identify clearly a common vocabulary. Using vertical experts can be a valuable technique to elaborate the understanding of needs and to clarify the meaning of words. The role of the requirements engineer is critical to the objective statement of requirements.

Key References and Suggested Readings

Michael Brassard and Diane Ritter. *The Memory Jogger II: A Pocket Guide of Tools for Continuous Improvement & Effective Planning.* **Salem, NH: GOAL/ QPC, 1994.** Also available at http://www.goalqpc.com. This pocket-size book is useful for process engineers and others involved in QI. It provides concise summaries of quality tools including the Gantt chart, control chart, flowchart, activity network diagram, check sheet, force field analysis, prioritization matrices, run chart, and scatter diagram. A tool selector chart that organizes the tools according to typical improvement situations is provided.

Jo Condrill and Bennie Bough. *101 Ways to Improve Your Communication Skills.* **Alexandria, VA: Goal Minds, 1998.** This book provides straightforward techniques to facilitate communication. It discusses *mind mapping*—a system of recording thoughts so that we employ both left-brain and right-brain thinking (p. 35). Condrill and Bough provide advice for speaking and writing, with appropriate emphasis on behavioral topics. They also provide a great list of sources for further reading (pp. 106–107).

Larry Constantine. *Constantine on Peopleware.* **Englewood Cliffs, NJ: Prentice-Hall, 1995.** Constantine provides insightful ideas concerning human issues in software development, including quality and productivity, teamwork, group dynamics, project management and organizational issues, interface design, human-machine interaction, cognition, and psychology. The book includes 30 articles. Among the topics discussed are group development (decisions, roles, space, time management), cowboys and cowgirls (teams and mavericks), work organization (seven different models), tools and methods (computer-aided software engineering, modeling, human-computer interface, methods), process improvements (visibility, reuse, just in time, quality), software usability (consistency/conventions, complexity, scope creep, languages, usability, objects), and brave new software (interfaces, wizards, future faces).

Michael Doyle and David Straus. *How to Make Meetings Work.* **East Rutherford, NJ: Berkeley Publishing, 1993.** Doyle and Straus observe that most organizations spend between 7% and 15% of their personnel budgets on meetings (this does not include time spent preparing for meetings or attending training programs or conferences). *Time spent attending a meeting is time taken away from other opportunities!* Doyle and Straus provide a set of tools and techniques to make groups more effective. They advocate the interaction method, which rests on four well-defined roles: the facilitator, the recorder, the group member, and the chairperson. They describe each of these roles and assert that 7 to 15 people is the ideal size for a problem-solving, decision-making meeting. Everyone should know what to expect before coming to a meeting. Doyle and Straus discuss how to make a presentation.

Roger Fisher and Scott Brown. *Getting Together: Building Relationships As We Negotiate.* **New York: Penguin Books, 1988.** Fisher and Brown provide a set of steps that address initiating, negotiating, and sustaining enduring relationships. A strong message is that each of us can make any relationship better if we make the choice to do so.

Milo O. Frank. *How to Run a Successful Meeting in Half the Time.* **New York: Simon and Schuster, 1989.** Frank provides suggestions for all aspects of meetings, offering ideas that will certainly be valuable if applied. We know from our experience that we waste a lot of time in meetings. Why not review these suggestions and make some improvements? Although this book is out of print, it is easily available through second-hand bookshops and the popular electronic booksellers. Meetings can be energizing, productive, and satisfying. Learn how to make them this way, and apply these suggestions to your daily work.

Steven Gaffney. *The Fish Isn't Sick . . . The Water Is Dirty.* **Training seminar.** Available at http://www.stevengaffney.com. This proactive one-day seminar teaches one how to clean up the communication water and establish honest, effective communication with anyone. Gaffney provides a process that has worked every time I've taken the opportunity to use it. He emphasizes the value of acknowledging the other people involved in our lives.

Charles Handy. *Gods of Management: The Changing Work of Organizations.* **New York: Oxford University Press, 1996.** This is an American edition of a book the author wrote in 1978 in England. It provides an insightful view of leadership styles and corporate cultures.

Watts S. Humphrey. *Why Don't They Practice What We Preach?* **1998.** Available at http://www.sei.cmu.edu/publications/articles/sources/practice.preach/index. html. I recommend this article to you for insights concerning why technical people do not use improved methods, even when there is clear evidence that the methods help and there is strong pressure to use them. This seems to be true regardless of the engineer's experience and training. Engineers tend to revert to their established ad hoc and informal practices. Only when they are convinced that a method works by seeing results will they even try a new method. Today's organizations have few role models that consistently demonstrate effective work habits and disciplines. This factor accounts for some of the reasons that industry results have not improved in spite of dramatic improvements in practices, methods, techniques, and tools. Practitioners are advised to read and reflect on Humphrey's insights so that we can develop ways to overcome our failure to take advantage of improvements. McConnell's *After the Gold Rush: Creating a True Profession of Software Engineering* is full of ideas and suggestions to help with this situation. McConnell notes in his epilogue that common development problems won't be avoided without our support.[8]

Otto Kroeger and Janet M. Thuesen (contributor). *Type Talk at Work: How the 16 Personality Types Determine Your Success on the Job.* **New York: Dell Publishing, 1993.** The authors explain how managers, executives, and workers can evaluate personality types and achieve improved job effectiveness. They provide suggestions for how to deal with individuals who are opposite of your type.

Six Sigma Qualtec. *QI Story: Tools and Techniques, A Guidebook to Problem Solving.* **3rd ed. Tempe, AZ: Six Sigma Qualtec, 1999.** This tiny reference book provides a concise and helpful description of the concepts of total quality management and an overview of the seven-step QI story. It also includes summaries of QI tools and techniques such as brainstorming, multivoting, the Pareto chart,

---

[8]McConnell, *After the Gold Rush,* p. 155. This is a great book, perhaps one of the best in software engineering. As noted earlier (Chapter 1), many of the tenets of the software engineering profession apply to systems engineering.

the Ishikawa (fishbone) diagram, countermeasures (solutions), cost-benefit analysis, barriers-and-aids analysis, graphs, histograms, process flowcharts, and control charts. Available from Six Sigma Qualtec, 480-586-2600.

Douglas Stone, Bruce Patton, and Sheila Heen. *Difficult Conversations: How to Discuss What Matters Most.* **New York: Penguin Books, 1999.** It's natural to avoid conversations that cause anxiety and frustration. This book provides an approach for having difficult conversations with less stress and more success. We all bring erroneous but deeply ingrained assumptions into our daily activities. This book provides valuable insights for anyone who works with others.

Gerald M. Weinberg. *Quality Software Management: Congruent Action.* **Vol. 3. New York: Dorset House, 1994.** This book deals with the ability to act appropriately in difficult interpersonal situations—an essential ability for successful software development managers. Weinberg uses simple but effective models to explain human behavior, and he uses examples from the software engineering industry to put these models in contexts familiar to software developers. He draws on his 40 years of work in the industry to discuss various styles of coping (especially under stress), selection of managers, the importance of self-esteem, how to transform incongruent behavior into effective actions, addictive behaviors, and how to create and manage productive teams. He addresses the important question of why people do things wrong when they know how to do them right.

Neal Whitten. *Becoming an Indispensable Employee in a Disposable World.* **Amsterdam: Pfeiffer & Company, 1995.** The author emphasizes the value of capitalizing on key personal traits, such as self-esteem and communication, noting that we mirror our self-expectations! He provides a step-by-step process to becoming a self-directed employee. He also addresses balancing our professional and personal lives. Recommended reading for everyone.

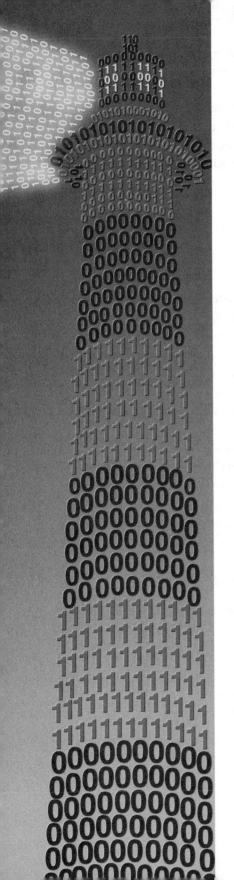

CHAPTER EIGHT

Select Familiar Methods and Maintain a Set of Work Products

Commit to the approach.
Establish and utilize a Joint Team responsible for the requirements.
Define the *real* customer needs.
Use and continually improve a requirements process.
Iterate the system requirements and architecture repeatedly.
Use a mechanism to maintain project communication.
Select familiar methods and maintain a set of work products.
Perform requirements verification and validation.
Provide an effective mechanism to accommodate requirements changes.
Perform the development effort using known, familiar proven industry, organizational, and project best practices.

This chapter shares industry experience concerning the effectiveness of methods and techniques to emerge the real requirements. Also, it urges you to maintain several working documents that *together* describe the set of requirements for your system under levels of configuration control (versions, change control, formal configuration management [CM]).

The Foundation for System Development

Using the joint team mechanism, customer and contractor technical representatives elicit, stimulate, analyze, and communicate customer needs, expectations, and **measures of effectiveness** (MOEs)[1] to obtain a better understanding of what will satisfy the real customer needs. As we have described, the *real requirements* are *not* those initially provided by our customers, nor are they the requirements that we, the development team, understand. Rather, the real requirements *emerge*[2] from concerted efforts by trained requirements engineers, engaged in meaningful communication with customers and users, to *discover* the real customer needs and expectations. The agreed-on needs, expectations, and MOEs form the basis for agreements between the customer and the contractor's engineering effort.

This chapter identifies a large number of methods and techniques that are available to support requirements engineering. In practice, only a few of these methods and techniques have proved most useful. A set of better requirements methods is recommended, based on industry experience. Also, it is recommended that several working documents be maintained that together describe the set of requirements for a system.

What Are the Candidate Methods and Techniques?

Methods and techniques utilized to emerge real requirements may include the following:

---

[1]MOEs are high-level indicators of how well the system performs its functions, defined in the terms and with the same dimensionality of the requirements document. For example, if we are dealing with a city's metro system, we may specify that a typical user during rush hour should not wait more than some period of time, on the average, for the next train.

[2]The word *emerge* (literally, "to become readily perceived, easily understood, and recognized") implies that requirements engineers should work with customers and users so that all can easily understand and recognize the real requirements. This is more proactive than to *discover* (literally, "to make known"). See Goguen, "Requirements Engineering as the Reconciliation of Social and Technical Issues," p. 168, for additional insights.

- Rapid application development (RAD)[3]
- Object-oriented methods
- Joint application design (JAD)
- Use cases (graphic **use case models** and accompanying textual representation of the use cases)
- Market surveys
- Questionnaires
- Customer and user interviews
- Limited capability/rapid prototyping
- Modeling[4]
- Finite-state machines
- State transition diagrams
- User-defined operational scenarios
- Process management
- Joint team meetings
- "Rules of conduct"
- Requirements elicitation methods
- Brainstorming and multivoting
- Quality function deployment (QFD)
- Interface control working groups
- Technical interchange meetings
- Operational scenarios obtained from users
- Prototypes
- Beta testing
- Observation of existing systems, environments, and work flow patterns
- MOEs
- Trade studies
- Mathematical techniques (design of experiments, sensitivity analysis, timing, sizing, Monte Carlo simulation)
- Requirements validation
- System capability concept
- Formal program reviews
- In-process reviews
- Status meetings
- Teleconferences
- Focus groups
- Storyboards

---

[3]Steve McConnell provides a concise definition and description of RAD: "RAD is an information-system-oriented set of practices that are somewhat adaptable to individual circumstances. RAD was defined with some precision when it was introduced in *Rapid Application Development* (Martin 1991) and refers to a combination of JAD sessions, prototyping, SWAT teams, time-boxed deliverables, and Computer-Aided Software Engineering (CASE) tools, all tied together with a fairly well-defined methodology. Because it is a collection of practices rather than a single practice, it can sometimes provide silver bullet-like gains within its specific areas of applicability. But RAD doesn't apply to any kind of unique software-custom, shrink-wrap, or systems software, for example, which tend to be the most problematic kinds. Outside of its origins in database-centered IS systems, RAD has become more of a rallying cry for faster development than a meaningful methodology." *Rapid Development,* p. 366. See also James Martin, *Rapid Application Development.* Bill Wiley provides insights and experience concerning RAD in *Essential System Requirements,* pp. 39–40.

[4]The subject of requirements modeling is beyond the scope of this book. See Beude, *The Engineering Design of Systems: Models and Methods;* Martin, *Systems Engineering Guidebook: A Process for Developing Systems and Products;* and Lubars, et al, "A Review of the State of Practice in Requirements Modeling." The CORE requirements tool has modeling capabilities—see http://www.vtcorp.com.

Input sources for new requirements could include

- Statement of work
- Contract
- Request for proposal, request for information, request for quote
- Environmental, legal, and other constraints
- Letters
- Informal communications

Documented results from the various methods for gathering the requirements information include

- Meeting minutes from requirements clarification meetings, JAD meetings, and other types of user meetings
- Updated working prototypes
- Requirements baselined in an automated tracking tool
- Updated operational concept definition
- Updated requirements document (RD)
- Updated functional description
- Updates to the requirements traceability matrix (RTM) tool based on requirements changes
- Validated systems requirements

Which Methods and Techniques Are Best?

A large set of candidate methods and techniques was just listed. In practice, which methods and techniques have proved best? Capers Jones, Chief Scientist, Software Productivity Research (SPR), Inc., has a comprehensive database for examining these questions. He has collected data from 1984 to 2000 from more than 650 organizations. Approximately 150 of these companies are in the Fortune 500 set, roughly 30 are government/military groups, and the data represent approximately 9,000 projects. The data address methods and techniques for the entire development process, not just requirements. Jones's data show that the most common problem with requirements is that they are incomplete.[5] The rate of

---

[5]Capers Jones, *Estimating Software Costs*, Chapter 17.

creeping requirements (changes after the initial set of requirements is defined) is a major problem.[6] Also, requirements and design defects outnumber code defects.[7]

Here is Jones's list of better requirements methods:[8]

Formal inspections (design and code)	Active quality assurance (>5% quality assurance staff)
JAD	Formal configuration control
QFD	**User satisfaction** surveys
Quality metrics using function points	Formal test planning
Quality metrics using IBM's orthogonal classification	Quality estimation tools
	Automated test tools
Defect removal efficiency measurements	Testing specialists
	Root-cause analysis
Defect tracking tools	

Figure 8-1 provides Jones's evaluation of selected methods in terms of effectiveness and cost.

Additional insights concerning defect prevention methods are provided in Figure 8-2.

Jones advises that the most effective defect prevention method for requirements defects is the construction of a working prototype, with disposable prototypes being much more effective than evolutionary prototypes.[9] Requirements defects are highly resistant to removal; however, formal requirements

---

[6]Ibid. The U.S. average is approximately 2% per month during the design and coding phases. The maximum amount of creep has sometimes topped 150%, so this is a major consideration. Prototyping plus methods such as JAD can reduce this rate to a small fraction, such as 0.5% per month. The fundamental root cause of changing requirements is because applications are expanding the horizon of the ways companies operate.

[7]Briefing by Capers Jones, *Software Quality in 2000: What Works and What Doesn't*, slide 11.

[8]Ibid, slide 19.

[9]Capers Jones, *Estimating Software Costs*, p. 432. Jones's data indicate that prototypes by themselves can reduce creeping requirements by between 10% and 25%.

Figure 8-1   Quality Method Effectiveness and Costs

METHOD	EFFECTIVENESS	COSTS
• Formal Inspections	Very High	High
• Defect Estimation	Very High	Low
• Defect Tracking	High	Low
• Formal Testing	High	High
• QA Organization	High	High
• Independent audits	High	High
• JAD and QFD	High	Low
• Prototyping	High	Low
• Test Case Tools	High	Medium
• Change Tracking	High	Medium
• Informal Walkthroughs	Moderate	Medium
• Informal Testing	Moderate	Medium
• TQM	Moderate	Medium
• ISO 9000-9004	Marginal	High

Figure 8-2   Relative Capability of Methods to Remove Various Types of Defects

	Requirements Defects	Design Defects	Code Defects	Document Defects	Performance Defects
JADs	Excellent	Good	Not Applicable	Fair	Poor
Prototypes	Excellent	Excellent	Fair	Not Applicable	Excellent
Structured Methods	Fair	Good	Excellent	Fair	Fair
Design Tools	Fair	Good	Fair	Fair	Fair
Blueprints & Reusable Code	Excellent	Excellent	Excellent	Excellent	Good
QFD	Good	Excellent	Fair	Poor	Good

inspections have been successfully utilized and deserve more widespread usage, in his view.[10]

Here are some additional comments from Jones concerning highly regarded approaches for requirements[11]:

A number of technologies have been developed [that] can either reduce the rate at which requirements change, or at least make the changes less disruptive. Following are the technologies with positive value in terms of easing the stress of creeping user requirements.

Joint Application Design

Joint application design or JAD is a method for developing software requirements under which user representatives and development representatives work together with a facilitator to produce a joint requirement specification which both sides agree to.

The JAD approach originated in Canada in the 1970s and has now become very common for information systems development. Books, training, and consulting groups that offer JAD facilitation are also very common. Compared [with] the older style of "adversarial" requirements development, JAD can reduce creeping requirements by almost half. The JAD approach is an excellent choice for large software contracts that are intended to automate information systems.

Prototypes

[Because] many changes don't occur until clients or users begin to see the screens and outputs of the application, it is obvious that building early prototypes can move some of these changes to the front of the development cycle instead of leaving them at the end.

Prototypes are often effective in reducing creeping requirements and can be combined with other approaches such as [JAD]. Prototypes by themselves can reduce creeping requirements by somewhere between 10% and about 25%.

---

[10]Ibid, p. 428. After requirements are "complete," downstream activities, such as design inspections, code inspections, and testing are not very effective in removing requirements defects. Indeed, once major defects are embedded in requirements, they tend to be immune to most standard forms of defect removal and are especially resistant to being found via testing. These data argue strongly for a major thesis of this book: that more time and effort need to be focused on the requirements process and on identifying the real requirements.

[11]Ibid, pp. 431–433.

Use Cases[12]

The use case technique deals with the patterns of usage that typical clients are likely to have and, hence, concentrates on clusters of related requirements for specific usage sequences. The advantage of the use case technique is that it keeps the requirements process at a practical level and minimizes the tendency to add "blue-sky" features that are not likely to have many users.

Change Control Boards

Change control boards are not exactly a technology, but rather a group of managers, client representatives, and technical personnel who meet and decide which changes should be accepted or rejected. Change control boards are often encountered in the military software domain and systems software domain, although they are not common for information systems. Such boards are most often encountered for large systems in excess of 10,000 function points in size.

Sabourin[13] advises that usage scenarios, storyboards, and static mockups are used effectively in requirements clarification for Web applications development. These techniques are becoming more mainstream, and they parallel prototyping and use cases.

Jones[14] has analyzed positive and negative factors that influence software productivity, indicating that there are at least 100 known factors that can influence the outcome of software projects. Figure 8-3 provides an analysis of the most positive and the most negative factors.

Jones notes that the influence of the negative productivity factors is not as well covered in the software literature as the influence of the positive factors. He feels that what is most interesting about these data is that the same factor—software reuse—can exert both the largest positive impact and the largest negative impact:

> The critical difference between the positive and negative influences of software reuse can be expressed in one word: Quality. The positive value of software reuse occurs when the reusable artifacts approach or achieve zero defect levels.

---

[12]See the discussion of use cases in Chapter 4.

[13]From Robert Sabourin's review comments of the manuscript for this book, September 13, 2000.

[14]Capers Jones, *Positive and Negative Factors That Influence Software Productivity*, p. 1.

Figure 8-3   Positive and Negative Factors That Influence Software Development Productivity

Impact of Positive Adjustment Factors on Productivity (Sorted in order of maximum positive impact)	
New Development Factors	**Plus Range**
Reuse of high-quality deliverables	350%
High management experience	65%
High staff experience	55%
Effective methods/process	35%
Effective management tools	30%
Effective technical CASE tools	27%
High-level programming languages	24%
Quality estimating tools	19%
Specialist occupations	18%
Effective client participation	18%
Formal cost/schedule estimates	17%
Unpaid overtime	15%
Use of formal inspections	15%
Good office ergonomics	15%
Quality measurement	14%
Low project complexity	13%
Quick response time	12%
Moderate schedule pressure	11%
Productivity measurements	10%
Low requirements creep	9%
Annual training of > 10 days	8%
No geographic separation	8%
High team morale	7%
Hierarchical organization	5%
Sum	800%

(continued)

Figure 8-3   Positive and Negative Factors That Influence Software Development Productivity (*continued*)

Impact of Negative Adjustment Factors on Productivity (Sorted in order of maximum negative impact)

New Development Factors	Minus Range
Reuse of poor-quality deliverables	−300%
Management inexperience	−90%
Staff inexperience	−87%
High requirements creep	−77%
Inadequate technical CASE tools	−75%
No use of inspections	−48%
Inadequate management tools	−45%
Ineffective methods/process	−41%
No quality estimation	−40%
High project complexity	−35%
Excessive schedule pressure	−30%
Slow response time	−30%
Crowded office space	−27%
Low-level languages	−25%
Geographic separation	−24%
Informal cost/schedule estimates	−22%
Generalist occupations	−15%
No client participation	−13%
No annual training	−12%
No quality measurements	−10%
Matrix organization	−8%
No productivity measurements	−7%
Poor team morale	−6%
No unpaid overtime	−0%
Sum	**−1067%**

The negative value of software reuse, on the other hand, will occur if the reusable materials are filled with errors or bugs. Imagine the result of reusing a software module in 50 applications only to discover that it contains a number of high-severity errors [that] trigger massive recalls of every application!

Note that software reuse encompasses much more than just source code. An effective corporate reuse program will include at least these five reusable artifacts:

Reusable requirements

Reusable designs

Reusable source code

Reusable test materials

Reusable user documentation

In order to gain the optimum positive value from software reuse, each major software deliverable should include at least 75% reused material, which is certified and approaches zero defect levels.[15]

Note that the cumulative results of negative adjustment factors are much larger than positive adjustment factors. This means that it is far easier to make mistakes and degrade productivity than it is to get things right and improve productivity.[16] This is an important finding that deserves attention and analysis. The methods to be used on any project and to be institutionalized for any organization should be selected carefully.

Use of Function Points for Software Estimation

Preparing estimates of the effort required to develop software is difficult.[17] It's recommended that for each organization or project a folder or database of

---

[15]Ibid, pp. 5–6.

[16]Ibid, p. 6.

[17]William Roetzheim's experience and work have convinced him that more projects are doomed by poor cost and schedule estimates than by technological, political, or team problems. "Few organizations understand that software estimating can be a science and that it is possible to predict accurately and consistently development life cycle costs and schedules for a wide range of projects," p. 66. See Roetzheim's four-part series in *Software Development Magazine* beginning in October 2000 with his article "Estimating Software Costs." The other three installments are "Project Cost Adjustments," "Dealing with Reuse," and "Creating the Project Plan."

the estimates developed be maintained, and each should work toward continuous improvement of the approach used to develop the estimates. Function point analysis (FPA) is a useful method. FPA is based on requirements and creates reasonably equivalent estimates when counted by different people at different times. The International Function Point Users Group (IFPUG) was established in 1986.[18] Trained and experienced analysts using the approach described in the current *IFPUG Function Point Counting Practices Manual* should perform FPA.

Quality Function Deployment

I found myself in an interesting dilemma in addressing this method. Mark Paulk encouraged me to provide more information about it. Capers Jones reported that QFD is not widely deployed or used. Richard Zultner reported widespread, effective use of QFD.

QFD began in the mid 1960s in Japan as a quality system focused on developing products and services that satisfy customers. Jones provides a description of QFD and a "status report" on its use in his book *Software Quality: Analysis and Guidelines for Success* (1997). He notes that QFD is a structured group activity that involves clients and product development personnel. QFD is sometimes called "the house of quality" because one of the main kinds of planning matrices resembles the peaked roof of a house. Only approximately a dozen of SPR's clients utilize QFD for software, and they are all high-technology manufacturing companies. The sample of QFD for software projects was less than 20 (out of 7,000) in 1997, and all were in environments providing fairly sophisticated quality control approaches. Jones concludes that the more recent experiences with QFD for software are favorable enough so that this methodology can be added to the list of approaches with good to excellent results, although the sample size is small enough so that caution is indicated.

Smith and Reinertsen, in *Developing Products in Half the Time* (1998), discuss *blitz QFD*. Bicknell and Bicknell's *The Road Map to Repeatable Success: Using QFD to Implement Change* provides a comprehensive review of QFD and shows how it can be used at all levels of an organization. Ramaswami of Global Technology

---

[18]See IFPUG's Web site, http://www.ifpug.org. An on-line demo of function points is available there. IFPUG may also be reached at 609-799-4900. Wiley provides a detailed discussion and example of function points in *Essential System Requirements*, pp. 138–179. He also discusses automated estimating tools and provides a representative list of them (pp. 155–157).

Operations in India has utilized QFD in several projects (see their Web site, http://www.gemedicalsystems.com/). Mark Paulk reports that nine organizations in the Software Engineering Institute's database of level 4 and 5 organizations use QFD—five in India and four in the United States.[19]

Zultner advises that the use of software QFD is growing. He has made presentations on software QFD at the QAI conference in Bangalore, at the European Organization for Quality conference in Budapest, and at the 2nd World Congress for Software Quality in Yokohama. He reports that some U.S. companies (such as Andersen Consulting) have been using software QFD on a global basis for years.[20] Zultner suggests reviewing the proceedings of the QFD symposia for the past 11 years and advises that the best way to start with QFD for software is blitz QFD.[21] Zultner believes no other tool, technique, or method even comes close to QFD for dealing with the "fuzzy front end of requirements definition." Zultner's[22] 1993 report on software QFD indicates that the most common error in software QFD is having the wrong items in the rows of the matrices.

> Typically, instead of customer needs, technical requirements are placed here. That leads to design alternatives (solutions) appearing in the columns. That is a perfectly reasonable matrix, but it is a design matrix. In order to get to the true customer needs [the real requirements], we must use other tools first, such as a customer voice table, an affinity diagram, a hierarchy diagram, and others. Starting a QFD project by jumping to the rows of customer needs is an excellent way to fail. It is not a shortcut to success. Understanding what problems and opportunities a customer has, their context, knowing why a customer would value a capability—those are true customer needs. (pp. 5–6)

In summary, concerning QFD, it appears that the fundamental issue is the same as with all other requirements methods: One must discover and emerge the *real* requirements in order for the method to be effective. See Chapter 4 for suggestions and recommendations for how to accomplish defining the *real* customer needs.

---

[19]E-mail communication to the author, March 30, 2000.

[20]E-mail communication to the author, September 27, 2000.

[21]See the QFD Institute's Web page, http://www.qfdi.org/. Zultner notes that the Bicknell and Bicknell book is out of print. He recommends two references on QFD: *Step-By-Step QFD: Customer-Driven Product Design* by John Terninko and *The QFD Handbook* by Jack Revelle and colleagues.

[22]Richard E. Zultner, *Software Quality Function Deployment*, pp. 5–6.

What Comprises the Requirements Specification?

Think of the following as the basis for your system's requirements specification:[23]

1. The database in your automated requirements tool. I trust that by now you are convinced that an automated requirements tool is required for a project of any size. Requirements must be classified (for example, rough requirements, those gathered from customers and users), reviewable requirements/requirements candidates (following analysis and clarification), accepted requirements (based on criteria provided in Chapter 6), prioritized requirements (following analysis and negotiation with the customer), rejected requirements, and requirements allocated to subsequent versions.[24] Attributes are assigned to each requirement reflecting its classification. The database provides the automated RTM,[25] which allows requirements to be tracked to other development activities.

2. The vision statement for the project (see Chapter 5).

3. The RD and other lists or descriptions of requirements provided by customers and users.

4. Lists of requirements met by related legacy (historical) systems.

5. The list of system-level (real) requirements evolved by the requirements manager/requirements engineers. This list should be considered "emergent" because the real requirements are discovered through the joint requirements analysis and elicitation work done together with the customers and users.

An excellent reference that clarifies the need to focus on essential requirements is an article by Neal Whitten.[26] Whitten makes several vital points, among them that one of our most common problems is taking on too much work—attempting to exceed requirements rather than meet minimum requirements. He believes that this contributes to several problems, including late deliveries,

---

[23]A template for a comprehensive requirements specification is available at http://www.atlsysguild.com/GuildSite/Robs/Template.html. The template can be used with popular requirements tools.

[24]Gerald Weinberg recommends these classifications. See "Just Say No! Improving the Requirements Process."

[25]Not to be confused with the commercial automated requirements tool RTM, marketed by Integrated Chipware, Inc.

[26]"Meet Minimum Requirements: Anything More Is Too Much," p. 19.

budget overruns, low morale, and poor quality. "Meet minimum requirements" means giving the client what he needs to be successful. Do not provide non-essential functionality. This can be addressed in future releases and new business opportunities.

Be sure to maintain appropriate configuration control of these requirements artifacts (revision histories, change control, formal CM). For example, a revision history page should provide

- The revision number or code for each change to the published information
- The date of each revision to the published information
- A short summary of the revisions made to the published information
- The name of the person responsible for the changes to the published information[27]

The Rationale for Prioritizing Requirements

Prioritizing requirements is a powerful and effective requirements practice that should be utilized on all projects. Step one is to convince your customer that prioritizing requirements is smart, is necessary, reduces risks, facilitates managing requirements changes and additions, provides a high return on investment, and requires customer involvement.

Common sense tells us that all requirements are not top priority. The real requirements should be grouped by relative importance.[28] We know from our experience that the requirements will change and grow during development. Therefore, consider high-priority real requirements for the initial release of the system and lower priority real requirements for later releases.

Hooks and Farry[29] provide an extensive discussion of the case for prioritizing requirements based on their many years of consulting experience. Among the reasons they site that prioritizing requirements contributes to an effective requirements process are the following:

1. Discussion of requirements priorities improves communication between the customer and the supplier. A prioritization effort involving both customer

---

[27]Dean Leffingwell and Don Widrig, *Managing Software Requirements: A Unified Approach*, p. 294.

[28]We discussed approaches and tools for prioritizing requirements in Chapter 4.

[29]*Customer-Centered Products*, pp. 202–211.

and developer perspectives facilitates separating essential from desirable, needs from wants, in a way not possible from only one side's perspective.

2. Prioritizing requirements may enable early delivery of functionality. Because most customers seek systems to improve their productivity and effectiveness, this can translate into improved results and competitiveness.

3. Prioritizing requirements facilitates trade-offs in the architecting and design activities and facilitates managing requirements changes as well as new and derived requirements.

4. Prioritizing requirements facilitates delivery of a useful product in spite of schedule and resource limitations. With requirements prioritization, one can put lower priority requirements in later versions or products. The product can be developed incrementally with the high-priority requirements in the earliest version. Prioritization helps avoid the "bailing" that often occurs just before delivery when partially implemented requirements are discarded in a frantic effort to save dwindling resources for finishing the critical system components.

5. Prioritization helps resolve requirements conflicts. The joint team can consider trade-offs to achieve the most customer-pleasing approach.

6. Knowing requirements priorities early provides options to reduce risks and can potentially avoid crises late in the development effort. Also, it preserves some flexibility for customers.

7. Prioritization helps a development manager control change and guides intelligent decision making.

8. In the absence of information concerning requirements priorities, developers tend to resolve trade-offs between ease of development and maintainability (for example, in ways that facilitate ease of development rather than real needs). The availability of the prioritized requirements provides insights and helps guide development activities. Including developers in the discussion of requirements priorities helps inform them and helps gain their support.

Hooks and Farry[30] recommend the following five-step approach to prioritize requirements:

1. Define priority classes. A numbering system of 1-2-3 works well.
2. Classify the requirements. Get a general sense of priorities jointly with your customer.

---

[30]*Customer-Centered Products*, pp. 207–209.

Figure 8-4   Requirements Prioritization Checklist

Have you:

Sold stakeholders on the benefits of requirements prioritization?
Defined priority classes?
Classified all requirements by priority?
Resolved the priority differences between stakeholders?
Created priority-based development schedules?
Maintained the priorities throughout development?

---

3. Resolve the differences. Build consensus on the requirements that different people prioritized differently.
4. Create priority-based development schedules.
5. Maintain the priorities. Revisit priorities as business needs change. Trade information provides new insights, requirements change, or new requirements develop. Sometimes new requirements change the priority of existing requirements.

The priority of the requirement is one of the attributes maintained in the automated requirements tool. This enables us to sort the requirements by priority. Requirements priorities must be reviewed and updated whenever the business context changes.

A related attribute is requirements stability. To what extent is the requirement likely to change? Highly volatile requirements may require special consideration (for example, a way to accommodate them in the architecture that facilitates accommodating change).

Figure 8-4 is a checklist to guide requirements prioritization.

Summary

Although a large number of methods and techniques to support requirements engineering is available, only a few have proved most useful. It's important for you to select methods and techniques that are familiar to the developers. Formal training in the use of the selected methods and techniques should be provided, particularly when they are new technologies. An organization should work toward the use of a common set of methods and techniques that have proved effective in your environment. Industry data concerning the effectiveness and cost of methods and techniques, as well as their relative capability to remove various types of defects, suggest that JAD, use of prototypes, use cases, and configuration control boards are very effective. Jones's data suggest that it is far easier to make mistakes and degrade productivity than it is to get things right and improve productivity. This is an important finding that deserves attention and analysis.

The methods and techniques to be used by a project and institutionalized for an organization should be selected carefully. Several working documents that together describe the set of the requirements for a system should be maintained. These include (1) the database in your automated requirements tool, (2) the vision statement for the project, (3) the RD, (4) lists of requirements met by related legacy systems, and (5) the list of system-level requirements. Prioritizing requirements is a powerful and effective requirements practice that should be utilized on all projects. It reduces risk, facilitates making trade-offs, helps deliver a useful product in spite of schedule and resource limitations, and improves communication with the customer and developers.

Key References and Suggested Readings

Barbara A. Bicknell and Kris D. Bicknell. *The Road Map to Repeatable Success: Using QFD to Implement Change.* **Boca Raton, FL: CRC Press, 1995.** The authors are associated with Bicknell Consulting, Inc., and have extensive experience applying the QFD methodology. Their book is a very comprehensive treatment of QFD, explaining not only how QFD can be applied to all levels of the organization, but also providing detailed guidance concerning how to create a QFD matrix, analyze it, and develop an integrated plan using it. They provide a nine-step approach to developing and using a QFD approach. A useful chapter concerning how to develop a pilot QFD program is provided. Several case studies and examples are provided.

Ian Graham. *Requirements Engineering and Rapid Development: An Object-Oriented Approach.* **Reading, MA: Addison-Wesley, 1998.** Graham has responsibility for software methods at Chase Manhattan Bank and believes that development should be done quickly and effectively. He provides practical advice concerning object modeling techniques. His approach complies with the principles of the Dynamic Systems Development Method that was developed by a consortium of 17 users in England. This method does not include or recommend techniques. See J. Stapleton, *Dynamic Systems Development Method: The Method in Practice*, Harlow, UK: Addison-Wesley, 1997.

IFPUG. *Function Point Counting Manual.* Current release. Westerville, OH. The use of function points as a measure of the functional size of information systems has grown rapidly. Function points are a more objective measure of software development than lines of code from the customer's point of view because of the characteristics of particular software languages. Recent releases of this manual have provided a consensus view of the rules of function point counting (IFPUG standard). The manual provides a discussion of the objectives and benefits of FPA, an overview of FPA, and function point counting procedures. Examples are provided to explain function point counting practices, concepts, rules, and procedures. Complementary IFPUG documentation is available, including an IFPUG brochure (with membership application), *Guidelines for Software Measurement, Application of Measurement Information, Quick Reference Counting Guide, Function Point Analysis Case Studies,* and IFPUG glossary. A list of instructors providing certified training courses is also available.

Michael Jackson. *Software Requirements & Specifications.* Wokingham, UK: Addison-Wesley, 1995. Jackson describes a large set of methods, including data flow diagrams, entity relationship span, frame diagrams, graphic notations, tree diagrams, and the top-down approach. He shares a set of principles and prejudices based on his 30 years in software development. His other books include *Principles of Program Design* (Academic Press, 1975) and *System Development* (Prentice Hall International, 1983).

Capers Jones. *Estimating Software Costs.* New York: McGraw Hill, 1998. This is a very thorough treatment of this subject. Jones worked for IBM and is founder and chairman of Artemis-SPR, Inc. (see http://www.spr.com). He has been collecting historical data and designing and building software cost estimating tools since 1971. Jones's awareness that there are hundreds of factors that determine the outcome of a project and his extensive database enable him to advise others concerning the factors that are the most critical.

Capers Jones. *Positive and Negative Factors That Influence Software Productivity.* Version 2.0. Burlington, MA: Software Productivity Research, Inc., 1998. This is an extremely insightful paper. Jones notes that software productivity is complex, with at least 100 known factors that can influence the outcome of software projects. The conclusions are derived from 2,000 software projects examined between 1993 and 1998. The requirements activity comprises an average of 8.42% of the total effort. Jones provides lists of factors that exert both positive and negative impacts on software productivity. The cumulative results of negative factors are much larger than those of the positive factors. This means that it is easier to make mistakes and degrade productivity than it is to get things right and improve productivity. Jones also provides data concerning the impact of positive and negative factors on maintenance productivity. He addresses "best in class" and "worst in class" companies. The most common pattern noted for both systems and software domains is projects and companies in which the technical work of building software (design and coding) is reasonably good, but project management factors and quality control factors are fairly weak.

James Martin. *Rapid Application Development.* **New York: Macmillan Publishing, 1991.** Martin provides a comprehensive treatment of RAD. He describes a requirements planning phase called *joint requirements planning* (JRP). JRP utilizes a workshop to examine goals, problems, critical success factors, and strategic opportunities to determine system objectives, departments and locations served, determination and prioritization of system functions, process flow, and a list of unresolved issues. The basic idea of JRP and JAD techniques is to select key end users and to conduct workshops that progress through a structured set of steps for planning and designing a system. This book is recommended reading for individuals considering the use of RAD techniques. Martin also provides an excellent discussion of metrics, tools, methodology, people, and management, as well as techniques including prototyping, data modeling, and others.

Mark C. Paulk. *A Comparison of ISO 9001 and the Capability Maturity Model for Software.* **Technical report CMU/SEI 94-TR-12. Pittsburgh, PA: Software Engineering Institute, Carnegie Mellon University, July 1994.** This report provides a detailed mapping between International Standard Organization (ISO) 9001 and the Capability Maturity Model (CMM). Paulk concludes that there is a strong correlation between ISO 9001 and the CMM, although some issues in ISO 9001 are not covered in the CMM, and some issues in the CMM are not addressed in ISO 9001. He believes that the biggest difference between the two standards is the emphasis of the CMM on continuous process improvement. ISO 9001 addresses the minimum criteria for an acceptable quality system. Both documents emphasize processes that are documented and are practiced as documented. However, Paulk concludes that a CMM level 1 organization could be certified as compliant with ISO 9001. If an organization is following the spirit of 9001, it seems probable the organization would be near or above CMM level 2. A CMM level 2 organization would have little difficulty in obtaining ISO 9001 certification.

Jack B. Revelle, John W. Moran, and Charles Cox. *The QFD Handbook.* **New York: John Wiley & Sons, 1997.** QFD uses a number of matrices that translate customer requirements into engineering or design requirements. Revelle and colleagues apply QFD to several areas such as ISO 9000, service design, and software design. A disk that supplies the QFD Pathway software tool package is packaged with the book.

Linda Rosenberg. *Writing High Quality Requirement Specifications.* **Tutorial presented at the 12th International Software Quality Week (QW'99). San Jose, CA. May 24–28, 1999.** The requirements specification establishes the basis for all of the project's engineering, management, and quality assurance functions. If the quality of the requirements specification is poor, it can create risks in all areas of the project. The tutorial addresses effective development of quality requirement specifications and provides ideas and methods that can be incorporated into the project plan. These produce a return on documentation effort and improved comprehension. See http://www.soft.com/QualWeek/QW99/qw99.abs.html.

John Terninko. *Step-by-Step QFD: Customer-Driven Product Design* **2nd ed. Boca Raton, FL: St. Lucie Press, 1997.** This is an excellent book that describes why to use QFD as a technique and provides a step-by-step guide for how to use it. The author provides suggested workshops and sample worksheets. An essential point is noted on page 3: "Once customer needs are understood . . ." In other words, one must know the *real* requirements prior to taking advantage of the QFD technique. Assuming use of the real requirements as the base, one can achieve reduced development time by a factor of 2 or 3 (that is, 1/2 to 1/3). The author notes that implementing QFD for new product designs requires a substantial initial investment of resources. Unfortunately, the book does not provide a system development or software development example. Rather, the examples of the application of QFD are limited to manufacturing. The book does discuss the origin and application of TRIZ, a Russian acronym that translates to Theory of Inventive Problem Solving (TIPS).

Jefffrey L. Whitten, Lonnie D. Bentley, and Kevin C. Dittman. *Systems Analysis and Design Methods.* **5th ed. Boston, MA: McGraw-Hill, 2000.** This popular textbook provides a comprehensive discussion of most information systems development topics. I particularly like the insight that classic, structured, and "modern" techniques are (or should be) mutually supportive, not mutually exclusive. The definitions of terms in the index help clarify an understanding of topics. The volume incorporates an adaptation of Zachman's *Framework for Information Systems Architecture* (color mappings to data, processes, geography, interfaces, and objects) so that in reviewing the figures, one can discern which is which. For each chapter Whitten and colleagues provide a set of suggested readings that seem to be well thought through.

Neal Whitten. "Meet Minimum Requirements: Anything More Is Too Much." PM Network (September 1998), p. 19. See also http://www.pmi.org. Whitten advocates committing to a project plan that includes only essential function, with a "closet plan" for nonessential function. Deliberately practicing meeting minimum requirements helps an organization or company be first-to-market, earn increasing credibility from its clients, and strongly posture its enterprise for taking on new business opportunities. USA. Phone: (610) 356-4600. Fax: (610) 356-4647.

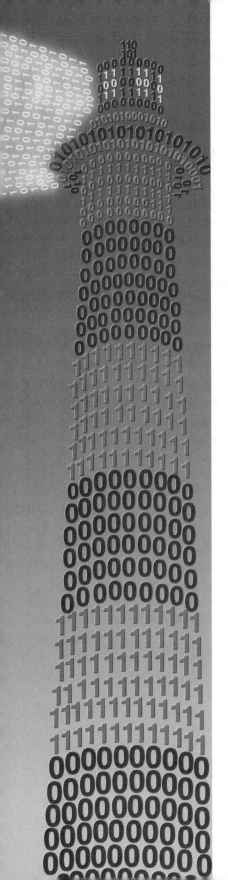

CHAPTER NINE

Perform Requirements Verification and Validation

Commit to the approach.
Establish and utilize a Joint Team responsible for the requirements.
Define the *real* customer needs.
Use and continually improve a requirements process.
Iterate the system requirements and architecture repeatedly.
Use a mechanism to maintain project communication.
Select familiar methods and maintain a set of work products.
Perform requirements verification and validation.
Provide an effective mechanism to accommodate requirements changes.
Perform the development effort using known, familiar proven industry, organizational, and project best practices.

This chapter describes the critical importance of validating that the real requirements have been met in the delivered system. It emphasizes the value of verification and validation (V&V) planning during requirements development and the value of a structured approach to testing that provides for test activities during requirements analysis. Pitfalls that have been experienced by practitioners are described, and suggestions are offered to overcome them. Clarification of terminology is provided. By including the Perform Requirements Verification and Validation effective requirements practice in your development process, you will confirm that the real requirements are met in your delivered system. The quality of the requirements can be improved, and costs and risks can be controlled by performing V&V planning early in your development process.

V&V Terminology

Some years ago, I attended an International Council on Systems Engineering requirements tutorial provided by Jeffrey O. Grady, author, presenter, and systems engineering consultant.[1] He took special effort to point out that the terms *verification* and *validation* are used differently among systems and software engineers. Figure 9-1 provides Grady's insight. See Grady's book, *System Validation and Verification,* Chapters 4 through 13, for a detailed description of the entire pathway from requirement to audit of the verification evidence.

It's important to note these differences and to be sure we know which is being used in our professional discussions and deliberations. Make the effort to understand how all parties on a program are defining V&V, particularly the contractor and the customer. We'll use the following terminology in this book:

Validation is a process for confirming that the real requirements are implemented in the delivered system.

Verification is a process for ensuring that the design solution satisfies the requirements.

---

[1]Grady is president of JOG System Engineering, Inc., in San Diego, California. He has authored several books, including *System Requirements Analysis* (McGraw-Hill, 1993), *System Validation and Verification* (CRC Press, 1997), *System Integration* (CRC Press, 1994), *System Engineering Planning and Enterprise Identity* (CRC Press, 1995), and *System Engineering Deployment* (CRC Press, 1999). See http://www.jogse.com.

Figure 9-1   Verification and Validation

- Validation is a process for proving that design risks presented by the requirements are minimized before a lot of money has been spent doing the design.
- Verification is a process for developing evidence that the design solution satisfies the requirements upon which it is based.
- The Software View:

  - Verification proves that the work of phase X is traceable to the work in phase X-1.
  - Validation develops evidence that the product complies with the requirements.

The Importance of V&V

The essential aspect is that we need to confirm that the real requirements are implemented in the delivered system.[2] Recall from Chapter 4 that an unverifiable requirement is a bad requirement. The outputs of the verification task are

- Documented verified requirements
- Updated requirements traceability matrix, because we want to track where in the design the requirement is satisfied
- Updated preliminary operational and system concept documents

V&V Planning

Hooks and Farry[3] encourage that V&V be addressed during requirements development, because this approach improves requirements quality, ensures that requirements support verification, provides a basis for estimating verification cost and schedule, and provides opportunities to control cost and risk. They identify words that flag unverifiable requirements and suggest possible substitutes you may be

---

[2]We note from Electronic Industries Association 632 that 9 of the 33 requirements for a sound system engineering process are V&V related.

[3]Ivy F. Hooks and Kristin A. Farry, *Customer-Centered Products,* Chapter 10.

able to use (Figure 9-2). They provide examples of unverifiable and verifiable requirements (Figure 9-3) and provide a checklist that summarizes verification-related questions that should be asked (Figure 9-4). Jeff Grady[4] concurs: Demanding that the same person who writes a product requirement also write the corresponding verification process requirement in approximately the same time frame reduces program risk more than any other one activity.

Figure 9-2   Certain Words Flag Unverifiable Requirements

Certain Words Flag Unverifiable Requirements	
Unverifiable Words	Possible Substitutes
flexible	• Add bending threshold or spring constant • Features that will cover anticipated changes from operational concepts
easy or user-friendly	• A maximum number of steps to perform an operation • An educational standard reference • A list of features found on similar popular products • Menus or prompts to guide user
accommodate	• Precise definition of accommodation from operational concepts
ad hoc	• List of features that support all uses anticipated in operational concepts
safe	• List of features that prevent harm from operator errors anticipated in operational concepts • References to specific safety standards
sufficient or adequate	• Quantities or other dimensions
usable	• Exact features needed
when required or if required	• Exact circumstances • Triggering events from operational concepts

[4]Jeff Grady, personal e-mail message providing review comments on the manuscript, April 2, 2000.

Unverifiable Words	Possible Substitutes
fast or quickly	• Minimum acceptable speed
portable	• Dimensions and weight • Description of desired carrying means • Operating systems that the software must run on
light weight	• Maximum acceptable weight
small	• Maximum acceptable dimensions
large	• Minimum acceptable dimensions
easily, clearly, or other "ly" words	• Quantities appropriate for the verb that the "-ly" word modifies (i.e., replace "fit easily" with "fit in X by Y by Z space")
maximize, minimize, optimize, or other "-ize" words	• Limits, greater than or equal to, less than or equal to

Figure 9-3   Examples of Unverifiable and Verifiable Requirements

Examples of Unverifiable and Verifiable Requirements	
Unverifiable	**Verifiable**
ABC shall support ad hoc queries.	• ABC shall retrieve up to five user-specified data items per user query. • ABC shall retrieve those records meeting the criteria in any legal Standard Query Language user query.
The ZZ database shall be flexible.	• The ZZ database shall have eight user-definable fields per record.
The sorting arm shall be flexible.	• The sorting arm shall elastically deform under loads of 0 to 75 pounds.
PQR shall clearly display safety warnings.	• PQR shall display safety warnings in yellow letters 1 ± 0.05 inch high and 0.5 ± inch wide.

(continued)

Figure 9-3   Examples of Unverifiable and Verifiable Requirements
              (*continued*)

The power supply shall be portable.	• The power supply shall weigh 25 pounds or less. • The power supply shall be less than or equal to 20 inches in each dimension. • The power supply shall have a carrying handle of the dimensions in drawing 12 of reference 4 (human factors standards).
The case shall accommodate contingency maintenance tools.	• The case shall have maintenance tool storage to hold all tools in drawing A.
The TMS shall handle deposits quickly.	• The TMS shall scan and record customer account number and amount from a single deposit slip in 2 seconds or less.
XYZ shall be user friendly.	• XYZ shall have controls labeled with their purpose in letters 0.3 ± 0.03 inch. • XYZ shall have controls positioned in the order (from left to right) of their use. • XYZ shall display menus of control options. • XYZ shall display prompts to remind the user of the next step. • XYZ shall use the display convention of product PQR. • XYZ shall have emergency stop controls colored red.
MNOP shall be safe.	• MNOP shall stop operation if a person comes within 10 feet of any moving component. • MNOP shall stop heaters if the vat temperature exceeds 100°C. • MNOP shall meet UL 544 Section 3.4 standards for temperatures on external surfaces.

Figure 9-4   Verification Planning Checklist

> *Have you:*
>
> Screened out or rewritten unverfiable requirements?
>
> Identified all verification stakeholders (customer, regulatory agencies)?
>
> Decided how each requirement will be verified?
>
> Decided when each requirement will be verified?
>
> Written requirements to cut time, cost, and special equipment required to verify your product?
>
> Built a verification matrix?

Verification Methods

The verification plan should define the methods to be used to verify compliance. The typical methods used are the following:[5]

Test—A test article is subjected to a controlled series of stimuli, and the article response is monitored and compared with a standard, expected, predicted result.

Analysis—A person (mentally or possibly augmented by a computer model or simulation) examines a design concept for compliance with requirements by understanding its elements and relations.

Demonstration—An article is manipulated in accordance with instructions and the outcome is compared with planned results.

Inspection—A person (aided by tools), machine, or special sensor compares the measured or observed characteristics of an object with a standard.

---

[5]Grady, *System Requirements Analysis*, p. 425. Note that MIL-STD-961D Appendix A replaces the word *inspection* with *examination*. With this update, all four methods are considered inspections. Some practitioners like to use simulation as another method because it is used frequently and does not fit easily into any of the other four methods.

V&V Techniques

Wallace and Ippolito[6] provide a discussion of V&V techniques including walk-throughs, performance testing, simulation, database analysis, algorithm analysis, functional testing, stress testing, interface testing, and others.

Using Traceability to Support Verification

A definition and guidelines for requirements traceability are provided in Figure 9-5. Leffingwell and Widrig[7] provide a comprehensive discussion of this topic,

Figure 9-5   Definition and Guidelines for Requirements Traceability

I. Definition and Benefits

A requirement is *traceable** if the following information is documented and available: the source of the requirement; why the requirement exists (rationale); what requirements are related to it; and how the requirement is met in the system design, implementation, and user documentation. Because requirements must be verified, traceability to test is required.

Benefits of maintaining requirements traceability include better customer satisfaction and lower system development costs (by avoiding effort on nonrequired capabilities, by reducing re-work, and by making testing more efficient). Experience has shown that investment in good requirements management practices is always cost-effective.

II. Guidelines for Requirements Traceability

A. Record requirements' sources and rationale.

A requirement's source can be a stakeholder need, an organizational quality standard, a specification, a statement of work,

---

[6]Wallace and Ippolito, "Verifying and Validating Software Requirements Specifications," pp. 396–403.

[7]Leffingwell and Widrig, *Managing Software Requirements*, pp. 333–346. Chapter 32 discusses validating the system, and Chapter 33 recommends using return on investment to determine the extent of the V&V effort.

technical documentation, incident reports, or other requirements. The rationale of a requirement summarizes the reasons why that requirement has been specified.

B. Use checklists for requirements analysis.

Checklist-based analysis incorporates our experience to check systematically each requirement to speed the analysis process. It reduces the chance of errors. It avoids rediscovering problems we have already encountered.

C. Prioritize requirements.

Assigning priorities helps stakeholders decide on the core requirements for the system. Priorities help focus negotiation meetings and help resolve disputes between stakeholders. This also helps designers to decide on the system architecture and helps to resolve design conflicts.

D. Provide standard templates for describing requirements.

E. Uniquely identify each requirement.

F. Define traceability policies.

Traceability policies define the information that should be maintained; the techniques to maintain it; and a description of how to handle and document exceptions.

G. Maintain a traceability manual.

H. Classify requirements using a multidimensional approach.

I. Use a data dictionary (a computer-maintained list of names with information about them).

J. Document the links between stakeholder requirements and the system. Linking the requirements to a system model increases the traceability of the system. When user requirements change, it is easier to assess the impact and estimate the costs of the proposed changes. Also, the development of a system model often reveals requirements problems.

K. Use a requirements tool/database to manage requirements and to maintain traceability.

---

*The ANSI/IEEE Standard 830-1984 definition of requirements traceability is "A software requirements specification is traceable if (i) the origin of each of its requirements is clear and if (ii) it facilitates the referencing of each requirement in future development or enhancement documentation."

including the use of traceability tools (see Chapter 31 of *Managing Software Requirements: A Unified Approach*).

A Structured Approach to Testing

William Perry[8] provides a structured approach to testing. Perry emphasizes that when testing is constrained to a single phase and confined to later stages of development, severe consequences (such as spending 50% of the project budget on testing) can develop. As noted early in this book, the later in the system development life cycle an error is discovered, the more costly the error. Therefore, verification should be incorporated into each activity of development.

> The verification activities that accompany the problem definition and requirements analysis phase of development are extremely significant. The adequacy of the requirements must be thoroughly analyzed and initial test cases generated with the expected (correct) responses. Developing scenarios of expected system use may help to determine the test data and anticipated results. These tests will form the core of the final test set. Generating these tests and the expected behavior of the system clarifies the requirements and helps guarantee that they are testable. Vague or untestable requirements will leave the validity of the developed product in doubt. Late discovery of requirements inadequacy can be very costly. A determination of the criticality of software quality attributes and the importance of validation should be made at this stage. Both product requirements and validation requirements should be established.[9]

Perry provides an entire chapter devoted to requirements testing (Chapter 5, pp. 66–98), noting that it is during this activity that most of the critical system decisions are made. "[Requirements] testing is designed to ensure the requirements are recorded properly, have been interpreted correctly and are reasonable, and that the requirements are recorded in accordance with guidelines, standards, and procedures."[10]

---

[8]*Effective Methods for Software Testing*, p. 20.
[9]Ibid, p. 22.
[10]Ibid, p. 66.

Recommendations

Here is a set of recommendations you can use to implement this effective requirements practice:

1. Establish the value of requirements verification through training.
2. Address requirements verification early, during requirements development. This provides opportunities to control cost and risk. The verification approach impacts the cost and effort required for verification.
3. Review your requirements to identify those that are not verifiable and take action either to create a verifiable requirement or to eliminate it from the real requirements.
4. As you plan each requirement's verification, tag it with the

   - Method (test, inspection, demonstration, analysis)
   - Level (component, subsystem, system)
   - Phase (design, manufacture, verification)

   Capture these data in your automated requirements tool and create a *requirements verification matrix*.[11] The verification method for each requirement is specified. Often the verification level is also specified.

5. Utilize familiar, proven verification methods and techniques.
6. Utilize your automated requirements tool to sort the requirements by verification method. This facilitates identifying duplication and other inefficiencies in your verification plan.

Pitfalls[12]

The key to successful requirements V&V is well-written requirements. Typically, verification is performed on the allocated or **B spec** requirements, although legally the A level must also be verified. Systems engineering and/or software development groups normally write these requirements. At an early point in a project, the group that will be validating the requirements is just beginning to form or may not even exist. When the requirements are written, the emphasis is

---

[11]See Martin, *Systems Engineering Guidebook,* for an extensive discussion and examples.

[12]With thanks to John Waters, requirements engineer, for sharing his requirements verification experiences.

on "how do I design . . ." rather than "how will I verify . . ." This is often compounded by a tight schedule and the writer's desire to complete this task so she can begin "the real work." As a result, the requirements that are written may be difficult for the test team to understand and evaluate, and they may be difficult to verify. This will almost certainly have a significant impact on requirements validation and may result in the system not being fully tested.

The following courses of action will help to avoid these pitfalls:

Full management support—Management needs to understand the importance of requirements V&V and fully support the development of a verifiable requirements baseline. They must be willing to take timely action during requirements development to preclude later and more painful problems that occur during testing. This includes slipping the schedule if required.

Timely assembly of the verification team—Don't wait until it is time to write the procedures to assemble the verification team. The team needs to be established early enough to understand the workings of the system.

Test team participation in requirements reviews—Include members of the test team who will be responsible for the verification.

User-friendly requirements tracking tool—Select an automated requirements tracking tool that has a reputation for being user friendly.

Indication of how the requirements can be verified—The requirement authors should include with each requirement one or two statements concerning how the requirements can be verified. This will not only encourage the author to think about how to verify the requirement but later will serve as a guide on how to write the verification procedure. These notes should be maintained in the automated tool along with the requirement.

Good communication—When the requirements have been written and approved, the author often feels that he has no further obligation. The only way to ensure that these requirements will be properly tested is through the continued participation of requirements authors.

Use of a group to control the baseline—Once the allocated requirements baseline is established, form a group to review any proposed changes and to control the baseline. The group should include engineering, software development, requirements management, verification, quality assurance, and configuration management representatives. No matter how well written the requirements are, changes always will be required.

A **truly independent requirements verification group**—Too often, the testers succumb to pressures to meet schedule. For example, a simple scenario works, so the requirement is considered verified. However, running the same scenario with slightly different parameters may result in a totally different outcome. This results in the system not being fully tested, leaving bugs undetected for later (and more costly) fixes.

Use of automated tools—The use of automated tools is an effective way to test the system more thoroughly.[13] Depending on the system to be tested, the tool may be as simple as a macro or script that mimics human interaction. The tool may inject hundreds of **transactions** into the system, simulating the future operational state. Problems that would never be detected during individual scenario tests will turn up.

Risk-based approaches to testing can help ensure reasonable (acceptable/ good enough) test coverage.[14]

Summary

It's important to make the effort to understand how all parties on a program are defining the terms *verification* and *validation*. We defined verification as a process for ensuring that the design solution satisfies the requirements. We defined validation as a process for confirming that the real requirements are implemented in the delivered system. The quality of the requirements can be improved, and costs and risks can be controlled by performing V&V planning early in the development process. Be alert for words that flag unverifiable requirements. Use of a verification planning checklist facilitates asking the right questions. V&V techniques include walkthroughs, performance testing, simulation, database analysis, algorithm analysis, functional testing, stress testing, and interface testing. A structured approach to testing can reduce costs. Requirements testing helps ensure that the requirements have been interpreted correctly, are reasonable, and are recorded properly. Proactive steps can avoid pitfalls in performing V&V.

---

[13]See Dustin and colleagues, *Automated Software Testing,* for a comprehensive treatment.

[14]See James Bach, "James Bach on Risk-Based Testing."

Key References and Suggested Readings

Barry W. Boehm. *Software Engineering Economics.* **Englewood Cliffs, NJ: Prentice Hall, 1981.** Boehm's book is a classic that identifies the factors most strongly influencing software costs and provides methods to determine the estimated costs of a software project. He presents the Constructive Cost Model and provides case study examples of its use. The book has an excellent section concerning people-related reasons for variability in software estimation (pp. 666–676).

Elfriede Dustin, Jeff Rashka, and John Paul. *Automated Software Testing: Introduction, Management, and Performance.* **Boston, MA: Addison-Wesley, 1999.** This book is a comprehensive, step-by-step guide to the most effective tools, techniques, and methods for automated testing. The Automated Test Lifecycle Methodology (ATLM) is a structured process for designing and executing testing that parallels the rapid application development methodology. The book provides guidance on all aspects of the testing process. A compact disk comes with the book that contains ATLM graphics in PDF, JPEG, EPS, and TIFF formats. There is extensive discussion of requirements-related testing topics.

Jeffrey O. Grady. *System Validation and Verification.* **Boca Raton, FL: CRC Press, 1997.** This book covers all aspects of V&V. Grady has extensive experience and provides practical methods for each aspect of the topics. The book is extensively illustrated with helpful explanatory figures.

Theodore F. Hammer, Leonore L. Huffman, and Linda Rosenberg. "**Doing Requirements Right the First Time.**" *CrossTalk,* **1998:20–25.** Hammer et al. address three critical aspects of requirements: definition, verification, and management. Project data collected from the National Aeronautics and Space Administration's Goddard Space Flight Center by the Software Assurance Technology Center (SATC) are used to demonstrate key concepts and to explain how to apply them to any project. SATC's Automated Requirements Measurement tool is used, and seven measures are developed (lines of text, imperatives, continuances, directives, weak phases, incomplete, and options). These metrics provide insight into the completeness of the test program and an understanding of the characteristics of the verification program.

James D. Palmer. "**Traceability.**" **In: R. H. Thayer and M. Dortman, eds.** *Software Requirements Engineering.* **Los Alamitos, CA: IEEE Computer Society Press, 1997: 364–374.** Palmer shows that traceability gives essential assistance in understanding the relationships that exist within and across requirements, design, and implementation. He points out that traceability is often misunderstood, frequently misapplied, and seldom performed correctly. This work is recommended reading for requirements engineers.

William Perry. *Effective Methods for SoftwareTesting.* **New York: John Wiley & Sons, 1995.** Perry provides extremely helpful guidance concerning verification and testing activities that need to accompany the problem definition and requirements analysis activities in a development effort. He emphasizes that failure to do this will result in much higher testing costs later in the project. He provides a detailed discussion of *requirements phase testing,* including recommendations for test tools (Walk-Through and Risk Matrix) and an extensive listing of application risks. Because testing during the requirements phase is a new concept to many development teams, Perry provides a requirements phase test process.

Delores R. Wallace and Laura M. Ippolito. "Verifying and Validating Software Requirements Specifications." In: Richard H. Thayer and Merlin Dortman, eds. *Software Requirements Engineering.* **2nd ed. Los Alamitos, CA: IEEE Computer Society Press, 1997: 389–404.** Wallace and Ippolito describe V&V activities and emphasize that V&V is a powerful tool for improving intermediate products such as requirements specifications, design descriptions, test cases, and test procedures. They provide descriptions of 28 test techniques and suggest strategies for choosing among them. A rich set of references is provided.

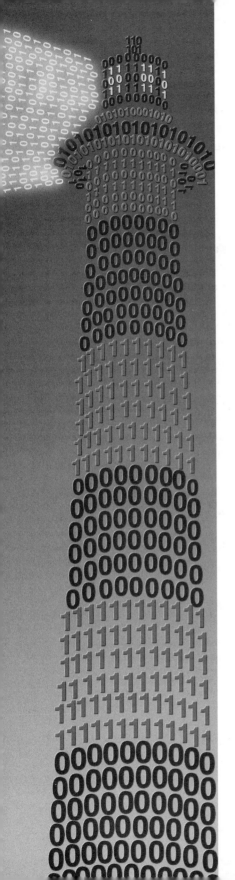

CHAPTER TEN

Provide an Effective Mechanism to Accommodate Requirements Changes

Commit to the approach.
Establish and utilize a Joint Team responsible for the requirements.
Define the *real* customer needs.
Use and continually improve a requirements process.
Iterate the system requirements and architecture repeatedly.
Use a mechanism to maintain project communication.
Select familiar methods and maintain a set of work products.
Perform requirements verification and validation.
Provide an effective mechanism to accommodate requirements changes.
Perform the development effort using known, familiar proven industry, organizational, and project best practices.

This chapter advises you to incorporate an effective mechanism to accommodate changes in requirements during the development process. This is a key component of an effective requirements process and is essential to maintain control of the project.

Why Such Emphasis?

Of all of the effective requirements practices, this one is among the most critical, perhaps second only to the need to discover and to emerge the *real requirements* (see Chapter 4). Capers Jones[1] reports that creeping user requirements is endemic to the software industry and that its severity is directly proportional to the size of the application. He believes that the real problem is inadequate methods, tools, and approaches for dealing with creeping requirements in a way that minimizes damage to the structure of the software, schedule slippage, and other related problems. Whitten[2] notes that one of the most common problems with projects is taking on too much work—attempting to exceed requirements rather than to meet minimum requirements. "Meeting minimum requirements" means providing the client what is needed. Don't provide unessential function. Whitten takes issue with the premise that meeting minimum requirements is unexciting and noncompetitive. He feels that *deliberately practicing meeting minimum requirements* helps an organization or company be first-to-market, earn increasing credibility from clients, and strongly posture their enterprise for taking on new business opportunities.[3]

The lack of an effective mechanism to deal with changes is a critical weakness in most system and software development efforts today. Without it, it's not possible to maintain control of the project.

Years ago, the conventional approach was to insist that the requirements be "frozen" before the development work proceeded. However, more recently, we've come to recognize that we can't hold requirements constant because the real world continues to change while we develop. We need other ways to deal with a changing world, or else the capabilities of our delivered systems will differ significantly from the real customer and user needs.

---

[1] *Assessment and Control of Software Risks,* p. 93.

[2] Neal Whitten, "Meet Minimum Requirements: Anything More Is Too Much," p. 19.

[3] Ibid.

Planning for Changes in Requirements

Requirement changes stem from numerous sources, including

- The expanded quantity of requirements associated with highly complex systems. Because of the large scope of a system, less rigor is applied to providing essential system function.
- The increased interaction and information sharing within and between systems.
- Poorly or loosely defined requirements from the onset (including failure to discover and to emerge the real requirements).
- Changes in business objectives and plans.
- Technology changes.
- Changes in law, policies, directives, and so forth.
- Customers and users who change their minds about things or learn of "neat" ways to do things.
- Developers who add their own special twists or even make requirements decisions.

With regard to technology changes, the rate of technology change continues to increase. Forward-looking system developers and integrators will utilize a technology change management (TCM) process to identify new technologies. New technologies should be piloted, applied, and reused when **technology insertion** supports the system and business objectives.[4] Figure 10-1 provides a context diagram for the TCM process.

We know from industry and our own experience that allowing requirements changes can jeopardize our ability to complete projects at all, let alone within budget and on schedule. It's important to plan on requirements changes because they are inevitable. A flexible or open architecture as discussed in Chapter 6 can help accommodate changes. An incremental or evolutionary life cycle may accommodate the needed changes. Also, having a mechanism to control and to prioritize requirements changes is critical.

---

[4]Note that TCM is a key process area for level 5 of the Software Capability Maturity Model (SW-CMM). See Paulk and colleagues, *Key Practices of the Capability Maturity Model*, pp. L5–17 through L5–30 for several suggestions concerning how to perform TCM. See also Daniel P. Petrozzo, *The Fast Forward MBA in Technology Management*.

Figure 10-1   TCM Process Context Diagram

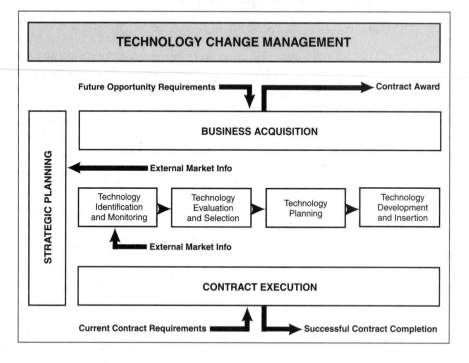

Successful completion of the system (meeting the defined customer valid requirements) may be jeopardized unless changes in requirements are dealt with via a win-win process for the customer and the developer. Changes in requirements can be an indicator of a poorly defined requirements set. Projects and organizations should develop over time metrics of the percent requirements volatility compared with budget and schedule overruns.[5] The anticipated impacts of changes in requirements are defined through analysis by the developers during the development process. The joint team considers whether the requested changes will be accommodated based on the impact analysis. Adjustments are made in the system or project architecture, design, budget, schedule, and staffing. Too often, developers are told to make changes in the requirements, architecture, and design without project management making concomitant changes in the budget, schedule, and staffing. This is one of the ways we allow projects to get out of control.

---

[5]Recall the discussion concerning requirements volatility and the recommended ceiling for this key metric in Chapter 3.

The Recommended Mechanism

Let's consider some characteristics of the needed mechanism. Perhaps most important, it must have both customer and system builder representation. The representatives must be decision makers who can represent their respective interests with good awareness of the big picture (what the system needs to do) as well as sensitivity to the technical work needed. They must be able to address the impacts of requirements changes, because the changes will affect the project schedule and the costs incurred. Requirements changes could well affect the design and the architecture and create rework. It's likely that staffing levels will be affected. The requirements change process must require that all change requests go through a single channel, thus the need for a mechanism that can balance enhanced capabilities as a result of new or changed requirements, with resulting impacts on the project itself. I have previously recommended that the joint team be utilized to maintain responsibility for the requirements throughout the development cycle. It is also the recommended mechanism to control requirements changes. Note in Figure 10-2, the requirements process macro (or high-level process), that the joint team maintains the responsibility for new requirements and requirements changes through the RE100 subprocess. An impact study[6] may be needed to evaluate the effect of the requested change.

Requirements Leakage

Weinberg[7] utilizes the term *requirements leakage* to refer to unofficial requirements added to the requirements specification where the requirements were not really needed. He has documented several sources of unofficial requirements (Figure 10-3). One study indicated that roughly half the requirements originated from unofficial sources!

---

[6]An impact study traces the effect of a requirement change to all affected requirements downstream to give project managers, change control managers and change control boards an indication of the scope of the change and then a means to track the changes and the subsequent testing/regression testing. Factors evaluated include the extent of change to the existing work, need for new work, alternatives, complexity, severity of the situation, impact on the schedule, cost incurred, and the relationship to other changes. Attributes such as defect description, source of change, stakeholders affected, risk, difficulty, team assigned, review team, requirements affected, importance to current release (data integrity, business need, risk), and estimated time required to implement the change are often kept as part of the control mechanism. A requirements change history is also an important part of the change management process.

[7]Gerald M. Weinberg, "Just Say No! Improving the Requirements Process," pp. 19–23.

Figure 10-2   **The Requirements Process Macro**

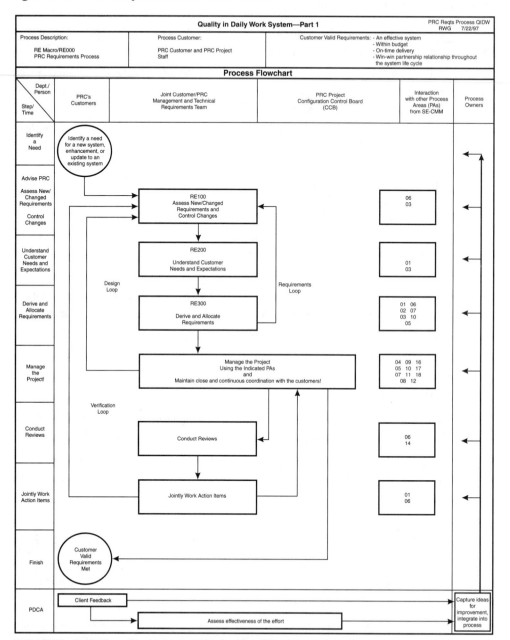

NOTES: 1. The PRC requirements (RE) process is characterized by partnership between the customer and PRC, by extensive communication and close and continous coordination, and by use of methods and tools to gain an increasingly more robust understanding of customer needs and expectations throughout the system life cycle.

       2. The project CCB consists of the project manager and the leads from all involved engineering groups. This is a mechanism to manage the project in a coordinated, effective manner. It could include a customer representative; be the "Joint Team," and on a small project even be one or two people.

       3. There are two entrance points to RE200: one from the initial assessment and another representing changes requested by the customer after the initial assessment.

       4. The composition of the members of the "Joint Team" may change over the course of the system development as different levels are defined and addressed.

       5. The requirements produced by the RE process will be impacted and changed by activities in the system architecture process.

Figure 10-3   Sources of Unofficial Requirements and Ways to Gain Control of Unofficial Requirements

1. Program plans (business plans)
2. Priority enhancements requested by marketing
3. Long experience in the industry
4. Looking at what's produced by more sophisticated software organizations
5. Enhancements mentioned by distributors who were overheard by programmers who were attending a sales meeting to support a demonstration
6. Enhancements requested by specific—usually large—customers
7. Enhancements requested by systems integrators or by management
8. Enhancements inserted by programmers with "careful consideration of what would be good for the customer" or as quick fixes
9. Enhancements inserted by contract programmers who then left, leaving no documentation
10. Mistakes that are made and shipped and then have to be supported
11. Features hardware engineers couldn't or wouldn't implement
12. Corrections to hardware faults
13. Change of scope in reaction to what competitors did
14. A mistake that was made in copying system drawings and is now a "feature"
15. Changes needed because of industry or international standards
16. "Easter eggs": stuff hidden in the code by programmers for their own amusement and activated only by "secret" and unlikely input combinations

Ways to Gain Control of Unofficial Requirements

1. Recognize that requirements come from many sources and know what those sources are.
2. Accept that these multiple interests are legitimate, but not necessarily guaranteed to have their way with the requirements.
3. Create an open, explicit negotiation process that will consider anybody's requirements ideas in the setting of priorities.
4. Develop a process to guarantee that all requirements come through a single channel—a funnel—if you like.

The sources of unofficial requirements are important. If unofficial requirements are not controlled, they render a requirements process ineffective. Knowing the source of each requirement is an important attribute, as noted in Chapter 5.

Attributes can be tagged to the requirements in the automated database/requirements tool, indicating which requirements are rough, in reviewable condition (requirements candidates), reviewed (for correctness and consistency), negotiated (for compatibility and priority), and rejected.[8] Weinberg suggests that the requirements database allow allocation of requirements to versions of the product to control the desire of various advocates to get "their" requirements met in the earliest possible version.[9] Use the joint team to prioritize the requirements. Address lower priority requirements in later versions of the products.

Focus on What Counts!

Smith and Reinertson[10] recommend focusing on what counts, which is product benefits, not features. Benefits refer to the necessary requirements. Certain features may be unnecessary to achieve product benefits, and imposing unnecessary features adds design constraints and increases costs. When designers concentrate on necessary requirements, they may be able to eliminate the need for unneeded features.

How Much Can Requirements Change?

The extent of requirements change depends on the development approach being used and the specific nature of the changes. If an incremental development approach is being used, change can be accommodated by assigning new or changed requirements to subsequent increments. As noted in Chapter 8, data provided by Capers Jones[11] indicate that the U.S. average rate of "creeping requirements" (changes after the initial set of requirements is defined) is approximately 2% per month during the design and coding phases. Jones emphasizes

---

[8]These categories are the ones suggested by Weinberg. Ibid, p. 21.

[9]Ibid, p. 23.

[10]Smith and Reinertsen, *Developing Products in Half the Time,* p. 97. They also recommend the use of off-site requirements workshops to write specifications jointly (see pp. 100–102).

[11]Capers Jones, *Estimating Software Costs,* p. 429.

that this is a major problem and that prototyping, change control boards (CCBs), the use case technique, and methods such as joint application design can reduce this rate to a small fraction, such as 0.5% per month.[12] Change in requirements is often referred to as *requirements volatility*, as previously mentioned. Many project managers don't pay careful attention to this key metric. This accounts for many of our problems in not being able to complete projects within budget and schedule. Note that a 2% monthly change in requirements equates to changing one quarter of the system each year. Accordingly, a reasonable target for an effective software development organization may be 0.5% requirements volatility per month. In a maintenance or sustained environment, a higher rate of change may be needed to remain effective.

Often, we see projects with requirements volatility far in excess of 24% per year.[13] The approach recommended in this book is that requirements changes be minimized[14] and agreed on with our eyes wide open and in a win-win partnership relationship as established in the partnering workshop and the project's plan for quality (see Chapter 2). Lacking this mechanism, we can practically guarantee that the project will be out of control soon after the development effort is initiated.

A Way to Deal with Requirements Creep Contractually

Jones[15] suggests a practical approach to dealing with changing user requirements: Include a sliding scale of costs in the contract itself.

---

[12]Ibid, pp. 432–434. The term *use cases* originated as a method for dealing with the requirements of object-oriented applications but has subsequently expanded toward a formal technique for dealing with requirements. See Geri Schneider and Jason P. Winters, *Applying Use Cases: A Practical Guide*.

[13]Because many projects don't even track this critical metric, how would they know? Jones advises that the maximum creep has sometimes exceeded 150%, so this is a major consideration (*Estimating Software Costs*, p. 429).

[14]Careful analysis of requests for requirements changes will eliminate many and place others in the hopper for future releases. Those remaining require careful scrutiny in the form of cost-benefit analysis, in which the effort for rework and the resulting cost and schedule impacts are assessed.

[15]This approach is extracted from Capers Jones, *Estimating Software Costs*, Chapter 17, pp. 434–435.

For example, suppose a hypothetical contract is based on an initial agreement of $500 per function point[16] to develop an application of 1,000 function points in size, so that the total value of the agreement is $500,000.

The contract might contain the following kind of escalating cost scale for new requirements added downstream:

Initial 1,000 function points	= $500 per function point
Features added more than 3 months after contract signing	= $600 per function point
Features added more than 6 months after contract signing	= $700 per function point
Features added more than 9 months after contract signing	= $900 per function point
Features added more than 12 months after contract signing	= $1,200 per function point
Features deleted or delayed at user request	= $150 per function point

Similar clauses can be utilized with maintenance and enhancement outsource agreements, on an annual or specific basis such as

Normal maintenance and defect repairs	= $125 per function point per year
Mainframe to client-server conversion	= $200 per function point per system

(Note that the actual cost per function point for software produced in the United States runs from a low of less than $100 per function point for small end user projects to a high of more than $5,000 per function point for large military software projects. The data shown here are for illustrative purposes and should not actually be used in contracts as the data stand.)

The advantage of the use of function point metrics for development and maintenance contracts is that they are determined from the user requirements and cannot be unilaterally added by the contractor.

---

[16]The use of function points for software estimation was discussed in Chapter 8. Function points are a measure of the complexity of the software.

One of the many problems with the older "lines of code" or LOC metric is that there is no objective way of determining the minimum volume of code needed to implement any given feature. This meant that contracts based on cost per LOC could expand without any effective way for the client to determine whether the expansions were technically necessary.

Function points, on the other hand, cannot be unilaterally determined by the vendor and must be derived from explicit user requirements. Also, function points can easily be understood by clients whereas the LOC metric is difficult to understand in terms of why so much code is needed for any given contract.

Other Recommendations

Implementation of the set of recommendations provided in Figure 10-4 will help control requirements changes.

Each of these recommendations is discussed in the following paragraphs.

1. Requirements engineers should maintain minutes of meetings, documenting changes in requirements, the resolution and rationale, and the affects of the changes. The impacts of changed requirements should be estimated and

Figure 10-4   Other Recommendations to Control Requirements Changes

1. Maintain minutes of meetings, documenting the changes in requirements, the resolution and rationale, and the impacts of the changes.
2. Maintain the set of work products that collectively comprise the requirements specification.
3. Agree on schedule and cost impacts.
4. Keep people informed.
5. Be proactive in considering impacts on staffing changes.
6. Don't try to take advantage of unproven or untrained processes, mechanisms, methods, techniques, or tools as requirements changes or new requirements show up.
7. Try not to allow your customer to force processes, mechanisms, methods, techniques, or tools on the project if they are not part of your trained, familiar, proven process.

documented. A mature systems organization will provide documented decisions and rationale so that people reviewing these decisions at a later date can have the benefit of the knowledge, long after some people have left the project. This habit makes us less "particular people dependent"; that is, more able to proceed without being dependent on the knowledge of certain individuals.

2. Requirements engineers should maintain the set of work products that collectively comprise the requirements specification. This topic was discussed in Chapter 8. If we don't take the time and effort to do this, the requirements baseline will be out of configuration management control.

3. The contractor and the customer should reach consensus concerning the schedule and cost impacts of requirements changes. This must be done in a win-win atmosphere, and the resulting requests for change should be processed in a timely manner. Agreements should be documented and actions should be closed promptly. There is a risk of losing control of the resources required to accomplish the new or changed requirement.

4. The joint team must keep the customer *and* the development team informed by advising them of requirements changes. It's important to keep everyone updated concerning the current requirements baseline because changes in the requirements impact all of the other activities and efforts going on within the project.

5. Project management must be proactive in considering impacts on staffing as a result of requirements changes. This goes beyond updating the staffing plan and requires consideration of additions and changes to the various engineering groups as needed to be responsive to new or changed requirements. In addition, training may be required, for example, to accommodate the use of new technologies.

6. Don't try to take advantage of unproven or untrained processes, mechanisms, methods, techniques, or tools as requirements changes or new requirements show up. This is a dangerous practice that often puts projects into difficulties.

7. Try not to allow your customer to force processes, mechanisms, methods, techniques, or tools on the project if they are not part of your trained, familiar, proven process. Sometimes customers "have heard" that such and such a process, mechanism, method, technique, or tool is "the way to go" or "better than 'older' approaches." For example, customers have stipulated that an object-oriented approach be used. Unless the project team has successfully

utilized object-orientated methods on previous projects, this approach could be challenging.

Summary

To maintain control of a project, it is essential to provide an effective mechanism to accommodate requirements changes during the development process. Industry experience indicates that there are several sources of requirements. Because the rate of technology change continues to increase, an organization is best served by having a TCM process. The joint team is an effective mechanism to control requirements changes. The role is consistent with the joint team's responsibility for the requirements throughout the development process. Applying several recommendations to help control requirements changes will facilitate project activities and reduce costs.

Key References and Suggested Readings

Mark C. Paulk, Charles V. Weber, Suzanne M. Garcia, Mary Beth Chrissis, and Marilyn Bush. *Key Practices of the Capability Maturity Model.* **Version 1.1. Pittsburgh, PA: Software Engineering Institute, Carnegie-Mellon University, 1993.** Also available at http://www.sei.cmu.edu/publications/documents/93. reports/93.tr.025.html. Many don't realize that the SW-CMM, version 1.1, is only 64 pages in length. *Key Practices of the CMM,* version 1.1, is much more extensive and describes the practices for each of the 18 key process areas. These are organized according to a set of common features: commitment to perform, ability to perform, activities performed, measurement and analysis, and verifying implementation. I have been applying these practices to projects and organizations for 12 years and have found them very helpful in improving the development process.

Daniel P. Petrozzo. *The Fast Forward MBA in Technology Management.* **New York: John Wiley & Sons, 1998.** This book is one from the Fast Forward MBA Series. Its aim is to facilitate the use of technology in an organization. Petrozzo provides examples of companies taking advantage of leading technologies and describes how to manage technology. An interesting section is provided concerning changing requirements. Two pitfalls identified by Petrozzo are (1) too large of an initial implementation and (2) dependence on outside providers of software, hardware, and expertise.

Preston G. Smith and Donald G. Reinertsen. *Developing Products in Half the Time.* **2nd ed. New York: John Wiley & Sons, 1998.** This book provides useful concepts, methods, and metrics for reducing the time required to develop products. In this new edition, Smith and Reinertsen have drawn on their experience in working with clients to provide practical tools to accelerate the development process. For example, they stress the value of partnering in off-site workshops to create specifications jointly.

Ian Sommerville. *Software Engineering.* **5th ed. Reading, MA: Addison-Wesley, 1995.** Sommerville is concerned that although there has been tremendous progress in software engineering, there has been a relatively slow diffusion of this progress into industrial practice. He perceives a need to transfer proven practices into everyday use. An extensive treatment of requirements and specifications is provided, with emphasis on a requirements engineering process. An emphasis on prototyping as being useful in validating the systems requirements is provided.

Ronald Starbuck. "How to Control Software Changes." *Software Testing and Quality Engineering (STQE) Magazine* **1/6 1999:18–21.** Starbuck provides a high-level change control process, describes the factors for how change requests are evaluated and explains the role of a CCB. He considers the business environment and the people involved and stresses the need for sponsorship. CCB infrastructure support includes policy (guiding principles), process (a flowchart), procedures (explaining how to accomplish the process steps), and authorization (agreement on what you are or are not empowered to do or not to do). The configuration management plan (CMP) defines how to use the process and procedures in the specific lifecycle situation, indicating who uses configuration management, what work products they use it on, and when they use it. An excellent, easily tailorable model for a CMP is *IEEE Standard for Software Configuration Management Plans* (IEEE Std 828, 1990).

Gerald M. Weinberg. "Just Say No! Improving the Requirements Process." *American Programmer* **(10) 1995:19–23.** Weinberg's view is that for many organizations, the principal barrier to higher quality is an inadequate requirements process. He suggests a four-step process: (1) measure the true cost and value of requirements, (2) gain control of the requirements inputs, (3) gain control of the requirements outputs, and (4) gain control of the requirements process itself.

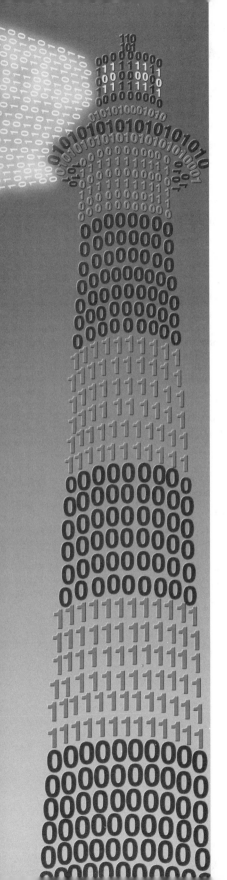

CHAPTER ELEVEN

Perform the Development Effort Using Known, Familiar Proven Industry, Organizational, and Project Best Practices

Commit to the approach.
Establish and utilize a Joint Team responsible for the requirements.
Define the *real* customer needs.
Use and continually improve a requirements process.
Iterate the system requirements and architecture repeatedly.
Use a mechanism to maintain project communication.
Select familiar methods and maintain a set of work products.
Perform requirements verification and validation.
Provide an effective mechanism to accommodate requirements changes.

Perform the development effort using known, familiar proven industry, organizational, and project best practices.

Requirements activities permeate the development process. This chapter discusses the relationship between requirements and project management, including the project environment. It emphasizes the critical importance of using familiar, proven practices, processes, mechanisms, methods, techniques, and tools during the system and/or software development effort. Many projects get into difficulties because they use unfamiliar and unproven practices, and others because the customer requires (or even insists on) use of methodologies in which the people doing the work are not trained and familiar. Also, project management is a critical skill that is not performed well on most projects. Finally, relatively few organizations embrace the concept of continuous improvement, in which a concerted effort is made to strengthen and improve processes and practices continually.

A thesis of this book is that identifying and managing the real requirements are critical factors in project success. This chapter addresses the environment in which the development work is performed. By *environment*, I mean the practices, processes, mechanisms, methods, techniques, and tools that are used to support the system or software development effort. Another critical factor in addition to the project environment is project management. Much has been written on this subject. However, based on industry results, we still don't manage projects well or even satisfactorily (as measured by completion within cost and schedule and by delivery of effective work products). This chapter provides several specific recommendations to provide a supportive environment and to facilitate effective project management. These recommendations may sound simple; however, it is amazing that, in practice, they typically are not utilized.

One of the key issues is the time and focus of the program or project manager (PM). She is called on by the organization to perform a host of activities that take time and attention away from managing the project. Some of these activities are

- Marketing
- Participation on proposal-writing teams
- Customer visits
- Professional conferences
- Management of off-site meetings
- Local or other volunteer activities
- Participation in company committees or teams

- Evaluation boards
- Recruiting efforts

The list goes on and on.

In one sense, by responding to all these needs asked by more senior managers, the PM is being very responsive and helpful. In another sense, the PM is being taken away from her project management responsibilities, jeopardizing project success.

What's All the Fuss?

According to Steve McConnell,[1] as of 1998, approximately two million people were working on roughly 300,000 software projects in the United States. Between one third and two thirds of these projects will exceed their schedule and budget targets before they are delivered. Of the most expensive projects, approximately half will eventually be canceled for being out of control, whereas others will be canceled in more subtle ways. The fuss, to my way of thinking, is that we can do better. We owe it to our customers, our organizations/employers, and the development team to work toward completing projects on time and within budget. Why not create an environment for the team that supports them in completing their work (empowers them) rather than frustrating them at every step? Moreover, the contribution to society achieved by performing development work better is potentially huge. For example, if we can avoid canceled projects, we can

- Save money
- Provide useful and usable products for customers
- Provide fulfilling employment for development teams

Recruiting and retention of technical people are major concerns. Based on projections, this situation will continue to worsen. By providing a supportive work environment and effective project management, we can create the situation in which people

- Are challenged
- Can learn

---

[1]Steve McConnell, *Software Project Survival Guide,* p. vii.

- Leave work most days feeling that they have accomplished something needed and important
- Feel appreciated
- Even have fun!

Such an environment fosters loyalty to employers and saves money.

What Can We Do About It?

Several recommendations are provided in support of this effective requirements practice:

1. Provide to the development team an understanding of the relevant business drivers and context as well as the policies, processes, and procedures to be used.
2. Utilize a practical, effective project management approach.
3. Ensure that selected members of the development team have domain knowledge.
4. Perform the development effort using known (trained), proven processes, mechanisms, methods, techniques, and tools.
5. Provide and utilize mechanisms to foster effective communication throughout the development team.
6. Utilize peer reviews and inspections to remove defects from processes and work products.
7. Ensure that configuration management is effective.
8. Foster an independent quality assurance (QA) role that proactively assists and supports the development team and provides value to the project.
9. Ensure that subcontractors are managed so that their contributions are effective.
10. Use appropriate, useful metrics to manage the project.
11. Ensure that a systematic approach to involving the customer in this entire effort is working.
12. Manage processes quantitatively. Also, use a defect prevention (DP) process, a technology change management (TCM) process, and a process change management (PCM) process. Perform extensive reinsertion and reuse throughout the organization.

Recommendations

Each of these recommendations is discussed in turn. The intent is to convince you that it is important to utilize familiar practices and to provide suggestions concerning what to do.

Provide to the Development Team an Understanding of the Relevant Policies, Processes, and Procedures to Be Used

In my consulting activities, I have seen countless project leaders expect their people to perform the development effort while they are basically clueless concerning the policies, processes, and procedures to be used. One can understand that project start-up is a confusing time. Staff is being recruited and assembled, physical facilities are being obtained and occupied, people are moving in, and equipment and furniture are being acquired. It's a time that is often characterized by general chaos. Organizations should develop, and improve over time, a *project start-up checklist* such as that provided in Figure 11-1. Also, materials and guidance should be readily available electronically, via a Web approach.

It's vital to provide orientation training to the entire development team concerning the policies, processes, procedures, mechanisms, methods, techniques, and tools they are to utilize. This can be accomplished in a way that fosters strong teamwork. My experience is that a trained and committed team can surmount the most ambitious projects.

Utilize a Practical, Effective Project Management Approach

There are a lot of training materials and books available on this subject. I recommend three to you:

The first is *How to Run Successful Projects II—The Silver Bullet* by Fergus O'Connell.[2] O'Connell is founder and chairman of ETP, an international training, consulting, and product development firm specializing in project management, located in Ireland. You may think that O'Connell is being a bit rash by suggesting that he has found the silver bullet.[3] O'Connell published his first book describing

---

[2] See http://www.etpint.com for more information.

[3] Fred Brooks's article in 1987 suggested that, despite advances in hardware and software technology, there seemed to be no way to ensure project success (no silver bullet). See "No Silver Bullet—The Essence and Accidents of Software Engineering."

Figure 11-1   Checklist for Project Start-up

Note: These are a set of suggested start-up activities. The order in which they should be addressed depends on the situation.

Action/Task	Resources Available
1. Request that someone be assigned to the project as advisor, mentor, and facilitator to access needed policies and to process capabilities, artifacts, and other resources.	
2. Establish an Engineering Process Group as a mechanism for policy-level management of the project's engineering activities.	Start this early, even if only a one- to two-person effort initially.
• Establish a quality improvement (QI) focus for the project.	Attend QI courses (MQI, QIDW, team leader).
3. Based on the statement of work, determine what type of project, system life cycle and processes are needed.	
• Utilize high-level processes as starters for sharing/discussion with the leads for their consideration in defining project processes.	Use a wall chart to track project deployment and use of the processes.
• Consider tailoring based on project needs.	Use tailoring white papers.
• Identify an approach for deploying project processes.	Utilize appropriate advisors.
4. Reuse the organization's process asset library (PAL) as a virtual PAL for the project.	
5. Review existing project plans (project management plan, software development plan, configuration management plan, quality assurance plan, and so on) to verify appropriate	Invite subject matter experts from other projects to help identify potential problems and improvements.

Action/Task	Resources Available
identification of tasks, sizing of the effort, and so forth.	
6. Review "videotapes list" to determine resources available for quick start-up training activities.	View videotapes of PRC Process Engineering Training Courses List
7. Initiate a risk management program.	
8. Initiate a peer reviews program.	
9. Create a "joint team" to be responsible for the requirements.	See the RE200 process description. Note also the availability of the PRC requirements transition package and the requirements management Web page.
10. Create a project configuration control board (CCB) to manage the project, consisting of all of the leads of the engineering groups.	The project CCB provides a mechanism for intergroup coordination and also for keeping the leads of all engineering groups aware of project decisions.
11. Consider training needs for project performers and schedule needed training.	
• Process engineering training	Supply vendor training.
• Training concerning methods, techniques, and tools to be utilized on the project	
12. Initiate project tracking and metrics activities.	

a structured project management approach in 1994. He then practiced the recommended steps on projects before writing his second edition in 1996. He confirmed that applying the ten steps works, hence the subtitle *The Silver Bullet*.

Figure 11-2 lists the ten steps of O'Connell's structured project management approach.

O'Connell describes these in his book and utilizes a probability of success indicator (PSI). Time management is integrated into the PSI. O'Connell disagrees

Figure 11-2   The Ten Steps of Structured Project Management

Planning the Project

1. Visualize what the goal is; set your eyes on the prize.
2. Make a list of the jobs that need to be done.
3. There must be one leader.
4. Assign people to jobs.
5. Manage expectations, allow a margin for error, have a fallback position.

Implementing the Plan/Achieving the Goal

6. Use an appropriate leadership style.
7. Know what's going on.
8. Tell people what's going on.
9. Repeat steps 1 through 8 until step 10.
10. **The Prize**

---

with the conventional wisdom that "software project management" is unique. See his "myths of software project management" in Figure 11-3.

O'Connell believes that to improve the project management side of your project, you need to use an approach that does the following:

1. Provides the ability to define the project goal clearly.
2. Provides a change control system.
3. Provides a way of ensuring that planned resourcing is achieved, and when it is not, that everybody is aware of the consequences (2, 4, 7, 8, and 9 will do this for you).
4. Provides a way of including contingency in the plan.
5. Enables the up-front production of project plans that predict a possible chaining together of all the jobs in the project.
6. Makes it clear that project managers are accountable for projects.
7. Ensures that the expectations of project participants aren't confined to a footnote in the plan but are a crucial element of the project planning progression and eventual success.
8. Provides simple and effective monitoring and control methods.

Figure 11-3   The Myths of Software Project Management

The Myths of Software Project Management

In our work with companies on project management, it is interesting how the same issues surface again and again. We publish them here under the title **The Myths of Software Project Management.**

(1) Software development is one of the most unpredictable things around.

Wrong. Software development is orders of magnitude more predictable than you think.

(2) If we told our customer/management what the real cost and delivery date of the project was, we would never win the business/get to do the project.

Perhaps. But do you think you would win the business if your customer/management always believed you when you told them what the delivery date and cost were? And if furthermore you *always* delivered on those commitments?

(3) Software project management is at best an uncertain science, at worst a black art. All we can do is to hire in or build up as much project management expertise as possible and hope that we win more than we lose.

Wrong. There is an absolutely correct way to run a project, which everyone involved in project management should know about.

(4) It's in the nature of the business that management/customers impose unreasonable deadlines.

It is, but have you ever stopped to wonder why they do it? It's because they don't believe you when you give them estimates. As a result they reckon that if they pin you to a tight deadline or resource constraint, they'll get it when they want it.

(5) Management or customers never believe us when we give them estimates.

Sure they don't. Generally speaking, you don't believe the estimates yourself. Either that or you have very little confidence in them. Why should they?

(continued)

Figure 11-3   The Rationale for Requirements Engineering (*continued*)

(6) But we can't have a great deal of confidence in our estimates. They're only guesses. Software estimating is hit and miss; we will never be able to do better than that.
Wrong. There are all sorts of methods available to do software estimation.

(7) Yes, but they involve us using COCOMO or something like that.
Wrong again. You have all the required information and methods already at your disposal.

(8) It's in the nature of software that projects will always require large amounts of overtime, blood, sweat, and tears to get them out the door.
Nuh uh. Doesn't have to be if you plan 'em properly.

(9) We always have a safety valve even if we wouldn't admit it publicly. We can always shorten the test phase and make up any shortcomings in future releases.
Sure you can. Have you ever calculated what this costs you?

(10) Software project management is a problem that will always be with us.
Nope. A solution exists, and you can start to implement it today.

9. Provides simple and effective reporting mechanisms.
10. Allows that when projects get into trouble, the source of the problem is looked for in the correct place.[4]

These guidelines may seem overly simplistic as presented here. Do yourself a favor: Get O'Connell's book and digest it before you draw your conclusions.

The second book that I recommend is *Software Project Survival Guide* by Steve McConnell. McConnell draws on a career's worth of experience to provide concepts and techniques to manage software projects effectively. A short test, called the Software Project Survival Test, assesses a software project's health.[5] McConnell provides survival concepts, with emphasis on well-defined processes. He notes that organizations that have explicitly focused on improving their

---

[4]See http://www.etpint.com/products.htm.

[5]The test is available in electronic form at http://www.construx.com.

development processes have, over several years, cut their time-to-market by approximately one half and reduced their costs and defects by factors of three to ten at an average cost of roughly $1,500 per developer per year![6]

McConnell advises that more attention be paid to project planning, tracking, risk management, and people dimensions such as aligning developers' interests with work assignments, showing appreciation, providing offices, and avoiding cubicles.[7] He suggests that keys to effective project management include being able to control changes; having an effective requirements process; providing a good architecture; being able to develop meaningful estimates for effort, cost, and schedule; providing a staged delivery plan; and performing technical reviews. He concludes: "Software project survival does not happen accidentally. The work that is required to make a software project succeed is not especially difficult or time-consuming, but it must be executed diligently from the first day of the project to the last." McConnell's approach is based on the Software Engineering Institute's (SEI's) Capability Maturity Model (CMM),[8] which he considers "a gold mine of hard-won industry experience in prioritizing implementation of development practices."[9] He recommends that the National Aeronautics and Space Administration Software Engineering Laboratory's *Recommended Approach to Software Development,* Revision 3, is a complementary reference that describes how to apply the practices to a specific project.[10] In a later article, McConnell emphasizes that it is possible to set up a project environment in which the goals of developers' creativity and the satisfaction of management objectives are in harmony. "Good project leadership puts a focus on process that allows programmers to feel incredibly productive. Developers, their project, and their organization all reap the benefit."[11]

The third book that I recommend is *Software Project Management: A Unified Framework* by Walker Royce. Royce helps us understand the shortcomings of

---

[6]McConnell, *Software Project Survival Guide,* p. 26.

[7]McConnell references DeMarco's and Lister's research in *Peopleware,* which found that productivity levels of developers who work in private offices can be as much as 2.5 times greater than the productivity levels of developers who work in open bays or cubicles. See also Jacqueline Vischer, "Will This Open Space Work?"

[8]Paulk and colleagues, *Capability Maturity Model for Software.* Note some additional advice concerning the CMM provided by Walker Royce in *Software Project Management,* pp. 387–390.

[9]McConnell, *Software Project Survival Guide,* p. x.

[10]This book is available free at http://sel.gsfc.nasa.gov/website/documents/online—doc.htm.

[11]McConnell, "The Power of Process," pp. 100–102.

several conventional practices. Figure 11-4 lists ten practices that are found on most projects.

Royce indicates how projects experience the impact of each practice (cost, schedule, and/or quality) and suggests an alternative practice. Another contribution is Royce's description of how artifacts evolve through three discrete states: the prototyping environment, the development environment, and the maintenance environment (Figure 11-5).

Figure 11-4   Modern Process Approaches for Solving Conventional Problems

Conventional Process: Top 10 Risks	Impact	Modern Process: Inherent Risk Resolution Features
1. Late breakage and excessive scrap/rework	Quality, cost, schedule	Architecture-first approach Iterative development Automated change management Risk-confronting process
2. Attrition of key personnel	Quality, cost, schedule	Successful, early iterations Trustworthy management and planning
3. Inadequate development resources	Cost, schedule	Environments as first-class artifacts of the process Industrial-strength, integrated environments Model-based engineering artifacts Round-trip engineering
4. Adversarial stakeholders	Cost, schedule	Demonstration-based review Use case-oriented requirements/ testing
5. Necessary technology insertion	Cost, schedule	Architecture-first approach Component-based development
6. Requirements creep	Cost, schedule	Iterative development Use case modeling Demonstration-based review
7. Analysis paralysis	Schedule	Demonstration-based review Use case-oriented requirements/ testing

Conventional Process: Top 10 Risks	Impact	Modern Process: Inherent Risk Resolution Features
8. Inadequate performance	Quality	Demonstration-based performance assessment Early architecture performance feedback
9. Overemphasis on artifacts	Schedule	Demonstration-based assessment Objective quality control
10. Inadequate function	Quality	Iterative development Early prototypes, incremental releases

Figure 11-5   Evolution of Project Artifacts

1. The *prototyping environment* includes an architecture test bed for prototyping project architectures to evaluate trade-offs during the inception and elaboration phases of the life cycle. This informal configuration of tools should be capable of supporting the following activities:

   • Performance trade-offs and technical risk analyses
   • Make/buy trade-offs and feasibility studies for commercial products
   • Fault tolerance/dynamic reconfiguration trade-offs
   • Analysis of the risks associated with transitioning to full-scale implementation
   • Development of test scenarios, tools, and instrumentation suitable for analyzing the requirements

2. The *development environment* should include a full suite of development tools needed to support the various process work flows and to support round-trip engineering to the maximum extent possible.
3. The *maintenance environment* should typically coincide with a mature version of the development environment. In some cases, the maintenance environment may be a subset of the development environment delivered as one of the project's end products.

Ensure That Selected Members of the Development Team Have Domain Knowledge

I recommend that several members of the development team have extensive domain knowledge. By domain knowledge, I mean that the individual has extensive experience and expertise in the functional areas being addressed by the system and/or with respect to specific capabilities required or needs of the customer. Sometimes such people are referred to as subject matter experts (SMEs). The reason for this recommendation is that such people have been involved in situations similar to those needed in the planned system. They have addressed some of the issues, they know the background and legacy (historical) systems, they are familiar with the organizations involved and the resources available, and they know some of the people who are involved as customers and in other key roles. In short, they have a knowledge base about the planned system. They have a perspective from which to consider new needs or enhanced capabilities.

This is not to suggest that the domain experts/SMEs will *dictate* the definition of the requirements, the design of the planned system, the selection of the methods and tools to be used, and so forth. Rather, they are an invaluable resource to the team because of their knowledge, experience, and expertise.

In particular, I recommend that one or more members of the requirements engineering group on the project be domain experts, preferably trained and familiar with the automated requirements tool to be used.

Perform the Development Effort Using Known (Trained), Proven Processes, Mechanisms, Methods, Techniques, and Tools

Industry experience has shown that development teams are more effective when they are using known (trained), proven processes, mechanisms, methods, techniques, and tools. This seems obvious. Why don't we do it?

Here are two reasons:

1. The customer insists that technologies, methods, or tools of which it has heard or previously bought into and deems advantageous be used. An example is a customer who insists that object-oriented (OO) technologies be used in spite of the fact that the development team is experienced primarily in structured development approaches.[12]

---

[12]Rational Corporation has made major investments in products to address requirements-related activities, which Rational refers to as the *Requirements Management Solution*. An example

2. Employers and project management are often concerned about training costs, which frequently wind up being an overhead cost rather than a cost that is reimbursed by the customer. There is a tendency to pretend that the team can learn methods, techniques, and tools via on-the-job training or from others who are familiar with them. It is an astute manager/organization who/that is willing to make an investment in the training and in the team. A related issue is that individuals need to feel that they are growing professionally. The practice of finding out what a technical performer is interested in learning, providing appropriate training, and assigning her to that area is one that fosters loyalty and commitment to the organization/employer. Not making this effort leads to frustration, a feeling that the employer is not willing to invest in his people and is not concerned with their professional development and reduced retention.

I have witnessed tremendous thrashing (lots of activity but not much progress) in my career in situations in which the members of the team were not familiar and trained in the processes, mechanisms, methods, techniques, and tools being used, and in which the customer or project management insisted on using unproven techniques. These situations defy common sense, which is always a good guide.

Royce has provided good insights for us in his book, *Software Project Management: A Unified Framework*. Figure 11-6 contrasts technologies used on successful and unsuccessful projects.

---

of a Rational product is Rational Suite Analyst Studio, which provides a Web-enabled elicitation capability; use case modeling; Rational RequisitePro for requirements management; Rational Rose for visual modeling; Rational ClearCase for configuration management (CM); and ClearQuest for change management. All this is provided on the basis of the Rational Unified Process (RUP). The RUP separates the terminology used by managers and developers. Developers concern themselves with work flows, which are the following typical activities: requirements gathering, analysis, design, and so on. Managers get a new set of terminology to describe the phases, which are not tightly linked to the work flows: inception, elaboration, construction, transition, and evolution (Kulak and Guiney, *Use Cases: Requirements in Context*, p. 140). The industry literature concerning OO, the Unified Modeling Language, and the RUP is growing rapidly. An early book on the topic was written by Ivar Jacobson and colleagues, *Object-Oriented Software Engineering*. See also the Addison-Wesley Object Technology Series, a collection of 30 recent, excellent books that provide guidance on all aspects of these technologies. The authors are established and are well known in systems and software engineering. See http://www.awl.com/cseng/otseries/. A special thank you to Hal Miller of Litton TASC for sharing his OO experiences and for helping me to clarify my own views. See Bruce F. Webster, *Pitfalls of Object-Oriented Development*, for an excellent set of recommendations.

Figure 11-6   Technologies Used on Successful and Unsuccessful Projects

Technologies on Unsuccessful Projects	Technologies on Successful Projects
No historical software measurement data*	Accurate software measurement*
Failure to use automated estimating tools*	Early use of estimating tools*
Failure to use automated planning tools*	Continuous use of planning tools*
Failure to monitor progress or milestones*	Formal progress reporting*
Failure to use effective architecture*	Formal architecture planning*
Failure to use effective development methods*	Formal development methods*
Failure to use design reviews	Formal design reviews
Failure to use code inspections	Formal code inspections
Failure to include formal risk management*	Formal risk management*
Informal, inadequate testing	Formal testing methods
Manual design and specification	Automated design and specifications
Failure to use formal configuration control*	Automated configuration control*
More than 30% creep in user requirements*	Less than 10% creep in user requirements*
Inappropriate use of Fourth-Generation Languages	Use of suitable languages
Excessive and unmeasured complexity	Controlled and measured complexity
Little or no reuse of certified materials	Significant reuse of certified materials
Failure to define database elements	Formal database planning

* Project management factors

Provide and Utilize Mechanisms to Foster Effective Communications Throughout the Development Team

Speaking of common sense, it would seem obvious that individuals throughout the team will be able to perform better and more effectively if they have an understanding of what's going on within the project effort. For example, it's likely that things I'm doing in requirements engineering impact (and are impacted by) things happening in other engineering groups (for example, systems engineering, software development, CM, integration and test, QA, independent verification and validation, documentation, project control, project management). We know from our experience (not only from our professional experience but also from our marriage, our children, and our relationships with others) that effective communication doesn't just happen. Effective communication requires sponsorship (including training), good interpersonal relations, teamwork, an open mind, and effort.

As emphasized in Chapter 7, we recommend that mechanisms be provided and utilized to foster effective communication throughout the development team. Examples of such mechanisms include the following:

1. Regular "brown bag" lunches at which one project group briefs the others concerning its current activities and plans. Invariably (in my experience), lightbulbs go off: "You're doing xyz? I didn't realize that! We are doing abc, which is related to what you're doing! We need to talk!"
2. Regular informal sessions at which the PM communicates to the project team such things as current status and activities concerning the customer, changes in requirements and the rationale for them, training needs and opportunities, project funding trends (budget and actual), special needs or initiatives as perceived by the PM or by one or more project groups, and so forth. The PM encourages questions and comments and is receptive (not defensive) to opinions being expressed, whether she agrees with them or not. The PM and other managers hang around after the sessions and otherwise make themselves generally available to receive inputs, ideas, suggestions, recommendations, comments, even criticism. Food could be provided. Such sessions may include recognition of the entire team, project groups, and/or individuals. Process improvement paraphernalia such as mugs, pocket guides, T-shirts, posters, pens with the project logo, and so forth could be provided to foster pride and morale.

3. Posting information (and keeping it current) in multiple visible locations around the project facilities. Examples of information that should be visible include

   - Project goals and objectives
   - Project schedule and current status
   - Project members by group
   - Relevant and useful metrics

4. Regular meetings with the customers. As noted previously, *keeping the customer involved and engaged throughout the project is a key to success.* Such meetings can be held at many levels and between related customer and project performers (for example, systems engineering, software engineering, QA, and CM). In addition, consider having the senior customer representative/sponsor (and other customer representatives) make a presentation informally and periodically to the project team. Such direct contact with the customer fosters a better understanding of why we're doing all this work, improves communications, provides greater motivation, and strengthens teamwork.

5. Formal internal training sessions to improve communications and relationships.

6. A facilitated session timed at the halfway mark of a project, during which the development team discusses what is working and what is not working at this point in the project. The project leader uses the information to redirect the project and to correct potential problems with personalities, management style, misunderstandings, schedule stress, and so forth.[13]

Utilize Peer Reviews and Inspections to Remove Defects from Processes and Work Products

Peer reviews are *a very effective method* for reducing the costs of a project. This is because peer reviews eliminate errors early and reduce rework. As noted earlier, rework is estimated at 45% of project costs industrywide.[14] Peer reviews come in

---

[13]With thanks to Bill Wiley for contributing his experience.

[14]An alternative that takes advantage of the subject matter expertise of domain experts is joint design sessions of users and analysts. This approach is effective and may make better use of the time available.

different flavors, from a simple approach to formal inspections.[15] PRC utilizes an internally developed peer review process based on the Software Capability Maturity Model (SW-CMM). It has been continuously improved during the past eight years to include a peer review handbook, checklists, peer review participant and moderator training, use of a personal defect checklist, and other capabilities. Peer review participant and peer review moderator training are available (each two hours in duration). Tom Gilb[16] strongly recommends a much more rigorous formal inspection approach. Peer reviews and inspections are recommended for all work products, not just for software, with one primary emphasis being *peer review of all requirements work products.*

The project should evolve a list of artifacts and work products for which a peer review or inspection is required. The attitude that the purpose of doing the peer review is to *help the author minimize defects* must be fostered. Defects are often referred to as *major* or *minor.* A **major defect** is one that precludes the effective use of the work product, such as a design deficiency or discovery of conflicting requirements. A **minor defect** is a format problem, spelling error, language usage problem, acronym or definition not provided or explained, or other cosmetic problem. (Engineers being engineers, we have very different opinions on what falls into different categories. It's important not to allow ourselves to become our own worst enemies. Members of project teams need to put values such as respect for one another, keeping an open mind, and looking to the greater good in front of "being right.") Recall the discussion of the traits of systems and software engineers in Chapter 1.

Tom Gilb[17] is an ardent advocate that rigorous, formal inspections should be used, rather than the peer review. The capability to perform "Gilb inspections"

---

[15]See Freedman and Weinberg, *Handbook of Walkthroughs, Inspections, and Technical Reviews.*

[16]See Gilb's courses and *Software Inspection* (by Gilb and Graham), and visit his Web site for more information, http://www.result-planning.com/. One can learn a lot from Gilb's books and his presentations, which are provided in the U.S. periodically.

[17]Gilb also advocates evolutionary delivery (EVO), requirements-driven management (RDM), and the use of impact estimation (IE) tables. For some intellectually challenging materials, see Gilb's Web site, http://www.result-planning.com/. See also "The Evolutionary Development Model for Software" by Elaine L. May and Barbara A. Zimmer. Gilb is currently writing another book on the subject of priority management. The manuscript is available for downloading at Gilb's Web site.

typically requires five days of formal training and a lot of rigor.[18] One advantage of the "Gilb approach" is that he advocates *sampling* of work products rather than review of the entire product. The idea is that by identifying defects in the first few pages, the author can utilize this feedback to address similar problems throughout the document or work product. My suggestion is to apply some of the characteristics of the Gilb inspection and his other techniques (EVO, RDM, and IE tables) as it makes sense for a project to do so.

We should not overlook having some of our work simply reviewed by one or two colleagues whose expertise in particular areas is valued. Following this practice before a formal peer review can save a lot of time and effort on the part of the several (three to seven) reviewers in a formal peer review.

Also, be advised of the tremendous value of a good peer review moderator. The moderator need not necessarily possess technical expertise in the area being addressed by the work product. Rather, he should possess superb facilitation skills and be well organized.

Ensure That Configuration Management Is Effective

As noted previously, there are three types of control:

1. Version control, in which the version number of a work product is tracked
2. Change control, for which we use change bars and so forth to indicate changes
3. Formal CM

Version control and/or change control are often applied to documents. Formal CM is most frequently referenced in connection with the code (sets of computer instructions) that comprise a baseline, although I recommend it for all requirements artifacts.

It's necessary to apply all three types to a project. It is alarming to note from industry experience how frequently projects lose all control by not providing

---

[18]Industry consultant Robert Sabourin trains and facilitates Gilb inspections. He advises that the basic training can be accomplished in four hours plus one example inspection. A mentor or champion is required to train moderators, scribes, and process administrators. Sabourin's experience is that Gilb inspections provide good value, for example, to inspect requirements against sources and to inspect all downstream work from requirements. Performing inspections can foster communication and gain buy-in. Inspections can be used to test artifacts that otherwise would be nearly impossible to test objectively. Inspections can be implemented with minimal impact on the normal work flow. See http://www.amibug.com.

CM. It's beyond the scope of this book to explain how CM should be implemented. The project requires people who have successfully implemented and deployed CM practices previously. This is not an area in which a project can afford to utilize junior people. Tremendous resources can be wasted and schedules jeopardized when CM is not used effectively.

Foster an Independent QA Role That Proactively Assists and Supports the Development Team and Provides Value to the Project

The performance of an effective QA role on a project is an art that requires an experienced, effective QA lead who has performed this role successfully on previous projects.

QA is not

- A service provided just prior to work products being delivered to our customers
- Limited to fixing format and spelling problems
- Unneeded or unnecessary
- The enemy
- To be feared or not trusted
- Overhead
- Too expensive

QA should be integrated effectively into the total project effort, and the QA lead and performers should be considered key members of the project team, equal to all other roles. QA should provide a proactive role and should participate (for example) in the design or tailoring and review of project processes. QA should perform periodic and event-driven reviews and audits of

- Organizational and project policies. Do we have them, and to what extent are they being complied with?
- Tailored organizational process/project processes. Are they available, documented, deployed, implemented, and being used?
- Training. Is required or desired training available and being provided, and what is its effectiveness?
- The processes, mechanisms, methods, techniques, and tools being used. Are they appropriate? Have users been trained? Are the performers familiar with them?
- The metrics used to track progress and to make adjustments/improvements. Is a set of effective measures available and used?

- The extent of senior management sponsorship. Is vocal and committed senior management support provided to the project?
- Periodic and event-driven reviews of project progress and status. Are they performed? Are action items assigned and action plans developed as a result of the reviews? Are action items and action plans tracked to completion?

In addition, project QA should be in regular dialog with customer QA. Perhaps most important, project QA should be the "eyes and ears" of senior management, ever vigilant to recommend steps that are in the best interests of the project and the organization.

Ensure That Subcontractors Are Managed So That Their Contributions Are Effective

An area in which many projects get off track relates to subcontractors. Let's be honest and direct: *Almost everyone wants to do a good job; that's human nature.* If I'm *not* doing a good job, it may be that I'm not fully aware of what I should be doing; or, possibly, I don't have the necessary motivation, experience, training, and/or authority to be effective in that role. Perhaps I'm underutilized, and I need additional challenge and responsibility.

So it is with subcontractor efforts. Let's accept the intentions of the subcontractor to do a good job. Why as an industry do we have such poor results in making effective use of subcontractors?

Here are some of the reasons, based on my own experience:

1. The subcontractor is viewed as a "taker" rather than as a valued member of the development team (for example, we assume that the subcontractor's only objective is to garner more business and revenue, rather than to contribute to the project).
2. The subcontractor has not been given needed background information and is crippled in performing well.
3. The subcontractor is physically located separately from the rest of the development team, jeopardizing effective communication and coordination.[19]
4. Insufficient efforts are made to foster strong teamwork and communication with the subcontractor.
5. Problems and issues are not addressed promptly, candidly, and with the certain expectation of change being required.

---

[19]Optimally, the entire development team should be collocated. Separate locations jeopardize team effort and success.

In other words, in my experience, prime contractors tend to create or cause the problems and issues that prevent the subcontractor from being an effective component of the team.

The SW-CMM[20] suggests an excellent set of criteria that facilitates good subcontractor performance (Figure 11-7). These criteria, if performed, will help implement this recommendation.[21]

Figure 11-7   Subcontractor Management Key Practices

The Purpose of Subcontractor Management

The purpose of Subcontract Management is to select qualified subcontractors and manage them effectively.

Subcontract Management involves selecting a subcontractor, establishing commitments with the subcontractor, and tracking and reviewing the subcontractor's performance and results. These practices cover the management of a software (only) subcontract, as well as the management of the software component of a subcontract that includes software, hardware, and possibly other system components. The subcontractor is selected based on its ability to perform the work. Many factors contribute to the decision to subcontract a portion of the prime contractor's work. Subcontractors may be selected based on strategic business alliances as well as technical considerations. The practices of this key process area address the traditional acquisition process associated with subcontracting a defined portion of the work to another organization. When subcontracting, a documented agreement covering the technical and nontechnical (e.g., delivery dates) requirements is established and is used as the basis for managing the subcontract. The work to be done by the subcontractor and the plans for the work are documented. The

(continued)

---

[20]Paulk and colleagues, *Capability Maturity Model for Software.*

[21]As in the case for all key process areas (KPAs) of the SW-CMM, *Key Practices of the Capability Maturity Model* provides much additional information and guidance concerning how to design, deploy, implement, and use the process (Paulk and colleagues). I suggest that this reference be utilized extensively in pursuing process improvement initiatives.

Figure 11-7   Subcontractor Management Key Practices (*continued*)

standards that are to be followed by the subcontractor are compatible with the prime contractor's standards.

The planning, tracking, and oversight activities for the subcontracted work are performed by the subcontractor. The prime contractor ensures that these planning, tracking, and oversight activities are performed appropriately and that the products delivered by the subcontractor satisfy their acceptance criteria. The prime contractor works with the subcontractor to manage the product and process interfaces.

The Goals of Subcontract Management

1. The prime contractor selects qualified subcontractors.
2. The prime contractor and the subcontractor agree to their commitments to each other.
3. The prime contractor and the subcontractor maintain ongoing communications.
4. The prime contractor tracks the subcontractor's actual results and performance against its commitments.

The Top-Level Activities Performed for Subcontract Management

1. The work to be subcontracted is defined and planned according to a documented procedure.
2. The subcontractor is selected based on an evaluation of the subcontract bidder's ability to perform the work according to a documented procedure.
3. The contractual agreement between the prime contractor and the subcontractor is used as the basis for managing the subcontract.
4. A documented subcontractor's development plan is reviewed and approved by the prime contractor.
5. A documented and approved subcontractor's development plan is used for tracking the activities and communicating status.
6. Changes to the subcontractor's statement of work, subcontract terms and conditions, and other commitments are resolved according to a documented procedure.

7. The prime contractor's management conducts periodic status/ coordination reviews with the subcontractor's management.

8. Periodic technical reviews and interchanges are held with the subcontractor.

9. Formal reviews to address the subcontractor's engineering accomplishments and results are conducted at selected milestones according to a documented procedure.

10. The prime contractor's quality assurance group monitors the subcontractor's quality assurance activities according to a documented procedure.

11. The prime contractor's configuration management group monitors the subcontractor's activities for configuration management according to a documented procedure.

12. The prime contractor conducts acceptance testing as part of the delivery of the subcontractor's products according to a documented procedure.

13. The subcontractor's performance is evaluated on a periodic basis, and the evaluation is reviewed with the subcontractor.

Note: This figure is adapted from the abridged practices of the *Key Practices of the Capability Maturity Model,* version 1.1. It deletes the word "software" and takes the view that these practices are effective for systems and software engineering.

Use Appropriate, Useful Metrics to Manage the Project

Inscribe onto your brain and on artifacts made available to project performers

The things that are measured and tracked are the ones that improve![22]

---

[22]The time in my life that I really came to understand this axiom was when our two older children were in college at the same time. The impact on our family budget was severe. I learned to manage and track our scarce resources very carefully.

As it is with family and personal budgets, so it is in project management. We need to identify a limited set of metrics or indicators to manage processes and the project. We need to engage the development team in the definition and selection of these metrics. We need to track them carefully. We need to make changes in how the project is being managed based on regular review of these indicators.

The two best references that I know concerning metrics in the vast metrics literature were written by Robert Grady[23] as he was creating, developing, implementing, and using a metrics program at Hewlett-Packard. Grady experienced the bumps and bruises that metrics programs do—most fail. Among the lessons learned are the need for senior management sponsorship of the metrics program, PM buy-in, and perseverance.

The $1 million question is: Which metrics should be used? Walker Royce provides the advice indicated in Figure 11-8 based on his two decades of experience. To this list I would add requirements volatility.

Many projects use (usually because they are required by contract to do it) an earned value (EV) approach to measuring cost expenditures over the project life cycle, sometimes referred to as *earned value analysis* (EVA). EVA is a general term for the formal cost/schedule status reporting (C/SSR) requirements defined by the U.S. Department of Defense.[24] Another related term is *cost and schedule control system criteria* (CSCSC). This involves a very detailed and work-intensive effort to measure budgeted and actual progress. Its major weakness for software projects is its inability to assess technical progress (percent complete) accurately and objectively. My experience as a member of a 100-person project team in support of a major government contract provides a testimonial. I witnessed a large expenditure of time and effort (not only on the part of the project control staff, but also on the part of all of the technical performers) to track budgeted and actual effort using a well-known and government-approved EV system. The approach did not work, because decisions concerning percent complete were

---

[23]Grady and Caswell, *Software Metrics: Establishing a Companywide Program*, and Grady, *Practical Software Metrics for Project Management and Process Improvement*. I recommend these to you for your study and application.

[24]The primary measurements used are the budgeted cost of work scheduled (BCWS), budgeted cost of work performed (BCWP), and actual cost of work performed (ACWP). From these, indicators are provided: Schedule Variance = BCWP – BCWS, and Cost Variance = BCWP – ACWP (a negative value indicates being over budget). Completion figures can be calculated as follows: budget at completion, the final value of BCWS, estimated cost at completion, and calculated cost at completion.

Figure 11-8   Overview of the Seven Core Metrics

Metric	Purpose	Perspectives
Work and progress	Iteration planning, plan vs. actuals, management indicator	SLOC, function points, object points, scenarios, test cases, SCOs
Budgeted cost and expenditures	Financial insight, plan vs. actuals, management indicator	Cost per month, full-time staff per month, percentage of budget expended
Staffing and team dynamics	Resource plan vs. actuals, hiring rate, attrition rate	People per month added, people per month leaving
Change traffic and stability	Iteration planning, management indicator of schedule convergence	SCOs opened vs. SCOs closed, by type (0,1,2,3,4), by release/component/subsystem
Breakage and modularity	Convergence, software scrap, quality indicator	Reworked SLOC per change, by type (0,1,2,3,4), by release/component/subsystem
Rework and adaptability	Convergence, software rework, quality indicator	Average hours per change, by type (0,1,2,3,4), by release/component/subsystem
MTBF and maturity	Test coverage/adequacy, robustness for use, quality indicator	Failure counts, test hours until failure, by release/component/subsystem

estimates by the technical performers, who were under great pressure to be "on schedule." The technical performers provided the data that management wanted to see. Finally, a point was reached at which it became obvious that the EV system didn't reflect reality. At that point, a decision was made to "rebaseline," that is, to start the EV data anew. This happened twice more over a three-year period on this same project. Bottom line: The substantial effort required to support the EV system was wasted, and project management lacked insight into the real schedule and financial status of the project. This example should not be interpreted to imply that EV systems aren't effective. I have seen them utilized effectively. However, one needs to have mechanisms in place to ensure that the data reported are real. For example, project management must encourage honesty and candor in reporting and must be willing to make adjustments in project activities based on the data. If management can't or won't deal with real data, no financial measurement system can help. Figure 11-9 explains the basic parameters of an EV system.

Figure 11-10 provides a case study of an innovative and effective use of EV from Litton Advanced Systems.[25]

I'll have more to say about the value of a PM being able to manage quantitatively later. *Suffice it to say, that without tracking useful metrics, we lack control of the project.*

Ensure That a Systematic Approach to Involving the Customer in This Entire Effort Is Working

The bottom line at delivery is: Do the customer and user find that the system works and meets their real needs?

To suggest that we could conduct a project development effort in a vacuum (without constant customer involvement) and expect to have a successful outcome is ridiculous. For one thing, customers' needs change while we are doing the development work. For another, decisions affect all aspects of the effort. To the extent

Figure 11-9   The Basic Parameters of an EV System

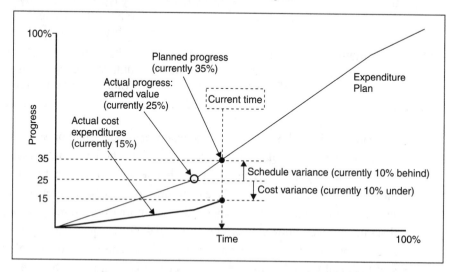

[25]With thanks to Dan Marchegiani, chief scientist, a member of the development team.

Figure 11-10   An Innovative Use of EV to Track Progress

Litton Advanced Systems used a simple system to measure earned value (EV) on a software design effort for a Navy Radar Warning System. The project was the higher order language upgrade to the AN/ALR-67E(V)2 Radar Warning System. The new software contained five computer software configuration items that were comprised of 30 computer software components (CSCs) and approximately 450 computer software units (CSUs). The project included the standard major milestones of requirements, preliminary design, critical design, code, unit test, and system test readiness reviews. The project also contained documentation artifacts, such as a system segment specification (SSS), an interface requirements specification (IRS), a system specification data dictionary (SSDD), a software requirements specification (SRS), software development folders for each CSC, unit test procedures for each CSU, a system test plan (STP), and a system test description (STD). The SSS contained approximately 1,500 requirements. The STD contained 624 system-level tests that verified all requirements. The tests were designed so that some tests could verify several requirements. The metrics used to determine EV were objective and did not require an opinion from the developing engineer. During the coding phase, each CSU was given a peer code walkthrough, reviewed by configuration management, quality assurance, software and system lead engineers, and Navy customer representatives. (As a side note, the Navy customer had representatives on-site for the entire development phase, and daily communication with them resolved many requirement and design issues quickly and expediently.) Each of the 450 CSUs was in one of three states: not submitted, reviewed and not accepted, or reviewed and accepted. The percentage of CSUs in each category was tracked and known by all members of the development team and customer at all times. During the test and integration phase, the metrics used were based on each of the 624 system-level tests in the STD. Each test was in one of three states: not tested, tested and failed, or tested and passed. Periodically, regression tests would be performed to ensure that new changes did not make a previously passed test failed. When this did happen, the status of the previously passed test case was

(continued)

Figure 11-10   An Innovative Use of EV to Track Progress (*continued*)

changed from passed to failed. The percentage of system test and integration completion was the percentage of currently passed tests over 624 total tests. At approximately one third of the way through the test phase, we were able to determine that the rate of new tests passing was linear and progressing at a rate of between 15 and 20 tests per week. The development team was able to predict within three weeks when the system testing would be completed and met their prediction. It was a good way for them to determine EV. Certainly, it was a lot better than asking the developer over and over when he was going to be done (knowing that the last 10% of the work takes 90% of the time).

that the customer is aware of and involved in these decisions, she will have a better understanding of the impacts on the delivered system.

McConnell[26] stresses this as a major theme of his works and also as a result of a career devoted to supporting customers with projects and developed systems.

It's common sense. But, we don't involve our customer. Why not? Here are some reasons from my own experience:

1. We fail to think of the project team as inclusive of our customers and users, and we fail to be proactive and to take specific steps and initiatives to involve the customer.
2. We're afraid the customer will find out too much about the problems we're having and the mistakes we've made, rather than seek their help in overcoming difficulties.
3. We are "too busy" to "take time out" to communicate and coordinate with our customer.
4. We fail to use mechanisms and development approaches that foster, encourage, and value customer involvement, such as requirements workshops, a joint team, prototyping, joint application development, and so forth.
5. We pretend "it's harder" when we involve the customer.
6. We think we can do it without the user.

---

[26]See Steve McConnell, *Software Project Survival Guide* and *Rapid Development*.

7. We believe customer involvement "costs too much money and time."
8. There are personality conflicts.
9. Our own management won't let us.

I recommend that the customer be involved extensively throughout the entire development effort.

Manage Processes Quantitatively. Also, Use a Defect Prevention (DP) Process, a Technology Change Management (TCM) Process, and a Process Change Management (PCM) Process. Perform Extensive Reinsertion and Reuse Throughout the Organization

At no time in my professional career did I come to appreciate this better than when senior management at PRC decided that we would be an SW-CMM level 5 Company by March 2000. Suddenly, the urging of our full-time process engineers for our PMs to consider and use quantitative methods became *required!* A combination top-down ("you need to do this") and bottom-up (working-level working group to figure out *how* it should be done) effort succeeded in less than nine months, with the PMs of the selected projects becoming *believers* in quantitative management! They enthusiastically expressed the business value of being able to manage quantitatively. The PMs were personally involved, and they became knowledgeable about the quantitative techniques and their utility. They were able to brief authoritatively explaining how statistical process control (SPC) (for example) enabled them to discover and implement improvements that had business value.

During the past several years, PRC has implemented a robust TCM process, another SW-CMM level 5 KPA. Again, the impetus for this improvement came from the corporate president at that time who believed that technology identification, application, insertion, and reuse are fundamental to PRC's strategic business objectives. He patiently mentored us in the development of the TCM process until at last he commented that he felt that the TCM process was "evolving and maturing."[27]

More recently, PRC has designed, deployed, and implemented a DP process. One must not confuse DP with peer reviews, discussed earlier. DP involves analyzing defects that were encountered in the past and taking specific actions to

---

[27]Len Pomata, President, Litton PRC, 1995.

prevent the occurrence of those types of defects in the future.[28] It involves systematically examining the data associated with a key activity, identifying categories of problems (or defects), doing root-cause analysis to identify the reasons for the defects, and taking corrective actions to prevent the defects from occurring.

A related SW-CMM level 5 KPA is process change management (PCM). PCM involves managing the organization's key processes and enabling and empowering continuous improvements to them. Richard Zultner, a respected consultant in the field of quality improvement, observes that an organization that actively practices continuous improvement can expect to become "world class" in approximately five years.

Technology reinsertion helps generate revenue and reuse (of processes, plans, work products, whatever), and saves time and money.

All of these areas reflect habits and attitudes of mature organizations. They are not the starting place for process improvement, but rather they help to facilitate and to understand and enjoy the benefits of process improvement as a result of improved return on investment of the work performed on our projects and in our organizations.

It's important to note that the work habits of the performers in a mature organization are also refined. Having a set of rules of how we are to treat one another is invaluable.[29] Action items are assigned and worked. Schedule milestones are met. People support one another. People respect and enjoy each other. They are fulfilled and most days leave work with a feeling of accomplishment. They have fun at work.

Musings on Project Management

Having considered an entire book full of effective requirements practices, suggestions, recommendations, and advice from countless industry practitioners and experts, it's interesting to reflect on the musings of a seasoned industry practitioner. The observations in Figure 11-11 reflect some of the practical limitations of our best efforts.

---

[28]Paulk and colleagues, *Key Practices of the Capability Maturity Model,* page L5-1.

[29]See PRC's rules of conduct, provided in Chapter 2.

Figure 11-11   Musings on Project Management

I'm grateful to have had the opportunity to support a software development contract recently. My involvement was originally in software metrics, but it has expanded somewhat to include technical interchange with
the subcontractor. The subcontractor is actually doing the majority of the
work, and we are acting as the prime contractor, but with little technical
involvement. It's been a good experience, and the length of time that I
have been involved, on and off, has allowed me to see the dynamics of
controlling a large project over a period of time. Although the project
has experienced problems, I think these problems highlight some fundamental guidelines we might keep in mind for project management and
process improvement.

1. Somebody has to be minding the store—all the time.

You cannot turn software engineers loose and hope they will do the
right thing. There are too many distractions and too many paths to follow, and they are too intelligent—they will find interesting things to do
on their own (which might not be the best things to do). Somebody has
to be there all the time, watching what they are doing. Preferably, this is
the project manager [PM], but if the project manager is not going to take
that responsibility, then the PM needs a surrogate to do it for them. This
continuous technical oversight needs to make sure that the software
engineers are doing the little things that are easy to drop: that software
is getting checked into the [configuration management] system, that testing is being done thoroughly and correctly, that the source code is getting documented, that peer reviews are taking place, that people are
communicating with one another. There are hundreds of little things like
these, that someone, somewhere, has to make sure get done. If no one is
there watching the store, the little things won't get done, and the little
things will add up and kill you.

What this might imply for our work in process improvement is that
we don't necessarily need more processes, but we need high-quality
processes that are "manageable"; i.e., ones that a manager, with a minimum of effort, can make sure are being done. The PM has way too

(continued)

Figure 11-11   Musings on Project Management (*continued*)

much to do already, and the processes need to make this job easier, not add burden. If the processes are too complicated or are not perceived to add value, they won't get done.

2. There is no substitute for technical knowledge.

Management theory is useful, but there is no substitute for having someone in charge who can evaluate technical issues and make informed decisions. Managers do not need to be experts in the field, but it helps immensely if they have enough technical knowledge that they can judge properly the value and the risks of the options being discussed. I think the risk portion of this evaluation is most important (see below). The real value of technical knowledge is to keep everyone honest. If the subordinates know that management has some idea of what they are talking about, they are less likely to color the truth. It is usually not that programmers intend to deceive, but none of us likes to admit we made a mistake or that the option we are proposing is really beneficial only to ourselves, and not to the project.

I think this implies that we need to keep our managers technically up to speed as well as trained in the latest management techniques. Perhaps we sometimes overstress management issues and fail to provide the technical training for managers that is essential for them to use properly the management training they are getting.

3. Mature people are more important than mature process.

Mature people are able to admit they made a mistake, take constructive criticism, and implement corrective action. Mature people are less likely to hide problems. No one likes to admit that he made a mistake or that he can't deliver on something he promised to deliver, but intellectual honesty is critical to the success of a complicated project. We can have mature processes, but if we don't have mature people using them, we don't have very much.

4. Software development is risky.

Sometimes I think our use of the term "software engineering" lulls us into the belief that this is a pure engineering discipline. Some parts of it are, but in implementing a software project, more often than not what we are really doing is research and development (R&D). Engineers can do R&D, but it really means we are doing research, not engineering. Anytime we are using a new platform, a new database product, a new language, a new methodology, a new anything, we are introducing much greater risks into the project. Our standards of testing and proof of concept must be higher than they would be on a typical engineering project. Basically, in an R&D mode, we have to assume that nothing works until proved that it works. This is different from the engineering mode where we can assume that if we follow a set of well-established mathematical procedures and processes, that things will work correctly every time. Management really needs to look at the big risks facing the project and assume that anything that they are doing for the first time represents major risk. The point is not to avoid risk, but to be able to recognize honestly the risks you are taking. The other point to recognize is that if you want a predictable schedule, you can't take too many of these risks all at once. Also, we have to recognize that risks are not additive: If you take too many big risks, they can compound one another so that finding out how to take remedial action can be many times more difficult than if you are dealing with a single major risk.

Summary

Because requirements activities permeate the development process, it is important to address best practices for the development effort. The project environment includes the practices, processes, mechanisms, methods, techniques, and tools that are used to support the development activities. Project management is a crucial factor. Your attention to several recommendations will enhance your project environment and facilitate project management.

The practices of effective communications, collecting requirements from various viewpoints, CM, QA, use of subcontractors, metrics, and systematically involving the customer in the entire project effort are proven ways to facilitate project success. Deployment and use of defect prevention, TCM, and PCM processes also support the achievement of better results. The ability to manage a project quantitatively reflects a mature approach. Reinsertion of technology, reuses of artifacts, and repeatability of processes save effort and money and help to ensure the development of leading-edge products. The habits and attitudes of the performers in mature organizations can help create a productive and enjoyable environment.

Key References and Suggested Readings

ABT Corporation. *Core Competencies for Project Managers.* **2000.** Available at http://www.tsepm.com/may00/art5.htm. The authors assert that core competencies of PMs should be divided into soft and hard skills. The soft skills (based on years of feedback from customers) include visible leadership, flexibility, sound business judgment, trustworthiness, possession of several effective communication styles, ability to act as a coach and mentor, active listening skills, ability to set and to manage expectations, ability to provide constructive project negotiations, ability to facilitate issue and conflict resolution, and ability to provide organizational and leadership skills. The hard skills include project definition, planning, and estimating and providing a control process.

Eliyahu M. Goldratt. *Critical Chain.* **Great Barrington, MA: The North River Press, 1997.** This is a business novel that introduces you to Goldratt's thinking processes. It is thought provoking and stimulating.

Eliyahu M. Goldratt and Jeff Cox. *The Goal.* **2nd rev. ed. Great Barrington, MA: The North River Press, 1992.** This is also a business novel considered by many to be a very important business book. It introduces the Theory of Constraints and emphasizes eliminating bottlenecks.

Robert Grady. *Practical Software Metrics for Project Management and Process Improvement.* **Englewood Cliffs, NJ: Prentice Hall, 1992.** This second book by Grady extends the concepts and examples in his first book based on the design and implementation of a software metrics program at Hewlett Packard. Grady states that if you are a PM or if you are involved in process improvement, this book is for you. Grady believes that the SEI CMM is a model that will help products move toward continuous process improvement—a key to our future. He also believes that a lot depends on what we believe we can do. He recommends that we use the techniques and ideas in the CMM, apply them to our projects, and use them to set continuous improvement goals for our project teams. He believes that we will be surprised at what it is possible to accomplish.

Robert Grady and D. Caswell. *Software Metrics: Establishing a Companywide Program.* **Englewood Cliffs, NJ: Prentice Hall, 1987.** This book provides the history, mechanics, and lessons learned from the example of the Hewlett Packard company's creation, design, development, and implementation of a successful software metrics program. Hewlett Packard, through its Software Metrics Council, determined to collect size, effort, schedule, and defects data initially. Grady and Caswell emphasize that the greatest benefits of collecting metrics are experienced by PMs through better understanding of the process that their team is following and through measurable indicators of project status.

Capers Jones. *Software Quality in 2000: What Works and What Doesn't.* **January 18, 2000.** Briefing available from Software Productivity Research, Inc., at http://www.spr.com. This is a comprehensive briefing based on the database of software projects maintained by Software Productivity Research, Inc., that includes 600 companies, 30 government and military groups, roughly 9,000 total projects, and data from 24 countries. Jones identifies practices that provide good-, mixed-, and minimal-quality results, thus suggesting approaches that provide the best return on the cost and effort invested.

Craig Kaplan, Ralph Clark, and Victor Tang. *Secrets of Software Quality.* **New York: McGraw-Hill, 1995.** Kaplan and colleagues report 40 innovations from IBM that address culture, leadership, process, and tools. There are many excellent suggestions for use in a forward-looking organization. A quality maturity assessment method that is based on the 1994 Malcolm Baldrige Quality Award criteria is provided.

Steve McConnell. *Software Project Survival Guide,* **Redmond, WA: Microsoft Press, 1998.** This is my favorite reference for providing advice, suggestions, and practical help for a systems or software project. McConnell provides a project survival test that gives insight into requirements, planning, project control, risk management, and personnel issues. He then proceeds to provide useful suggestions and survival checks in each area. One can't help being helped by this book. See also http://www.construx.com/stevemcc/.

Fergus O'Connell. *How to Run Successful Projects II—The Silver Bullet.* **2nd ed. New York: Prentice Hall, 1996.** O'Connell is a principal of ETP, The Structured Project Management Company, in Ireland. He presents a straightforward approach for project management consisting of ten steps, with emphasis on project planning and tracking and use of an automated project-tracking tool such as Microsoft Project. He presented this approach in the first edition of his book and then tried it with the companies with which he was consulting—it worked! Hence the unfortunate subtitle *The Silver Bullet.* O'Connell uses a PSI indicator to evaluate the status and probability of success of a project. This is highly recommended reading for every PM and anyone with management responsibilities. See http://www.etpint.com/.

Lawrence H. Putnam and Ware Myers. *Measures for Excellence: Reliable Software on Time, Within Budget.* **Upper Saddle River, NJ: Yourdon Press, 1992.** Putnam and Myers emphasize the life cycle model and provide a simple software estimating system. They provide a glossary of more than 100 terms used in quantitative software management. They explain how conceptual work like software development has been found to progress according to a mathematical curve known as the *Rayleigh distribution.* This formula helps to understand what happens when you compress a schedule, estimate new projects, and add people to a late project, as well as to be able to project the number of defects remaining in a work product. Study of this book facilitates understanding of reliability.

Walker Royce. *Software Project Management: A Unified Framework.* **Reading, MA: Addison-Wesley, 1998.** An excellent read. "Key Points" are provided at the beginning of each chapter, summarizing the main themes. Royce gives attention to project economics, including improving processes and team effectiveness. He provides a management process framework, with emphasis on iterative process planning. He suggests seven core metrics and describes tailoring of processes (including an example of a small-scale project versus a large-scale project). Useful appendixes include The COCOMO Cost Estimation Model, Change Metrics, CCPDS-R Case Study, and Process Improvement and Mapping to the CMM.

Rob Thomsett. *Third Wave Project Management.* **Upper Saddle River, NJ: Yourdon Press, 1993.** This is a useful handbook that encourages use of updated management ideas and techniques for project initiation, planning, estimation, and risk assessment. Thomsett believes that the emergence of new development techniques such as joint requirements planning, joint application design, and rapid application development require a more dynamic and real-time project management approach than is typically used. They require a new focus on team formation, structure, and management, based on pressures for increased productivity, fewer people, and more client-oriented service.

Bruce F. Webster. *Pitfalls of Object-Oriented Development.* **New York: M&T Books, 1995.** This is a superb book that describes pitfalls, not only for OO development but for development in general. Webster candidly shares his wealth of experience, describing each pitfall and noting symptoms, consequences, detection, extraction, and prevention for each one. This is a valuable read for any developer or manager.

Ed Weller. "Practical Applications of Statistical Process Control." In: *Proceedings of the 10th International Conference on Software Quality.* This is an excellent article that explains how to use SPC to improve project success. Applying quantitative methods and SPC to development projects can provide a positive cost-benefit return. Quantitative analysis of inspection and test data is used to analyze product quality during test and to predict postship product quality for a major release. The processes used, decisions made using the project's data, and the results obtained are described. Weller advises that the following questions be asked about any metric or analysis technique: (1) Is it useful, and does it provide information that helps make decisions? (2) Is it usable, and can we reasonably collect the data and do the analysis?

Neal Whitten. *Managing Software Development Projects: Formula for Success.* **2nd ed. New York: John Wiley & Sons, 1995.** Whitten's focus is on practical, easy-to-implement solutions to common problems he has found in consulting with organizations. Formerly with IBM, Whitten has managed a variety of projects. Among the areas addressed are personnel, quality, project scheduling and tracking, product requirements, and product quality and usability. Managers will find many helpful lessons.

PART III

What to Do Next

Part III consists of one chapter, Chapter 12, that describes how to proceed based on the information provided in this book. Common issues (things that are typically in the way) are described. The key importance of the customer is emphasized. Requirements are viewed as a key driver of any systems or software effort. How to finance improvements in the requirements process is discussed. The increasingly competitive business environment is noted. It is asserted that increased management awareness of the importance of the requirements process and stronger management commitment to it are needed. The value of a few useful metrics is emphasized. The "people aspects" of technical projects are addressed, and the importance of the project environment in which they work is emphasized. I suggest that you approach the effort to improve the requirements process in the order of the practices presented here. A requirements checklist to facilitate organizing and carrying out the needed activities is provided. A facilitated goal-setting session involving your customers and the development team is recommended to achieve consensus on critical aspects, including a "shared vision" and a set of "rules of conduct" for the team to which all members of the team agree. Guidelines for systems development based on requirements considerations are provided. A description of how a requirements process facilitates effective project performance is provided. I suggest that no matter where you are in the life cycle of your project, progress is achievable and desirable.

CHAPTER TWELVE

How to Proceed

This chapter provides suggestions concerning how to proceed. I'll assume you agree that the practices recommended in this book are useful and that you believe that many of the recommendations provided in the preceding chapters are practical and doable, and will help you save effort, time, and money. But where do you begin? What should you do to get started from where you are now?

My experience in consulting with organizations is that almost everyone is sincerely committed to doing a good job. Also, funds are usually available for training—a critical ingredient in project success. Management wants to do the right set of things (or at least have the right set of things done), and the technical development team is thirsting for the opportunity to demonstrate its expertise and capabilities. Techniques and automated tools abound. There is a lot of activity.

Why, then, can't we make it happen?

Common Issues

Here is a list of some of the things that are in the way of an effective approach based on my experience:

1. There is no clearly defined goal and set of objectives for the project. Sure, there is a lot of information around, and yes, there are many opinions of what the project is all about. But there is no clearly defined goal and set of

objectives. You could say that the requirements for the project are not clear at the highest level. Whatever information is available is understood differently by various developers. This should not be a surprise, for each of us is the sum of our own experiences—all different!

2. Communication is confused. The leader of the effort is consumed by activities that take him away from "leading the technical development team." Hence, there is no real leader. Other managers involved in the project have strong views, but there is no consensus among them, just strongly held views. The individual managers can't seem to win the others over to their point of view, so they just keep moving with their own perspective. Everybody is busy. People are too busy to communicate effectively.

3. The project lacks mechanisms

   - For achieving a shared vision of the project
   - For fostering effective teamwork
   - For creating a "win-win partnership relationship" between the customer and the supplier
   - For resolving issues
   - For joint responsibility for the requirements
   - For communication among the project team and with the customers and users
   - For sharing information, such as working groups to define best practices
   - For gaining consensus on practices, processes, mechanisms, methods, techniques, and tools
   - For reviewing work products early
   - For prioritizing requirements

4. The requirements process is not defined, documented, trained, understood, and used. There always is a process; it is whatever is being done at the time. It most often is not a defined process, nor is it documented, trained to all of the participants, understood by all of the performers. The opportunity for making improvements to the process is not available or used.

5. No effort has been made to identify the real requirements. The project and the technical development team are proceeding with whatever the customers and users of the needed system have provided them (stated requirements), based on their understanding of what the customers and users meant. No effort is made to achieve a common understanding or to address "real" needs and expectations as discussed in this book (real requirements).

6. Proven, effective practices, such as the ten advocated in this book, are not implemented or used. It's not that industry, program and project managers, and individual performers/developers don't know what to do; rather, we don't make the effort to apply (practice) what we know is better! (From Watts Humphrey's perspective, we don't practice what we preach.) This observation seems to defy logic. However, from our experience, we know that it is true.

7. Most important, the project exists in its organizational setting, with all of the politics, bureaucracy, organizational complexity, and inertia that go with it. There is a lack of a quality improvement (QI) ethic, a commitment to support each other, a set of rules of conduct concerning how to treat one another, and a commitment to teamwork and continuous improvement.

Sound familiar? Take comfort that you and your project are not alone. I see this everywhere. It energizes my own efforts in working with organizations because there is *a lot* of opportunity for improvement.

Key Factors in Addressing These Issues

The Customer

The customer is critical. We must find ways to establish and maintain effective communication with our customer and users. We must gain trust and create and maintain a win-win environment in which the agreed-on definition of success is important to everyone involved. This needs to be emphasized every day by the project manager and the development team. Actions to strengthen teamwork and to evolve win-win partnership relationships are a great starting point.

Requirements as a Key Driver to Any Systems or Software Effort

The requirements provide the basis for all of the follow-on development work. Therefore, the requirements are a key driver of the needed work. Consider each effective requirements practice in the context of your current work. Prepare a requirements plan (see Chapter 5). Provide an opportunity to consider requirements-related activities, efforts, methods, tools, and so forth, based on the specific situation.

Financing Improvements in the Requirements Process

Industry data show that requirements-related problems result in waste equal to more than one third total project costs. The challenge for development organizations is to channel a portion of this waste into improvement activities that continuously improve results. Because managers can be expected to be more supportive of process improvement efforts when savings are measured, the availability of cost-effectiveness data for specific improvement initiatives will facilitate gaining sponsorship from management at all levels.

Survival of the Fittest

The systems and software suppliers that address issues and solve problems are the ones that will survive in an increasingly competitive business environment. Frameworks such as the Capability Maturity Model (CMM) and Pressman's Process Advisor[1] have provided our industry the ability to evaluate practices and undertake continuous improvement. Increasingly, customers seek evidence of systems and software engineering proficiency such as CMM level. The CMM facilitates useful comparisons of suppliers.

Management Awareness and Expectations

Increased management awareness of the importance of the requirements process and stronger commitment to its use are needed. This requires the personal involvement of the project manager to

- Articulate the issues and vision to the project staff
- Set specific objectives
- Provide adequate resources for requirements-related activities
- Track progress and results
- Provide the environment in which developers are empowered, productive, effective, and fulfilled

Improvements in requirements practices should take place within the context of an ongoing continuous improvement program implemented in a total quality management framework.

Metrics

As I've said, the things that are measured and tracked are the ones that improve. Decide on a few useful metrics and utilize them. It is truly enlightening to experience projects that effectively use peer reviews, defect prevention techniques,

---

[1]See http://www.rspa.com/pa/index.html.

quality improvement tools,[2] and quantitative management techniques such as statistical process control.

The Development Team

The project is its people. How are things going for them? Ask them! *The project performers possess a wealth of information and ideas for improvement.* If you've experienced turnover, find out why and take action. Project management *must* provide the environment to allow its people to be effective. We must demonstrate by our actions that

- We care
- We value people's opinions
- We'll take action to address concerns

In short, we must empower the development team—give them what they need to be effective, committed, and helpful performers.

Where to Start

I encourage you to approach the effort in the order of the effective requirements practices presented in this book:

1. Gain commitment. Establish a team environment. Commit to a shared vision of project success.
2. Determine the real requirements. It's apparent from Chapter 4 that the real requirements *emerge* and are *discovered* via the concerted effort of contractors and customers *working together* in a win-win effort to complete the system development effort successfully and effectively. Align the work required with the budget and schedule available.
3. Establish mechanisms, such as the joint team and others noted earlier in this book.
4. Define, document, train, and use a requirements process. Make improvements to it as you learn what works and what doesn't. Industry experience suggests that spending 8% to 14% of total project cost on the requirements process results in the best outcomes, as measured by total project costs versus planned expenditures.

---

[2]A concise, easy-to-use summary of QI tools is *QI Story: Tools and Techniques, A Guidebook to Problem Solving,* by Six Sigma Qualtec. A similar useful pocket-size book is *The Memory Jogger II* by Brassard and Ritter.

5. Iterate the system requirements and the architecture repeatedly. Utilize available technical expertise with domain knowledge to collaborate on an effective implementation.

6. Improve communications among the project team. Provide individuals the wherewithal to improve relationships through appropriate, professional training. The existence of good relationships is the foundation for teamwork. An empowered team can accomplish anything it sets out to do.

7. Manage the project. Perform the development effort using known, proven industry, organizational, and project best practices. If you are using new methods or tools, invest in training so that the developers become familiar with their capabilities. Plan some time for them to familiarize themselves with the capabilities and the use of the new method or tool.

8. Select a set of techniques that work for you in your environment. Become familiar with them over time. Proceed deliberately, and don't pretend there are silver bullets.

9. Manage changes to requirements and new requirements during the development life cycle.

10. Verify and validate that the real requirements are met.

Figure 12-1 provides a checklist that will help organize and carry out the requirements-related activities. Tailor this to your environment and approach.

Figure 12-1   Requirements Activities Checklist

Action	Person Responsible	Completion	
		Plan	Actual
1. Has a Partnering Process Workshop been conducted?			
• Customer and contractor aligned?			
• Has a systematic approach to involve the customer in the entire development process been developed and documented?			

Action	Person Responsible	Completion	
		Plan	Actual
• Have mutually agreed goals and objectives been determined?			
• Has a "win-win" partnership relationship been committed to by both customer and developer?			
• Has an operating charter been created?			
• Has "success" of this project been defined?			
• Is there "joint responsibility" for requirements?			
• Has an action plan that provides dates and formats for deliverables been established, documented, and agreed on?			
• Has a Team Risk Management Plan been developed?			
• Barriers to success identified?			
• Countermeasures proposed?			
• Risks identified?			
• Risk mitigation plans developed?			
• One individual identified to manage each risk?			
• Has a "Plan for Quality," providing operating guidelines for the Project Team been written?			
2. Has a Requirements Plan (RP) been written?			
• Does the RP provide a suggested strategy and recommended approach to elicit, identify, analyze, define, specify, prioritize, derive, partition, allocate, track, manage, and verify and validate the system requirements?			

(continued)

Figure 12-1   Requirements Activities Checklist (*continued*)

Action	Person Responsible	Completion Plan	Actual
• Have the guidelines for system development based on requirements considerations been developed and trained?			
3. Has a Joint Team been formed?			
4. Has a requirements process to be used throughout the system life cycle been defined?			
5. Are the requirements engineers assigned to the project trained and familiar with the practices, processes, mechanisms, methods, techniques, and tools to be used; and do they have application domain knowledge?			
6. Have appropriate techniques to be used to elicit real customer needs been selected, and has training been provided?			
7. Have the requirements and the architecture to allow discovery of impacts of each on the other and to enable both the requirements and the architecture to evolve been iterated?			
8. Has an extensive effort utilizing domain subject matter experts and a variety of techniques been performed to elicit customer needs?			
9. Has an automated requirements tool that provides for requirements traceability and use of requirements attributes been			

Action	Person Responsible	Completion Plan	Actual
selected and purchased? Has formal training concerning how to utilize the tool been provided?			
10. Have the real customer requirements been documented, prioritized, and agreed to by the customer and the developer?			
• "Project champion" identified? • Initial Operational Concept Definition developed? • Requirements Workshop conducted? • Peer reviews and inspections of requirements work products conducted? • Rationale for *why* each requirement is needed documented?			
11. Have the derived requirements (those requirements that are logically inferred and implied as essential to system effectiveness) been defined and documented?			
• Have the derived requirements been explained to the customer? Does the customer concur?			
12. Has a detailed operational concept of the system, the users, and the system environment been developed and documented?			
13. Have the requirements been partitioned into groups and allocated to the components of the planned system to support synthesis of solutions?			

(continued)

Figure 12-1   Requirements Activities Checklist (*continued*)

Action	Person Responsible	Completion Plan	Actual
14. Have the requirements associated with external and internal interfaces been identified and documented?			
15. Have the requirements been analyzed to ensure that they are verifiable by the methods?			
16. Are the activities of the steps of the requirements-related work documented to provide a written record of why decisions were made?			
17. Is a mechanism such as a project configuration control board used to manage the project and to maintain effective communication and intergroup coordination among all involved groups on the project?			
• Are regular meetings held?			
18. Has formal configuration control been required for all requirements outputs and products?			
19. Has a set of work products that collectively comprise the requirements specification been developed?			
• Requirements database			
• Functional documents			
• Requirements traceability matrix (RTM)			
• Requirements document			
20. Have the requirements been verified?			
• RTM updated?			
• Preliminary operational concept updated?			
• System concept updated?			

Action	Person Responsible	Completion Plan	Actual
21. Has an effective mechanism to accommodate changes in requirements during system development been provided, and is it effective?			
22. Is the development effort using known, proven practices, processes, mechanisms, methods, techniques, and tools being performed?			
23. Are peer reviews and inspections of work products conducted extensively?			
24. Is configuration management (CM; version control, change control, and formal CM) conducted effectively?			
25. Is the independent quality assurance role performed effectively?			
26. Are subcontractor efforts effectively integrated into the project work program and managed effectively?			
27. Are appropriate metrics collected, tracked, analyzed, and utilized to manage project activities?			
28. Are well-structured, well-trained teams performing the software development work?			
29. Have results of requirements engineering work been captured and the benefits dependents-related activities checklist been analyzed?			

(continued)

Figure 12-1   Requirements Activities Checklist (*continued*)

Action	Person Responsible	Completion Plan	Actual
30. Has a Team Risk Management Plan been developed, and is it used effectively?			

How to Prioritize Needed Efforts

Gain consensus among the project team concerning the project goal and objectives. Involve your customer in a work session of the project performers to establish an action plan. An outside facilitator, not invested in any particular point of view, can be a big help. Call it a "partnering workshop," a "goal-setting session," a "requirements workshop," a "facilitated team-building meeting," or whatever works for you in your environment. Achieve consensus on the following:

1. Who are the members of the team (all should be there or at least be represented)? You may be surprised to find out that some of the team members don't know one another!

2. What is the goal of the project effort? Be forewarned that there will be different opinions about this. Drive to consensus, drawing on the extensive knowledge in the room. Don't allow the most vocal participants to dominate the conclusions. The critical need here is to gain a shared vision of project success.

3. What top-level customer needs and expectations must be met? Establish the joint team that will determine and agree on the real requirements and be responsible for them throughout the development effort or take responsibility for them immediately if you are mid project.

4. Prepare a set of "rules of conduct" for the team to which all members of the team agree. The time, effort, and investment in the project can be made much more effectively and efficiently by using this mechanism. The idea is to create the environment in which people want to support one another: Treat each other as customers.

5. A set of actions that are needed to move the team forward (each action should be accompanied by the name of the individual who will accomplish it

and the date it will be completed). The sum is the Project Action Plan. The discussion will clarify the actions that are critical (highest priority) for the success of the team. Establish a tracking system and ways to remind people that are helpful, well received, and effective.

6. A set of mechanisms that will facilitate keeping the team moving effectively toward the project goal, for example, how to maintain effective communications among the project team members.

7. The project team's expectation that it requires a leader who is committed to the project performers. No complex effort can be accomplished without a leader.[3] The leader needs to view her role as an enabler of the things that need to get done for the project to be successful. The project performers are her customers too.

Figure 12-2 provides a set of guidelines for system development based on requirements considerations. Consider them in connection with your current approach.

Figure 12-2   Guidelines for System Development Based on Requirements Considerations

1. Developers must be trained not to add any features or capabilities beyond those stated in the approved requirements. Industry experience is that developers add capabilities, increasing the scope of the product and adding to the effort required throughout the system life cycle.

2. Methods such as requirements workshops (conducted as needed), storyboards, requirements reviews, idea reduction, role playing, and prototyping should be used. See Leffingwell and Widrig, *Managing Software Requirements* (Addison-Wesley, 2000), for a lot of experience and suggestions.

3. "What if" questions should be asked, focusing on the boundary conditions, exceptions, and unusual events.

(continued)

---

[3]For clarification on the critical role of the project leader, read Chapter 3 in *How to Run Successful Projects II*, by Fergus O'Connell.

Figure 12-2   Guidelines for System Development Based on
Requirements Considerations (*continued*)

4. A careful manual review and analysis of the complete set of requirements, supported by the user and utilizing appropriate automated tools, will be needed to ensure consistency in the requirements set.

5. Developers, customers, and other stakeholders need to rank the individual requirements in terms of their importance to the customer. This technique helps to manage the project scope. Requirements should also be ranked in terms of their stability. This is only a beginning to defining the releases of the product. Data dependencies must be considered as well. See Bill Wiley, *Essential System Requirements* (Addison-Wesley, 2000), Chapters 8 and 9, for a discussion of data/process interaction and transition to physical design.

6. One of the most difficult requirements challenges is writing the requirements detailed enough to be well understood without overconstraining the system and annoying users with details intended to remove ambiguity. Here are some guidelines:

   • Use natural language whenever possible.
   • Use pictures and diagrams to illustrate the intent.
   • When in doubt, ask for more information.
   • Augment specifications with more formal methods when it is critical not to be misunderstood (life-and-death situations or grave consequences of erroneous behavior).
   • Train people to recognize the problem and the solution.
   • Use diagrams and structured pseudocode to describe complex technical specifications.

7. We *know* that the requirements will change for several reasons:
   A. External factors
      1. Change in the problem (the business) we are attempting to solve.
      2. Users change their minds.
      3. The external environment has changed, creating new constraints and/or opportunities (for example, the availability of the Internet and the World Wide Web).

     4. The very existence of the new system causes the requirements for the system to change!

  B. Internal factors

     1. Failure to discover the real requirements during the initial requirements-gathering effort.

     2. Failure to create a practical process to help manage changes.

  C. Requirements leakage

     1. Direct user/customer requests to programmers.

     2. Functionality inserted by programmers "because it's a good thing."

8. Change must be managed. Here are some guidelines:

  A. Recognize that change is inevitable, and provide methods to deal with it.

  B. Baseline the requirements.

  C. Establish a single channel to control change (such as the joint team).

  D. Use a change control system to capture changes. Keep requirements under vigorous configuration management.

  E. Manage changes hierarchically so that the downward ripple effect of a change will be highlighted by the traceability in the requirements tool.

  F. Industry data show that a change of 30% in the requirements results in *doubling* of the costs of the project. The joint team is critical to providing joint customer and contractor responsibility for the requirements and for the impacts of any approved changes.

Figure 12-3 summarizes how a requirements process facilitates effective project performance. Use this to help motivate action to define, document, train, and use a requirements process. You may start by documenting the process now being used. Do this in a group environment of six to eight people who are very familiar with what is actually being done. As you document it, the group will identify several suggestions for improving the process. Eureka! You're doing continuous improvement!

**Figure 12-3   How a Requirements Process Facilitates Effective Project
Performance**

- Provides a documented, proven process
- Joint responsibility is fundamental—"Joint Team"
  - Partnering approach—unleash the power of teamwork at the project kickoff
    - Establish a mutual commitment to succeed.
    - Develop a shared vision of project objectives to create common goals.
    - Identify, analyze, plan, track, and control project risks.
    - Develop an issue resolution ladder.
    - Create a Project Management Plan.
    - Perform joint evaluations of plans and progress.
- Major emphasis on clarifying what the requirements really are
  - Expend 8% to 14% of total project costs on *the requirements process*.
  - Provide a description of what is needed. Develop and document the project scope (customer needs, goals and objectives, mission definition, operational concept, customer requirements, constraints, schedules, budgets, authority, responsibility).
  - Clarify and document requirements using proven methods.
    - Elicit, stimulate, analyze, and communicate customer needs.
    - Suggested methods: brainstorming, joint application design, meetings, prototyping, modeling, use cases, trade studies, requirements validation, focus groups, storyboards, and reviews.
    - *Understand customer needs and expectations.*
    - Prioritize requirements. All requirements are not equal. Find out which requirements are most important to the customer.
    - Partition like requirements, derive requirements, and identify interfaces.
    - Allocate requirements to functional partitions, interact with clarification of the system architecture, and iterate.
    - Conduct requirements reviews and inspections. The cost to find defects during the requirements phase dwarfs the cost of finding errors later in the system life cycle.

- Manage the project using a mechanism such as a configuration control board to maintain effective communication between and among all project performers. Provide and maintain effective intergroup coordination.
- Utilize an automated requirements tool to document and maintain control of requirements; to allocate requirements to the system components; to provide traceability of requirements to design, code, and test; to enable verification; to track builds and baselines; to maintain change history and rationale for changes; and to enable customer suggestions and ideas to be submitted, evaluated, and priced.
- Perform project tracking utilizing useful metrics such as requirements volatility.

Relationship of the Recommended Effective Requirements Practices to the CMM

We've observed earlier that the CMM is a proven framework for process improvement. What is the relationship of the effective requirements practices advocated in this book to the CMM framework? Figure 12-4 provides a mapping of the effective requirements practices to the CMM for Software (SW-CMM).[4] This mapping will help organizations and projects using this book to support their process improvement program when they are utilizing the CMM framework. Note that all of the effective requirements practices map to CMM key practices. A key process area (KPA)[5] key and a common features[6] key are provided to help interpret the applicable CMM key practices.[7]

---

[4]With thanks to Mark Paulk for most of the effort that went into creating this figure.

[5]A KPA of the SW-CMM is a cluster of related activities that, when performed collectively, achieve a set of goals considered important for establishing process capability.

[6]The subdivision categories of the CMM KPAs. The common features are attributes that indicate whether the implementation and institutionalization of a KPA are effective, repeatable, and lasting. The CMM common features are commitment to perform, ability to perform, activities performed, measurement and analysis, and verifying implementation.

[7]The CMM key practices are the activities that contribute most to the effective implementation and institutionalization of a KPA. For example, a written organizational policy is required for each of the 18 KPAs, reflecting the organization's commitment.

Figure 12-4   Mapping of the Effective Requirements Practices to the SW-CMM

Effective Requirements Practice	Applicable Software Engineering Institute Capability Maturity Model
1. Commit to the approach.	RM.AB.1,3,4 RM.CO.1 IC.AB.1,2 IC.AC.1,3
2. Establish and utilize a Joint Team responsible for the requirements.	RM.AC.1,3 RM.VE.1 IC.AB.3,4,5
3. Define the *real* customer needs.	RM AB.2 IC.AC.1
4. Use and continually improve a requirements process.	RM KPA (all Key Practices)
5. Iterate the system requirements and the system architecture repeatedly.	RM.AB.1 PE.AC.2
6. Use a mechanism to maintain project communication.	RM.AC.1 IC.CO.1 IC.AB.1 IC.AC.1,2
7. Select familiar methods and maintain a set of work products.	RM.AC.2,3 IC.AB.2
8. Perform requirements verification and validation.	RM.VE.3 PE.AC.2
9. Provide an effective mechanism to accommodate requirements changes.	RM.AC.3
10. Perform the development effort using known, proven industry, organizational, and project best practices.	IC.AB.2

KPA Key
RM, requirements management
IC, intergroup coordination
PE, software product engineering

Common Features Key
AB, ability
AC, activity
CO, commitment
VE, verification

But I Have So Many Things to Do . . .

Systems and software engineering practitioners (managers and performers or developers) often feel overwhelmed. There is so much to do! Our days are often ones that have many more demands than time available to meet them. We often ask ourselves: Of all of the things I should do, which ones *must* I get done today?

Figure 12-5 provides a great list of bad excuses related to requirements definition and management. Perhaps reviewing this list will help motivate you to take some of the actions, suggestions, and recommendations offered in this book to implement effective requirements practices. We know from our experience that all too often we don't take the time that is required to do something correctly but wind up doing things over. Capitalize on industry experience that on the average, 45% of project effort is rework. As I have said, by capitalizing on the implementation and use of effective requirements practices, we can reallocate wasted time and money to our advantage.

Figure 12-5   Bad Excuses Related to Requirements Definition and Management

1. The users don't know what they want.
2. We don't need people from the field to be involved in defining system requirements because we have people in the program office with domain experience.
3. We won't do any prototyping of the user interface until we've finished design, because coding shouldn't begin until design is finished.
4. We can't ask the user; we're too far down the road.
5. We are at the leading edge of technology. We can certainly figure out how to run a mailroom better than the low-skilled people who work there.
6. This is an OO project, so we never stop iterating among requirements analysis, design, and coding.
7. Future users were involved in requirements definition—they reviewed the A-spec written by the development contractor.
8. The system-reliability and safety requirements were allocated to software by the systems engineers because software is very flexible, and these requirements would be too hard to implement in hardware.

(continued)

Figure 12-5   **Bad Excuses Related to Requirements Definition
and Management** *(continued)*

9. There are no software engineers on the engineering team for this embedded system (software engineers are not real engineers).

10. This is evolutionary development. We'll identify security and safety requirements after we tenth incremental release.

11. This is evolutionary development, so we won't have stable requirements until eighteen months after project start.

12. We have experienced a lot of requirements volatility, and it's all the government's fault.

13. We trace requirements only to the Computer Software Configuration Item (CSCI) level because the buyer requires only functional, allocated, and product baselines to be under configuration control.

14. We can't do requirements traceability because the CASE tools we are using don't support it.

15. Our requirements traceability information is not up to date because it takes a lot of time to do this manually.

16. How could we have known before integration test that modifying this algorithm would have anything to do with the response time to that user request?

17. We do exhaustive regression testing for every change to the operational software because you can never know everything the change might affect.

18. How could we have known that errors in that code module would cause secure data to be transmitted in the clear?

19. We can't be sure that system requirements are mapped correctly into software requirements because we used different CASE tools for systems engineering and software design.

20. We can't use a rigorous methodology for systems requirements definition because functional people are defining these requirements and they are not technical.

21. We award the Systems Engineering Technical Assistance (SETA) contract to the lowest bidder because that contractor only defines requirements.

22. We are using leading-edge concurrent engineering methods to define CSCI external interface requirements in parallel with designing the CSCI.
23. There was no way to know for sure before integration test that the database stored all the data needed by the application software, because we used different CASE tools to design the database and the application software.
24. There is no top-down requirements traceability because this is the Demonstration and Validation Phase.

What If We Are "Further Along" on Our Project?

It may be that your project is well along in the system development life cycle. You may be thinking that because your project has been underway for several months or years, you can't be helped by these ideas. You may believe that it's too late for the project to be helped! *My experience is that these issues are preventing progress in projects, no matter at what point they are in the system development life cycle. It is never too late to commit to needed improvements.* My suggestion is to get the members of the project team in a setting with your customer where a candid discussion of current efforts can be held. Identify areas that seem to be in the way, and *take action* to address them. Consider which of the practices, recommendations, and suggestions can help.

A lot of what I am talking about here has to do with commitment, the topic of Chapter 2. Lacking real commitment to do anything in life, where are we? Without clear intent, it's not going to happen. It's about deciding what we really want to happen, creating a plan to achieve it, and (in concert with the others involved) taking the set of actions required to make it happen.

Summary

Review your project environment to determine issues that are in the way. Address them by applying effective practices including recommendations and suggestions based on industry experience to help you make your systems and software project efforts more successful. Start by undertaking an improvement effort in the order of the effective requirements practices presented in this book. Gain consensus among the project performers concerning project goals and objectives. Involve your customer. Consider utilizing a partnering workshop to achieve a shared vision of success and to create a set of rules of conduct to provide a productive environment. Building systems and software is difficult. Although spectacular things have been accomplished, as an industry we don't yet have an enviable record of achievement. It's my hope that these ideas will contribute to improving our track record and that, in particular, they help you.

Key References and Suggested Readings

Frederick P. Brooks, Jr. *The Mythical Man-Month.* **Anniversary ed. Reading, MA: Addison-Wesley, 1995.** This is probably the most cited software project management book of all time. In the first edition of this book (1975), Brooks drew on his experience as the project manager for the IBM/360 computer family and then for OS/360 to provide propositions concerning software engineering and programming. One assertion was that the man-month is mythical as a measure of productivity. In his twentieth anniversary edition (1995) of this book, Brooks notes that he was struck by how few of the propositions have been critiqued, proved, or disproved by ongoing software engineering research and experience! Chapter 16 reprints "No Silver Bullet: Essence and Accidents of Software Engineering," a 1986 paper that was reprinted in 1987 in IEEE *Computer* magazine. This paper predicted that the next decade would not see any single development in either technology or management technique that by itself would provide even one order of magnitude of improvement in productivity, reliability, or simplicity. Brooks's position 20 years later is still that software development is difficult.

Alan M. Davis. *Software Requirements: Objects, Functions, and States.* **Rev. Upper Saddle River, NJ: Prentice Hall PTR, 1993.** This book provides a good discussion of "what is a requirement?" It also provides a survey of techniques, including object-oriented problem analysis, function-oriented problem analysis using data flow diagrams, and state-oriented problem analysis. It has a detailed discussion of the attributes of a software requirements specification and a very exhaustive (772 sources) annotated bibliography as of 1993.

James A. Highsmith III. *Adaptive Software Development: A Collaborative Approach to Managing Complex Systems.* **New York: Dorset House, 1999.** As characterized by Ken Orr, the message of this book is that large information systems don't have to take so long to develop, they don't have to cost so much, and they don't have to fail. This is hard to disagree with. The recommended solution is a radical form of incremental development. Recommended techniques include using customer focus groups, versioning, **time-boxed** management, and active prototyping in combination. The book is advertised to provide a framework to build independent subprojects in small, short-term pieces. Adaptive cycles are mission driven, component based, iterative, time boxed,[8] risk driven, and change tolerant. Highsmith advocates the *optimization paradox,* basically denying that process improvement (for example) could have any beneficial effect (p. 187). Another theme of the book that is also hard to disagree with is that collaboration enables organizations to generate emergent results (p. 126). Highsmith asserts that "active partnerships are required" (p. 158). He believes that inspections (encompassing reviews, inspections, and walkthroughs) have the most consistently proven track record of all software engineering techniques implemented since 1980. Chapter 7, Why Even Good Managers Cause Projects to Fail, is insightful.

Watts S. Humphrey. *Introduction to the Personal Software Process.* **Reading, MA: Addison-Wesley, 1997.** This excellent book provides the background and approach for implementing the Personal Software Process (PSP). The PSP is a methodology based on process improvement principles that enables developers to develop high-quality products consistently and efficiently. The PSP is offered in a course that teaches developers to measure and to manage the quality of their work using defect density, **defect removal** rate, and yield versus productivity to analyze size, time in phase, defects, and schedule measures. Experience has shown that a serious commitment to the PSP is required, that management support is essential, and that transition to practice must be actively managed. Humphrey's earlier book, *A Discipline for Software Engineering,* also addresses the PSP. See also the article by Ferguson and colleagues titled "Results of Applying the Personal Software Process."

Watts S. Humphrey. *Managing Technical People: Innovation, Teamwork, and the Software Process.* **Reading, MA: Addison-Wesley, 1997.** Humphrey had nearly 50 years of experience working with technical people when he wrote this book. As he notes, history is a marvelous teacher as long as we are willing to learn. The key is to understand and to respect people and to follow sound management

---

[8]*Time boxed* refers to a technique that forces trade-offs in the context of short delivery cycles. See James Highsmith, *Adaptive Software Development.*

principles, applying them with a healthy sprinkling of common sense. This book adds several chapters to Humphrey's earlier book, *Managing for Innovation: Leading Technical People,* including one concerning the process improvement strategy and describing its power. Topics include respect for the individual, motivating technical and professional people professional discipline, developing technical talent, managing innovative teams, and managing change.

Ravi Kalakota and Marcia Robinson. *e-Business: Roadmap for Success.* **Reading, MA: Addison-Wesley, 1999.** This book facilitates understanding how electronic business (e-business) impacts current business strategies, applications, and models. Kalakota and Robinson have extensive experience in e-commerce and e-business. A thesis is that technology is now a cause and driver in forming business strategy and that e-commerce is enabling organizations to listen to their customers and to become the cheapest, the most familiar, or the best. An interesting concept is *customer relationship management*—an integrated sales, marketing, and service strategy that depends on coordinated actions.

Mitch Lubars, Colin Potts, and Charles Richter. "A Review of the State of the Practice in Requirements Modeling." In: *Proceedings of IEEE International Symposium on Requirements Engineering.* **Los Alamitos, CA: IEEE Computer Society Press, 1993: 2–14.** The authors conclude that it is not easy to make specific recommendations concerning how to improve requirements practices. They observe from other studies that accurate problem domain knowledge is critical to the success of a project, and requirements volatility causes major difficulties during development. Lubars and colleagues encountered several cases of customer-generated ("stated") requirements documents that were hundreds of pages long: "But verbosity does not imply clarity of understanding." Many customer-specific projects employ several domain specialists. Their survey indicated that no companies really know how to assign and to modify priorities or how to communicate those priorities effectively to project members. They observed several times that a "small" change to the requirements caused a large change to the design. The customer/developer partnership is preferred to foster interaction and to promote consensus. Few projects used any particular requirements method. In no case did the researchers find a coherent relationship between requirements analysis and project planning. Requirements engineers did not know how their project managers estimated costs or scheduled milestones. An important finding is that software professionals are notoriously undercapitalized relative to professionals in other engineering or manufacturing fields.

Steve McConnell. *After the Gold Rush: Creating a True Profession of Software Engineering.* **Redmond, WA: Microsoft Press, 1999.** McConnell's easy-to-read style prevails in this excellent analysis of the status of software engineering today and what should be done. He puts the state of current practices into context and notes that each of us has a choice: to stay with "code-and-fix development practices" or to venture boldly toward a true profession. McConnell made his choice years ago, as is evident from his many important contributions, ministering as he does in a practical manner to the needs and welfare of our industry and humankind. It's time for each of us to read this book, digest it, and join him.

Steve McConnell. *Rapid Development.* **Redmond, WA: Microsoft Press, 1996.** This is another of McConnell's great books—a testimony to why process improvement is never finished! McConnell takes the view that rapid development is not a "glitzy methodology," but rather the use of good practices, time, and effort to achieve an effective development process. He advocates: (1) choosing effective practices rather than ineffective ones, and (2) choosing practices that are oriented specifically toward achieving your schedule objectives. After a discussion of the major topics in development (including partnering), McConnell proceeds to discuss 43 best practices. This is recommended reading for anyone involved in the development process.

Fergus O'Connell. *How to Run Successful High-Tech Project-Based Organizations.* **Boston, MA: Artech House, 1999.** In this book, O'Connell leverages his six years of success of his company, ETP (Eyes on the Prize), Inc., in helping to change the behavior of the people running projects and organizations. He applies his structured project management approach to organizations. The focus is on causing people to do the things that create results in customer satisfaction, reduced time-to-market, gaining market edge, increased revenue, and increased profits.

Peter Senge, Art Kleiner, Charlotte Roberts, Richard Ross, George Roth, and Bryan Smith. *The Dance of Change.* **New York: Doubleday, 1999.** This book is full of ideas concerning organizational change. It provides a vision of growth and prosperity based on the concept of the learning organization. It is a valuable resource for a leader seeking new possibilities.

Paul A. Strassmann. *The Squandered Computer: Evaluating the Business Alignment of Information Technologies.* **New Canaan, CT: The Information Economics Press, 1997.** Strassmann believes that U.S. companies are excessively overspending on computers and that there is no demonstrable relationship between computer spending and corporate profits. He points out that overhead costs of U.S. firms have grown faster than revenues or profits, and he feels that computers have not increased worker productivity. He asserts that 31% of computer projects are canceled and that 53% overrun their budgets. Strassmann believes that the computer trade press has a tendency to popularize examples of excellence in computer usage that disregard financial results. He believes that the cyclical investment pattern for computers is as much a reflection in shifts in organizational power as the result of technological innovation. He provides 152 recommendations for what to do (pp. 389–400). This book is clearly not representative of everyday thinking, and for that reason it is provocative and challenges us to evaluate our "typical" approach.

R. H. Thayer and M. Dorfman, eds. *Software Requirements Engineering.* **2nd ed. Los Alamitos, CA: IEEE Computer Society Press, 1997.** This is a valuable resource that includes a collection of informative articles on topics including what is a requirement; system and software engineering requirements elicitation techniques, including use cases; requirements methodologies and tools; traceability; requirements and quality management; and life cycle models. Two Institute of Electronic and Electrical Engineers standards (IEEE *Recommended Practice for Software Requirements Specifications* and "Guide for Developing System Requirements Specifications") and a comprehensive software requirements engineering glossary are provided.

Gerald M. Weinberg. *Quality Software Management.* **Vol. 4. Anticipating Change. New York: Dorset House Publishing, 1997.** This is the fourth and last volume in a series by Weinberg titled *Quality Software Management.* Weinberg's focus in this book is on how to create a supportive environment. His tenet is that management creates the environment in which the development work is performed. Without improving management, spending on methodologies, tools, application packages, and even training won't help. Based on my own experience, it's hard to disagree with this view. There are two chapters that specifically focus on requirements principles and process.

Karl E. Wiegers. *Creating a Software Engineering Culture.* **New York: Dorset House Publishing, 1996.** This book provides lots of suggestions and ideas based on Wiegers' experience at Eastman Kodak Company. He provides practical approaches to support process improvement and development efforts, and he identifies culture builders and culture killers that are important to consider.

Epilogue

The time is here for practitioners in the systems and software development profession to decide that we stand for excellence. Our objective is to deliver effective systems, on time and within budget. These goals are within our grasp; we have the wherewithal to meet them.

This challenge is as much one to management as it is to technical performers. Yet, we developers know when things aren't working:

- When there is no process
- When the practices being used don't work
- When the methods and tools are not proved, familiar, and trained
- When the opportunity for continuous improvement is absent

It is our responsibility to inform "management," to make sure management knows what we need to be effective in our work, and to insist that our work environment is effective. Dr. Deming explained that the "workers" are powerless when they lack a work environment conducive to quality and to productive work.

So, it is up to us. First we need to decide what we want. Then we need to turn our focus to making it happen. Let each and every one of our days move us in that direction.

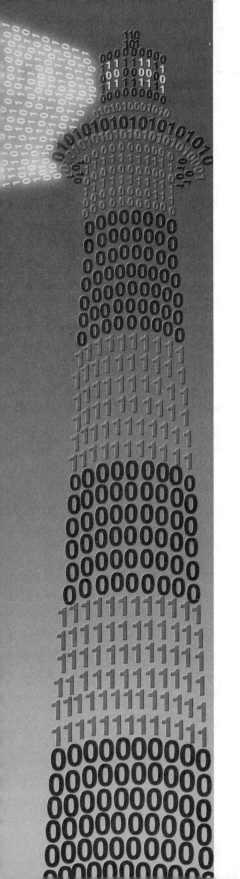

List of Acronyms

ABD	Architecture Based Design
ACM	Association for Computing
ACWP	actual cost of work performed
AHP	Analytic Hierarchy Process
AI	Action Item
AKA	Also Known As
ANSI	American National Standards Institute
AP	Action Plan
API	Application Program Interface
ARC	Assessment Requirements for CMMI
ARM	Automated Requirements Measurement (software used at NASA)
ATAM	Architecture Tradeoff Analysis Method
ATLM	Automated Test Lifecycle Methodology
AW	Addison-Wesley
BAC	Budget at Completion
BCWP	Budgeted Cost of Work Performed
BCWS	Budgeted Cost of Work Scheduled
C2	Command and Control
C3I	Command, Control, Communications, and Intelligence
C4ISR	Command, Control, Communications, Computers, Intelligence, Surveillance, and Reconnaissance
CAC	Calculated Cost at Completion
CAIV	Cost as An Independent Variable

CARE	Computer Aided Requirements Engineering, a requirements tool by SOPHIST Technologies
CASE	Computer-aided Software Engineering
CAT	PRC Center for Applied Technology
CBA	CMM-based Appraisal
CBA IPI	CMM-based Appraisal for Internal Process Improvement
CCB	Configuration Control Board
CCPDS-R	Command Center Processing and Display System-Replacement
CD	Compact Disk
CDR	Critical Design Review
CIO	Chief Information Officer
CM	Configuration Management
CMM	Capability Maturity Model
CMMI	Integrated Capability Maturity Model
CMP	Configuration Management Plan
CMU	Carnegie Mellon University
CMWG	Configuration Management Working Group
COCOMO	Constructive Cost Model
COE	Common Operating Environment
Comms	Communications
CONOPS	Concept of Operations
CORBA	Common Object Request Broker Architecture
COTS	Commercial Off-the-Shelf
CRM	Customer Relationship Management
CSC	Computer Software Component
CSCI	Computer Software Configuration Item
CSCSC	Cost and Schedule Control System Criteria
C/SSR	Cost/Schedule Status Reporting
CSU	Computer Software Unit
CV	Cost Variance
CVR	Customer Valid Requirement
DARPA	US Defense Advanced Research Projects Agency
DBA	Database Administrator
DBMS	Database Management System
DID	Data Item Description
DII	Defense Information Infrastructure
DISA	Defense Information Systems Agency

DoD	Department of Defense
DoD-STD	DoD Standard
DOORS	Dynamic Object Oriented Requirements System
DP	Defect Prevention
DSDM	Dynamic Systems Development Method
EAC	Estimate at Completion
EASE	Expert Assistant Software Engine
EIA	Electronic Industries Association
EIA G-47	The EIA Committee on System Engineering
EPG	Engineering Process Group
EPI	Engineering Process Improvement
EPIC	Enterprise Process Improvement Collaboration
EPIP	Engineering Process Improvement Plan
EPS	Encapsulated PostScript (a format)
ETP, Inc.	A company headquartered in Ireland
EV	Earned Value
EVA	Earned Value Analysis
EVO	Evolutionary Delivery
FD	Functional Document
FFRDC	Federally Funded Research and Development Center
FP	Function Point
FPA	function point analysis
FY	Fiscal Year
GCPR	Government Computer-based Patient Records
GOTS	Government Off the Shelf Software
GSFC	Goddard Space Flight Center (NASA)
GUI	Graphical User Interface
HCI	Human Computer Interface
HOL	High Order Language
HP	Hewlett Packard
HR	Human Relations
I&T	Integration and Test
IC	Intergroup Coordination
ICASE	Integrated Computer-aided Software Engineering
ICD	Interface Control Document
ICRE	IEEE Conference on Requirements Engineering
IE	Impact Estimation

IEEE	Institute of Electrical and Electronic Engineers
IFPUG	International Function Point Users Group
ILS	Integrated Logistics Support
IM or ISM	Integrated (Software) Management
INCOSE	International Council on Systems Engineering
IPI	Internal Process Improvement
IPT	Integrated Product Team
IT	Information Technology
ISO	International Standards Organization
IRD	Interface Requirements Document
IRS	Interface Requirements Specification
IS	Information System
ISO	International Standards Organization
ITA	Information Technology Architecture
IV&V	Independent Verification and Validation
JAD	Joint Application Design
JPEG	Joint Photographic Experts Group (a format)
JRP	Joint Requirements Planning
J-STD	Joint Standard
JT	Joint Team
KPA	Key Process Area
KSLOC	Thousands of Source Lines of Code
LAN	Local Area Network
LOC	Lines of Code
MIL	Military
MIL STD	Military Standard
MIS	Management Information System
MLT	Metrics Lead Team
MNS	Mission Needs Statement
MOE	Measure of Effectiveness
MQ	Maturity Questionnaire
MQI	Managing Quality Improvement (a course offering at PRC)
MS	Microsoft
NASA	National Aeronautics and Space Administration
NCOSE	National Council on Systems Engineering
NDIA	National Defense Industrial Association
NIST	National Institute of Standards and Technology

NT	Windows NT (New Technology)
NTIS	National Technical Information Service
OBE	Overcome by Events
OCD	operational concept definition
OD or OPD	Organizational Process Definition
OEG	Other Engineering Groups
OF or OPF	Organizational Process Focus
OLAP	Online Analytical Processing
OMG	Object Management Group
OO	Object Oriented
OOSE	Object Oriented Software Engineering
ORB	Object Request Broker
ORD	Operational Requirements Document
ORR	Operational Readiness Review
OSD/AT&L	Office of the Secretary of Defense, Acquisition, Technology, and Logistics
OT	Object Technology
PA	Process Area
PAL	Process Asset Library
PAL	Purpose, Agenda, and Limit (in connection with a meeting)
PCM	Process Change Management
PD	Process Description
PDF	Portable Document Format (a format)
PE	Project Execution (AKA Project Tracking)
PI	Process Improvement
PIP	Process Improvement Plan
PM	Program Manager, Project Manager
PMI	Project Management Institute
PMP	Program Management Plan
POSIX	Portable Operating System Interface
PP	Project Planning or Program Plan
PR	Peer Review
PREVIEW	Process and Requirements Engineering Viewpoints
PSI	Probability of Success Indicator
PSP	Personal Software Process
PT	Project Tracking
QA	Quality Assurance

QAP	Quality Assurance Plan
QFD	Quality Function Deployment
QI	Quality Improvement
QIDW	Quality In Daily Work (also referred to as "Process Management")
QM	Quantitative Management
QMB	Quality Management Board
QSS, Inc.	Quality Systems & Software (vendor of the DOORS requirements tool), acquired by Telelogic in 9/00.
QW	Quality Week (an international conference)
RAD	rapid application development
RD	Requirements Document
RDM	Requirements-Driven Management
RE	Requirements or Requirements Engineering
ReqPro	Requisite Pro by Rational Corporation
RFC	Request for Change
RFI	Request for Information
RFP	Request for Proposals
RFQ	Request for Quote
RM	Requirements Management
RMP	Risk Management Plan
RMUG	Risk Management Working Group
ROI	return on investment
RP	Requirements Plan
RSEB	Reuse-Driven Software Engineering Business
RT	Requirements Tracer, a requirements tool by Teledyne Brown Engineering
RTM	Requirements Traceability Matrix
RUP	Rational Unified Process
RWG	Requirements Working Group
S&PE	PRC's Systems and Process Engineering Organization
SA	System Architecture
SAR	System Acceptance Review
SATC	Software Assurance Technology Center
SCAMPI	Standard CMMI Assessment for Process Improvement
SCE	Software Capability Evaluation
SCO	Software Change Order
SDF	Software Development Folder

SDLC	System Development Life Cycle
SDP	Software Development Plan
SE	Systems Engineering
SECAM	Systems Engineering Capability Assessment Model
SECAT	Systems Engineering Capability Assessment & Training, Inc. (a company headquartered in La Mirada, CA)
SECM	Systems Engineering Capability Model
SE-CMM	System Engineering Capability Maturity Model (EPIC)
SEI	Software Engineering Institute
SEL	Systems Engineering Laboratory (NASA)
SELT	PRC's Systems Engineering Lead Team
SEMP	System Engineering Management Plan
SEP	System Engineering Process
SEPG	Systems and/or Software Engineering Process Group
SGS	Satellite Ground Stations
SIM	PRC's System Integration Manual
SLATE	A requirements tool by TD Technologies, Inc.
SLC	Systems Life Cycle
SM	Subcontract Management
SME	Subject Matter Expert
SOW	Statement of Work
SPA	Software Process Assessment
SPC	Statistical Process Control
SPE or PE	Software Product Engineering
Spec	Specification
SPI	Software Process Improvement
SPIN	Software Process Improvement Network
SPIP	Software Process Improvement Plan
SPR	Software Productivity Research, Inc.
SRR	System Requirements Review
SRS	System or Software Requirements Specification
SS	System Specification
SSDD	System Specification Data Dictionary
SSS	System Segment Specification
STD	Standard
STD	System Test Description
STMC	Litton Industries' Software Technology Management Conference

STP	System or Software Test Plan
STQE	Software Testing & Quality Engineering (a periodical). See http://www.stqemagazine.com/
Sub	Subcontractor
SV	Schedule Variance
SW	Software
SWAT	Strategic Weapons Attack Team
SW-CMM	Capability Maturity Model for Software
SWE	Software Engineering
TA	Technical Architecture
TAFIM	Technical Architectural Framework for Information Management
TASC, Inc.	A systems integration company that is part of Litton Industries (Litton-TASC)
TBD	To Be Determined
TBI, Inc.	Technology Builders, Inc., vendors of the CaliberRM requirements tool
TCM	Technology Change Management
TCP/IP	Transmission Control Protocol/Internet Protocol
TIFF	Tagged Image File Format
TIM	Technical Interchange Meeting
TL	Team Leader
TOC	Table of Contents
TOG	The Open Group
TOGAF	The Open Group's Architectural Framework
TP	Training Program
TQM	Total Quality Management
TRM	Technical Reference Model
TSP	Team Software Process
UML	Unified Modeling Language
URL	Uniform Resource Locator
US	United States
USC	University of Southern California
V&V	Verification and Validation
WAN	Wide Area Network
WBS	Work Breakdown Structure
WMA	Washington Metropolitan Area (chapter of INCOSE) See http://www.incose-wma.org/info/

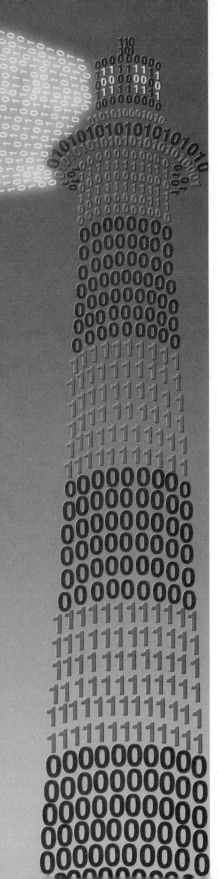

Glossary

Application: The use of capabilities (services and facilities) provided by an information system to satisfy a set of user requirements, such as word processing.

Architecture: The underlying structure of a system.

Architecture baseline: The underlying structure of a system associated with a particular product or release.

Architecture framework: A description of a family of related architectures that allows an individual architecture to be created by selection from and modification of the components. An architectural framework describes an information system in terms of a model comprised of a set of conceptual building blocks. It shows how the building blocks fit together.

Artifact: A document representing the result of effort. Artifacts are often referred to as examples of work products needed to provided evidence in support of assessments.

A spec: Common name for the system specification or segment specification as defined by MIL-STD-961. See Martin, *Systems Engineering Guidebook*.

Attribute: A characteristic of a requirement that is useful in sorting, classifying, and/or managing requirements.

Bad fixes: Secondary defects injected as a by-product of defect repairs.

Baseline: A specification or product that has been formally reviewed and agreed on and thereafter serves as the basis for further development. It is changed only through formal change control procedures.

Bottom up: Putting lowest level system components together, one level at a time. Between each level's integration, the results are tested to make it work.

Brown Bag: An informal lunchtime meeting.

B spec: Common name for the development specification as defined by MIL-STD-961. This specification has several subtypes. B1 is for a prime item. B2 is for a critical item. B3 is for a noncomplex item. B4 is for a facility or ship modification. B5 is equivalent to a software requirements specification and its associated interface requirements specification. A functional specification is a special version of the B spec that lists the requirements for a particular functional definition. See Martin, *Systems Engineering Guidebook*.

Business requirements: The essential activities of an enterprise. Business requirements are derived from business goals (the objectives of the enterprise). Business scenarios may be used as a technique for understanding business requirements. A key factor in the success of a system is the extent to which the system supports the business requirements and facilitates an organization in achieving them.

Business scenario: A technique that can be used to understand an enterprise or organization. A business scenario describes the business process, application, or set of applications; the business and technology environment; the people who and the computing components that execute the scenario; and the desired outcome of proper execution.

Business system: Hardware, software, policy statements, procedures, and people that together implement a business function.

Buyer: An organization that procures a system from a supplier.

Client: An application component that requests services from a server.

Commercial-off-the-shelf (COTS): An item of hardware or software that has been produced by a contractor and is available for general purchase.

Communications network: A set of products, concepts, and services that enable the connection of computer systems for the purpose of transmitting data and other forms (for example, voice and video) between the systems.

Complexity: The degree to which a system has requirements, a design, and/or an implementation that is difficult.

Concurrent engineering: Physically collocated cross-functional teams of engineers from many disciplines working together. Some equate this simply to systems engineering. It seeks to address negative aspects of specialization.

Configuration management: A discipline that applies technical and administrative direction and surveillance to (1) identify and document the functional and physical characteristics of a configuration item, (2) control changes to those characteristics, and (3) record and report changes to processing and implementation status.

C spec: Common name for the product specification as defined by MIL-STD-961. This specification has several subtypes. C1 is for a prime item. C2 is for a critical item. C3 is for a noncomplex item fabrication. C4 is for an inventory item. C5 is equivalent to a software product specification. See Martin, *Systems Engineering Guidebook*.

Customer: The person with the funds to pay for the project or its end product. The customer is not necessarily the user.

Customer need: The set of requirements desired by a customer.

Database: A structured or organized collection of information that may be accessed by a computer.

Data dictionary: A repository of information describing the characteristics of data used to design, monitor, document, protect, and control data in information systems and databases.

Data warehouse: A collection of integrated subject-oriented databases designed to support the decision support system function.

Decomposition: Breaking apart the attributes of a customer need (the requirements of a system) so that they can be addressed.

Default: Command that is automatically executed if none is specifically indicated.

Defect: A variance from a desired product attribute.

Defect Prevention: Technologies and techniques (for example, statistical process control) that minimize the risk of making errors in deliverables.

Defect removal: Activities that find and correct defects in deliverables.

Defect removal efficiency: The ratio of development defects to customer defects.

Derived requirement: A requirement that is further refined from a primary source requirement or from a higher level derived requirement or a requirement that results from choosing a specific implementation or system element.

Design: The process of defining the architecture, components, interfaces, and other characteristics of a system.

Development: The process of transforming a design into hardware and software components.

Distributed database: A collection of information that is dispersed over a network of interconnected computers.

Domain expert: An individual who has been working in a particular field for an extensive period of time and who is trained in that area. A domain expert is often referred to as a subject matter expert.

Enterprise: The highest level in an organization.

Event: A change in a system's environment that creates a response/set of actions.

Feasibility study: An analysis that provides an initial understanding of the cost, viability, high-level technical architecture, and requirements of a capability or system

Framework: A basic structure of ideas or a frame of reference.

Function: A useful capability provided by one or more components of a system.

Functional architecture: The framework for developing applications and defining their interrelationships in support of an organization's information structure. It identifies the major functions or processes an organization performs and their operational interrelationships.

Functional document: A comprehensive collection of the characteristics of a system and the capabilities it will make available to the users. It provides a detailed analysis of the data the system will be expected to manipulate. It may include a detailed definition of the user interfaces of the system.

Function point: A measure of the complexity of software development.

Gold plating: Adding features and capabilities to systems when not required by the system specification or the real requirements.

Graphical user interface: A computer program designed to allow a user to interact easily with a computer, typically by using a mouse or a pointing device to make choices from menus or groups of icons.

Hardware: Physical equipment.

Heuristic: Involving or serving as an aid to learning, discovery, or problem solving by experimental and especially trial-and-error methods (assumptions).

Hot swap: To replace a board, component, servlet, or server application with a new one while the system is running, without shutting down the system.

Information system: The computer-based portion of a business system.

Information technology (IT): Applied science utilizing hardware and software to support transfer of ideas.

Institutionalization: The building of an infrastructure and corporate culture that support methods, practices, and procedures so that they are the ongoing way of doing business, even after those who originally defined them are gone.

Integrated product team (IPT): A group that includes customers and developers and that blends perspectives into a functioning or unified whole. The joint team recommended in this book is an example of an IPT.

Integration and test: The activity in which modules of a system are combined according to the technical specification, and the interfaces between the modules are examined critically to ensure that expected results are achieved. The results of testing provide the basis for acceptance or rejection of the system.

Interface: The interaction or communication between independent systems or components of systems.

Interoperability: The ability of two or more systems or components to exchange and use information.

Iterate: To repeat a sequence of operations to yield results that are successively closer to a desired result.

Life cycle: The period of time that begins when a system is conceived and ends when the system is no longer available.

Life cycle model: A framework of processes and activities concerned with evolving a system that also acts as a common reference for communication and understanding among the participants in the effort.

Major defect: A problem that precludes effective use of a work product, such as a design deficiency or discovery of conflicting requirements.

Manifest: A term used in Canada instead of *project charter* or *project vision document*.

Measures of effectiveness (MOEs): High-level indicators of how well the system performs its functions, defined in the terms and with the same dimensionality of the requirements document. For example, if we are dealing with a city's metro system, we may specify that a typical user during rush hour should not wait more than some period of time, on the average, for the next train.

Mechanism: A way to get something done or to achieve a result.

Method: A way, technique, process, plan, mechanism, body of skills or techniques, discipline, practice, system, model, framework, capability, or procedure for doing something.

Methodology: A body of methods, rules, and postulates employed by a discipline; a particular procedure or set of procedures.

Middle out: Working upward to integrate major elements (such as government-furnished equipment) and downward to decompose into component subsystems simultaneously.

Minor defect: A problem that doesn't preclude effective use of a work product, such as a formatting issue, spelling error, language usage problem, or acronym or definition not provided or explained.

Objectory: The object factory for software development; an object-oriented method developed by Ivar Jacobson at Objective Systems in Sweden. See Jacobson, *Object-Oriented Software Engineering*.

Open architecture: Construction of the underlying structure of a system in a way that allows additional capabilities to be added with little or no adjustment.

Open system: People, machines, and methods organized to accomplish a set of specific functions that implement sufficient specifications for interfaces, services, and supporting formats to enable properly engineered applications software to (1) be ported with minimal changes across a wide range of systems, (2) interoperate with other applications on local and remote systems, and (3) interact with users in a style that facilitates user portability. Open systems are vendor independent.

Portability: The ease with which a system or component can be transferred from one hardware or software environment to another.

Practice: The performance of work activities repeatedly so as to become proficient; the usual way of doing something to produce a good result.

Prioritized requirements: Categorization of the real requirements into subsets according to criticality of need for a system or capability.

Process: A set of activities that results in the accomplishment of a task or the achievement of an outcome.

Process capability: The range of expected results that can be achieved by following a process.

Process description: A document that describes a process, including (for example) its purpose, customers, customer requirements, entrance criteria, inputs, outputs, exit criteria, tasks involved, and who is responsible for each, measurement indicators, resources needed, and version.

Process flowchart: A diagram that shows a step-by-step series of actions through a procedure using connecting lines and a set of standard symbols adopted by an organization.

Process model: A framework for identifying, defining, and organizing the functional strategies, rules, and processes needed to manage and support the way an organization does or wants to do business. The process model provides a graphical and textual framework for organizing the data and processes into manageable groups to facilitate their shared use and control throughout the organization.

Project: An undertaking focused on developing or maintaining a product. Typically a project has its own funding, accounting, and delivery schedule.

Project champion: An advocate who is very familiar with the set of real customer needs for a system and who provides an active role in the development effort, facilitating the tasks of the development team.

Project or program manager (PM): The person who has total business responsibility for a project and is ultimately responsible to a customer.

Protocol: A set of rules governing network functionality.

Prototyping: A technique for building a quick and rough version of a desired system or parts of that system. The prototype illustrates the capabilities of the system to users and designers. It serves as a communications mechanism to allow reviewers to understand interactions with the system. It enables them to identify problems and to consider ways to improve a system. It sometimes gives an impression that developers are further along than is actually the case, giving users an overly optimistic impression of completion possibilities!

Quality: Meeting real customer needs.

Quality culture: The presence of an attitude of continuous improvement and customer satisfaction throughout an organization.

Quality function deployment (QFD): A methodology originally conceived in Japan in the 1970s that provides an opportunity for the user and the developer of a system to understand requirements more fully and to prioritize them.

Rational Unified Process: A methodology advocated by Rational Software, Inc.

Real requirements: The subset of stated requirements that reflects the verified needs for a particular system or capability.

REQ FLOW: How a requirement flows through an organization or department.

REQ MULTIPLEXING: The assignment of business requirements to the right project or projects. One requirement manager can multiplex requirements between many projects.

Requirement: A necessary attribute in a system; a statement that identifies a capability, characteristic, or quality factor of a system in order for it to have value and utility to a user.

Requirements allocation: Assignment of requirements to architectural components of a system (for example, a hardware or software configuration item, training, or documentation); sometimes referred to as *flowdown.*

Requirements analysis: A structured (organized) method to understand the attributes that will satisfy a customer need.

Requirements baseline: The set of requirements associated with a particular release of a product or system.

Requirements definition: A detailed description, in general rather than functional terms, of the attributes needed in a system.

Requirements derivation: To obtain requirements for a system from sources provided by the customer.

Requirements document: A repository of the attributes in a system.

Requirements elicitation: The process of emerging requirements based on information provided by the customer.

Requirements engineering: An area within the broader field of systems and software engineering that focuses on the requirements process.

Requirements leakage: The addition or leaking in of unofficial requirements to the requirements specification when the requirements are not really needed.

Requirements management: Tracking requirements status and change activity and tracing requirements to the various phases and products of the development effort.

Requirements process: A full system life cycle set of actions concerning the necessary attributes of systems. The requirements process involves understanding customer needs and expectations (requirements elicitation), requirements analysis and specification, requirements prioritization, requirements derivation, partitioning and allocation, requirements tracing, requirements management, requirements verification, and requirements validation.

Requirements traceability: The ability to map the customer need to the requirement (connectivity) or to map a parent requirement to a child and vice versa. The ability to trace a requirement throughout the system development process, from requirements specification to design, to system component development, through testing and system documentation. This is absolutely critical for all systems.

Requirements verification: Independent assurance that requirements are addressed and met in a system.

Requirements verification matrix: An analysis that shows the verification method for each requirement.

Risk: The possibility of suffering loss.

Robust architecture: An underlying structure of a system that can readily meet and adapt to real requirements.

Role: A set of defined responsibilities that may be assumed by one or more individuals

Rules of engagement: A term used in Canada to describe the roles and responsibilities for project decision makers, including requirement prioritization and escalation procedures.

Scalability: The capability to grow to accommodate increased workloads.

Security: Services that protect data, ensuring its confidentiality, availability, and integrity.

Senior management: A role sufficiently high in the organization that the primary focus is on the long-term vitality of the organization.

Software quality: Software that combines the characteristics of low defect rates and high user satisfaction.

Specification: A document that describes technical requirements and verification procedures for items, materials, and services; an output of the requirements analysis process.

Stakeholder: Anyone who has an interest in a system or in its possessing qualities that meet particular needs.

Stated requirements: Requirements provided by a customer at the beginning of a system or software development effort; should be distinguished from real requirements.

Subject matter expert (SME): An individual who has been working in a particular field for an extensive period of time and who is trained in that area; often referred to as a *domain expert.*

Supplier: An organization that contracts with a buyer to provide a system.

SWAT team: A group tasked to provide a fast-action cure for a problem.

System: An integrated set of people, products, and processes that provides a capability to satisfy a customer need.

System life cycle: The set of activities involved in understanding a customer need; defining and analyzing requirements; preparing a design; developing a system; testing, implementing, operating, and maintaining it; and ending in its retirement.

Systems engineering: (1) A technical and management discipline that translates a customer need into a system that meets the customer need. Another source states system engineering is the iterative but controlled process during which user needs are understood and evolved into an operational system. The role of systems engineering is technical authority on a project; single interface to customer and project; architecture and system design; requirements derivation, allocation, and interpretation; and others (check SE-CMM key process area list).

Systems engineering: (2) (According to the CMM) The selective application of scientific and engineering efforts to transform an operational need into a description of the system configuration that best satisfies the operational need according to the measures of effectiveness; to integrate related technical parameters and to ensure compatibility of all physical, functional, and technical program interfaces in a manner that optimizes the total system definition and design; and to integrate efforts of all engineering disciplines and specialties into a total engineering effort.

Tailoring: The activity of modifying, elaborating, or adapting a process or document for another use. Reuse of tailored artifacts saves time and money and is an advantage of a process-oriented approach.

TCP/IP gateway: Transmission Control Protocol/Internet Protocol gateway. A device, or pair of devices, that interconnects two or more networks or subnetworks, enabling the passage of data from one (sub)network to another.

Teamwork: Proactive support of one another; necessary for success of any significant undertaking. Physical colocation facilitates teamwork and may be a prerequisite to success.

Technical performance measures: Indicators of how well the system works and how well the requirements are met; estimates or measures of the values of essential performance parameters. TPMs are used to evaluate the impact on cost, schedule, and technical effort.

Technical reference model (TRM): A structure that allows the components of an information system to be described in a consistent manner.

Technical specification: A comprehensive collection of the details of how a system will be implemented, including the technical architecture (hardware and software), decomposition of the system into subsystems, identification of common modules that will be developed, and other details requiring definition to allow development of the system.

Technique: A set of rules to follow to accomplish a task, a treatment of technical details, a body of technical methods, or a method of accomplishing a desired aim.

Technology insertion: Adding new technology to a system throughout the system life cycle.

Time-boxed: A technique that forces trade-offs in the context of short delivery cycles. See Highsmith, *Adaptive Software Development*.

Tool: Something used to facilitate performing an operation or practicing a process or activity.

Top down: Breaking down a system (decomposing) into component subsystems; often referred to as a *structured approach*.

Trade study: An analysis of alternative courses of action in which a balancing of factors, all of which are not obtainable at the same time, is performed.

Transaction: Interaction between a user and a computer in which the user inputs a command to receive a specific result from the computer.

Unified Modeling Language (UML): A general-purpose notation (a way to document) that describes the static and dynamic behavior of a system; not a design method or a development process.

Use case: A picture of actions a system performs, depicting the actors.

Use case driven: Describing the behavior of a system based on how the users interact with the system.

Use case model: A description of the functional behavior of a system that includes all the actors and all the use cases through which the actors interact with the system.

User: The individual or group that uses a system in its environment.

User friendly: Easy to use.

User perspective: The view the user wants, needs, prefers, is happy with, and can use.

User satisfaction: Clients who are pleased with a vendor's products, quality levels, ease of use, and support.

Validation: A process for confirming that the real requirements are implemented in the delivered system.

Venn diagram: An illustration that employs circles to represent the relationships between and among sets (groups of objects that share something in common).

Verification: A process for ensuring that the design solution satisfies the requirements.

Verification methods: The approaches used to perform verification: test, inspection, demonstration, and analysis.

View: A perspective of a system such as the functional, implementation, or physical view.

Workbench: A suite of development tools.

Work product: Something produced or created as a result of systems or software development activity.

Credits

Figure 1–1 from Paulk. *The Capability Maturity Model: Guidelines for Improving the Software Process.* © 1995 Addison-Wesley Publishing Company, Inc. Reading, Massachusetts. p. 9. Reprinted by permission of Addison Wesley Longman.

Figure 1–2 from "Benefits of CMM-Based Software Process Improvement." Reprinted with permission from SEI Technical Report, CMU/SEI-94-TR13, August 1994.

Figure 1–3 from Grady, J.O. *System Validation and Verification.* © 1997 CRC Press, Boca Raton, Florida. p. 24. Reprinted by permission of the publisher.

Figure 2–1 from Jack Hayes, PRC Program Manager.

Figures 2–2, 2–3, 2–4, and 2–5 from Carr/Hurtado/Lancaster/Markert/Tucker, *Partnering in Construction: A Practical Guide to Project Success.* © American Bar Association, Chicago, Illinois. pp. 2-13, 122, 126 and 153. Reprinted with permission.

Figure 2–6 from Charles Markert. Used with permission.

Figures 2–7, 2–8 and 2–9. © 2000. Reprinted with permission from Litton PRC, McLean, Virginia.

Figure 3–1 from Leffingwell, D., "Estimating Typical Project and Rework Costs." © 2000. Dean Leffingwell. Reprinted with permission.

Figure 3–2 from "Uses of Requirements throughout the Lifecycle." Course title: Writing Better Requirements. © 2000. Telelogic AB, Oxford, United Kingdom. Reprinted with permission.

Figure 6–1 from "Processes for Engineering a System." EIA/IS [Interim Standard]-632. © December 1994. Adapted from Figure 3, page 8. Reprinted with permission.

Figure 6–2 from PRC System Architecture Flowcharts. © 2000. Reprinted with permission from Litton PRC, McLean, Virginia.

Figure 6–3 from "Processes for Engineering a System."ANSI/EIA632. © 1998. Consolidated from the discussion in Table 6.3, page 62. Reprinted with permission.

Figures 6–4 through 6–8 from "Introduction to the Architecture Development Method." The Open Group Architecture Framework (TOGAF), Version 6 (Document Number 1910). © The Open Group, 2000 and Published Electronically by the Open Group. December 2000. Available at http://www.opengroup.org/public/arch/ Reprinted with permission.

Figure 7–1 from PRC System Flowcharts. © 2000. Reprinted with permission from Litton PRC, McLean, Virginia.

Figure 7–2 from Litton PRC. Reprinted with permission from Litton PRC, McLean Virginia.

Figure 8–1 and 8–2 from Jones, C. "Software Quality in 2000: What Works and What Doesn't." © 2000. Reprinted with permission from Capers Jones.

Figure 8–3 from Jones, C. "Software Quality in 2000: What Works and What Doesn't." © 2000. Combination of two tables from "Positive and Negative Factors That Influence Software Productivity". Reprinted with permission from Capers Jones.

Quote on page 193: Leffingwell/Widrig *Managing Software Requirements*. © 2000. Addison Wesley Longman, Inc. Reading, Massachusetts. p. 294. Reprinted with permission of Addison Wesley Longman.

Figure 8–4 from Hooks, I. and Farry, K. *Customer-Centered Products*. © 2000. p. 210. Alstair Literary Agency, New York. Used with permission.

Figure 9–2, 9–3 and 9–4 from Hooks, I. and Farry, K. *Customer-Centered Products*. © 2000. pp. 162, 163, and 169. Alstar Literary Agency, New York. Used with permission.

Figure 10–1 from Guenterberg, S., et al. Litton PRC's Technology Change Management Program: The Continuing Quest for Aligning People, Technology, and Strategy. Proceedings from Managing Software Innovation

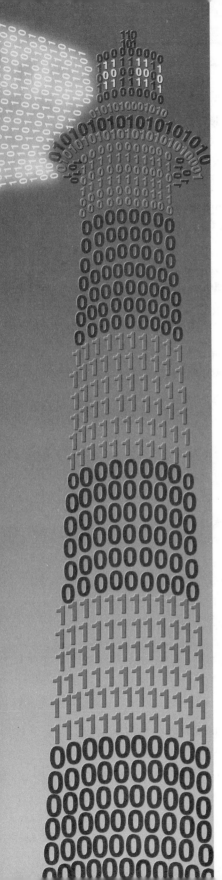

Bibliography

ABT Corporation. *Core Competencies for Project Managers.* 2000. Available at *http://www.tsepm.com/may00/art5.htm.*

Adams, James L. *Conceptual Blockbusting: A Guide to Better Ideas.* 3rd ed. Reading, MA: Perseus Books, 1986.

Adhikari, Richard. "Development Process Is a Mixed-Bag Effort." *Client/Server Computing* 1996:65–72.

Andriole, Stephen J. *Managing System Requirements: Methods, Tools, and Cases.* New York: McGraw Hill, 1996.

Bach, James. "James Bach on Risk-Based Testing: How to Conduct Heuristic Risk Analysis." *Software Testing and Quality Engineering (STQE) Magazine* 1999:1(6)23–29.

Bachmann, Felix, Len Bass, Gary Chastek, Patrick Donohoe, and Fabio Peruzzi. *The Architecture Based Design Method.* Technical report CMU/SEI-2000-TR-001, ESC-TR-2000-001. Pittsburgh, PA: Software Engineering Institute, 2000.

Bass, Len, Paul Clements, and Rick Kazman. *Software Architecture in Practice.* Reading, MA: Addison-Wesley, 1998.

Bennis, Warren, and Patricia Ward Biederman. *Genius: The Secrets of Creative Collaboration.* Reading, MA: Perseus Books, 1997.

Bicknell, Barbara A., and Kris D. Bicknell. *The Road Map to Repeatable Success: Using QFD to Implement Change.* Boca Raton, FL: CRC Press, 1995.

Boehm, Barry W. *WinWin Spiral Model and Groupware Support System.* University of Southern California, 1998. Available at *http://sunset.usc.edu/ research/WINWIN/index.html.*

Boehm, Barry W. *Software Engineering Economics.* Englewood Cliffs, NJ: Prentice Hall, 1981.

Boehm, Barry, Alexander Egyed, Julie Kwan, Dan Port, Archita Shah, and Ray Madachy. "Using the WinWin Spiral Model: A Case Study." *IEEE Computer* 1998:31(7)33–44.

Boehm, Barry W., and Kevin J. Sullivan. *Software Economics Status and Prospect.* Information and Software Technology 1999:41(14)937.

Boehm, B.W., and Hoh In. "Identifying Quality-Requirements Conflicts." *IEEE Software* 1996:13(2)25–35.

Booch, Grady, James Rumbaugh, and Ivar Jacobson. *The Unified Modeling Language User Guide.* Reading, MA: Addison-Wesley, 1999.

Brassard, Michael, and Diane Ritter. *The Memory Jogger II: A Pocket Guide of Tools for Continuous Improvement & Effective Planning.* Salem, NH: GOAL/QPC, 1994. Also available at *http://www.goalqpc.com.*

Brodman, Judith G., and Donna L. Johnson. *The LOGOS Tailored CMM for Small Businesses, Small Organizations, and Small Projects.* Needham, MA LOGOS International, Inc. 1996. Also available at *http://www.tiac.net/ users/johnsond.*

Brooks, Jr., Frederick P. *The Mythical Man-Month.* Anniversary ed. Reading, MA: Addison-Wesley, 1995.

Brooks, Jr., Frederick P. "No Silver Bullet—The Essence and Accidents of Software Engineering." *Computer* 1987:20(4)10–19.

Bruggere, T. "Software Engineering Management, Personnel, and Methodology." In: *Proceedings of the Fourth International Conference on Software Engineering.* Munich: IEEE Computer Society Press, 1979:361–368.

Buede, Dennis M. *The Engineering Design of Systems: Models and Methods.* New York: John Wiley & Sons, 2000.

Buzan, Tony. *The Mind Map Book: How to Use Radiant Thinking to Maximize Your Brain's Untapped Potential.* New York: Plume, 1996.

Capability Maturity Model Integration (CMMI) Project. Available at *http://www.sei.cmu.edu/cmmi/.*

Carr, Frank, Kim Hurtado, Charles Lancaster, Charles Markert, and Paul Tucker. *Partnering in Construction: A Practical Guide to Project Success.* Chicago, IL: American Bar Association Publishing, 1999.

Carr, Marvin J., Suresh L. Konda, Ira Monarch, F. Carol Ulrich, Clay F. Walker. *Taxonomy-Based Risk Identification.* Technical report CMU/ SEI-93-TR-6. Pittsburgh, PA: Software Engineering Institute, Carnegie-Mellon University, 1993.

Condrill, Jo, and Bennie Bough. *101 Ways to Improve Your Communication Skills.* Alexandria, VA: Goal Minds, 1998.

Connell, John L., and Linda Shafer. *Structured Rapid Prototyping: An Evolutionary Approach to Software Development.* Englewood Cliffs, NJ: Yourdon Press, 1989.

Constantine, Larry. *Constantine on Peopleware.* Englewood Cliffs, NJ: Prentice-Hall, 1995.

Curtis, Bill, Herb Krasner, and N. Iscoe. "A Field Study of the Software Design Process for Large Systems." *Communications of the ACM* 1988: 31(11)1268–1287.

Curtis, Bill, William E. Hefley, and Sally Miller. *People Capability Maturity Model.* Pittsburgh, PA: Software Engineering Institute, Carnegie-Mellon University, 1995.

Cusumano, Michael, and Richard Selby. *Microsoft Secrets: How the World's Most Powerful Software Company Creates Technology, Shapes Markets, and Manages People.* New York: Free Press, 1995.

Davis, Alan M. In: Thayer R. H., and M. Dorfman, eds. *Software Requirements Engineering.* 2nd ed. Los Alamitos, CA: IEEE Computer Society Press, 1997: Foreword vii.

Davis, Alan M. *Software Requirements: Objects, Functions, and States.* Rev. Upper Saddle River, NJ: Prentice Hall PTR, 1993.

Davis, Alan, Scott Overmyer, Kathleen Jordan, et al. "Identifying and Measuring Quality in a Software Requirements Specification." In: Thayer R. H., and M. Dorfman, eds. *Software Requirements Engineering.* 2nd ed. Los Alamitos, CA: IEEE Computer Society Press, 1997:164–175.

DeGrace, Peter, and Leslie Hulet Stahl. *Wicked Problems, Righteous Solutions.* Englewood Cliffs, NJ: Yourdon Press, 1990.

DeMarco, Tom, and Timothy Lister. *Peopleware: Productive Projects and Teams.* 2nd ed. New York: Dorset House Publishing, 1999.

Deming, W. Edwards. *Out of the Crisis.* Cambridge, MA: MIT Center for Advanced Engineering Study, 1986.

Doyle, Michael, and David Straus. *How to Make Meetings Work.* East Rutherford, NJ: Berkeley Publishing, 1993.

Dreon, Barbara E. *CMM Level 3: How Do I Get There from Here?* Version 1.1. McLean, VA: Litton PRC, June 28, 2000.

Dustin, Elfriede, Jeff Rashka, and John Paul. *Automated Software Testing: Introduction, Management, and Performance.* Boston, MA: Addison-Wesley, 1999.

Electronic Industries Alliance (EIA). *ANSI/EIA 632, Processes for Engineering a System.* Arlington, VA: EIA, 1998.

Electronic Industries Alliance (EIA). *EIA/IS 731, Systems Engineering Capability,* Arlington, VA: EIA, 1998.

Engineering Process Improvement Collaboration (EPIC). *A Systems Engineering Capability Maturity Model.* Version 1.1. Pittsburgh, PA: Software Engineering Institute, Carnegie-Mellon University, 1995. Also available at *http://www.sei.cmu.edu/pub/documents/95.reports/pdf/mm003.95.pdf.*

Ensey, Nancy, Penny Waugh, and Barbara Dreon. *Peer Review Meeting Form.* McLean, VA: Litton PRC, 1999.

Ferguson, Pat, Watts S. Humphrey, Soheil Khajenoori, Susan Macke, and Annette Matvya. "Results of Applying the Personal Software Process." *IEEE Computer* 1997:30(5)24–31.

Fisher, Roger, and Scott Brown. *Getting Together: Building Relationships As We Negotiate.* New York: Penguin Books, 1988.

Fisher, Roger, and William Ury. *Getting to Yes.* New York: Penguin Books, 1991.

Fowler, Jim. *Tool-Heavy Software Development.* Presented at the Litton Software Technology Management Conference. Dana Point, CA. February 28–March 2, 2000.

Fowler, Priscilla, Malcom (Mac) Patrick, Anita Carleton, and Barbara Merrin. "Transition Packages: An Experiment in Expediting the Introduction of Requirements Management." In: *Proceedings of the Third IEEE International*

Conference on Requirements Engineering (ICRE). Los Alamitos, CA: IEEE Computer Society Press, 1998:138–145.

Fowler, Priscilla, Mac Patrick, and Ralph Young. *Using Transition Packages to Accelerate the Adoption of Software Processes.* Presented at the National SEPG Conference. Atlanta, GA. March 1999.

Frame, J. Davidson. *Managing Projects in Organizations.* Rev. ed. San Francisco, CA: Jossey-Bass Publishers, 1995.

Frank, Milo O. *How to Run a Successful Meeting in Half the Time.* New York: Simon & Schuster, 1989.

Freedman, Daniel P., and Gerald M. Weinberg. *Handbook of Walkthroughs, Inspections, and Technical Reviews.* 3rd ed. New York: Dorset House Publishing, 1990.

Gaffney, Steven. *The Fish Isn't Sick . . . The Water Is Dirty.* Training seminar. 1998. Available at *http://www.stevengaffney.com.*

Gause, Donald C., and Gerald M. Weinberg. *Are Your Lights On? How to Know What the Problem REALLY Is.* 2nd ed. New York: Dorset House Publishing, 1989.

Gause, Donald C., and Gerald M. Weinberg. *Exploring Requirements: Quality Before Design.* New York: Dorset House Publishing, 1989.

Gibbs, W. Wayt. "Trends in Computing: Software's Chronic Crisis." *Scientific American* September 1994. Available at *http://www.di.ufpe.br/~java/gradu-acao/referencias/SciAmSept1994.html.*

Gilb, Tom. *Principles of Software Engineering Management.* Wokingham, UK: Addison-Wesley, 1988.

Gilb, Tom, and Dorothy Graham. *Software Inspection.* Reading, MA: Addison-Wesley, 1993. Also available at *http://home.c2i.net/result-planning/.*

Glass, Robert L. *Software Runaways: Lessons Learned from Massive Software Project Failures.* Upper Saddle River, NJ: Prentice Hall PTR, 1998.

Goddard Space Flight Center. *Recommended Approach to Software Development.* Rev. 3. National Aeronautics and Space Administration (NASA) Software Engineering Laboratory's (SEL) series, SEL-81-305. June 1992. Available at *http://sel.gsfc.nasa.gov/website/documents/online-doc.htm.*

Goguen, Joseph A. "Requirements Engineering as the Reconciliation of Social and Technical Issues." In: Jirotka, M., and J. Goguen, eds. *Requirements*

Engineering: Social and Technical Issues. San Diego, CA: Academic Press, 1994: 165–199.

Goguen, Joseph A., and Charlotte Linde. "Techniques for Requirements Elicitation." In: Thayer, Richard H., and Merlin Dorfman, eds. *Software Requirements Engineering.* 2nd ed. Los Alamitos, CA: IEEE Computer Society Press, 1993:Chapter 3, pp. 110–122.

Goldratt, Eliyahu M. *Critical Chain.* Great Barrington, MA: The North River Press, 1997.

Goldratt, Eliyahu M., and Jeff Cox. *The Goal.* 2nd rev. ed. Great Barrington, MA: The North River Press, 1992.

Grady, Jeffrey O. *System Validation and Verification.* Boca Raton, FL: CRC Press, 1997.

Grady, Jeffrey O. *System Requirements Analysis.* Tutorial presented at the INCOSE Symposium. Boston, MA. July 1996.

Grady, Jeffrey O. *System Requirements Analysis.* New York: McGraw-Hill, 1993.

Grady, Robert. *Practical Software Metrics for Project Management and Process Improvement.* Englewood Cliffs, NJ: Prentice Hall, 1992.

Grady, Robert, and D. Caswell. *Software Metrics: Establishing a Company-wide Program.* Englewood Cliffs, NJ: Prentice Hall, 1987.

Graham, Ian. *Requirements Engineering and Rapid Development: An Object-Oriented Approach.* Reading, MA: Addison-Wesley, 1998.

Guenterberg, Sharon, et al. "Litton PRC's Technology Change Management Program: The Continuing Quest for Aligning People, Technology, and Strategy." In: *Proceedings of the Managing Software Innovation and Technology Change Workshop.* Pittsburgh, PA: Software Engineering Institute, 1999.

Hadden, Rita. "How Scalable Are CMM Key Practices?" *CrossTalk* 1998: 11(4)18–23. Also available at *http://www.ppc.com.*

Hadden, Rita. *Now What Do We Do?* Presented at the Society for Software Quality (SSQ) Roundtable 1998. Washington, DC. January 26, 1998. For more information, call Project Performance Corporation at 301-601-1810, or contact Rita Hadden at *rhadden@ppc.com.*

Hammer, Theodore F., Leonore L. Huffman, and Linda Rosenberg. "Doing Requirements Right the First Time." *CrossTalk* 1998:11(12)20–25.

Handy, Charles. *Gods of Management: The Changing Work of Organizations.* New York: Oxford University Press, 1996.

Harwell, Richard. "Systems Engineering Is More Than Just a Process." In: Martin, James N. *Systems Engineering Guidebook.* Boca Raton, FL: CRC Press, 1996:249–255.

Harwell, Richard, Erik Aslaksen, Ivy Hooks, Roy Mengot, and Ken Ptack. "What Is a Requirement?" In: Thayer, R. H., and M. Dorfman, eds. *Software Requirements Engineering.* 2nd ed. Los Alamitos, CA: IEEE Computer Society Press, 1997:23–29.

Hatley, Derek, Peter Hruschka, and Imtiaz Pirbhai. *Process for System Architecture and Requirements Engineering.* New York: Dorset House, 2000.

Henderson, Lisa G. R. "Requirements Elicitation in Open-Source Programs." *CrossTalk* 2000:13(7)28–30.

Herbsleb, James, Anita Carlton, James Rozum, Jane Siegel, and David Zubrow. *Benefits of CMM-Based Software Process Improvement: Initial Results.* Technical report CMU/SEI-94-TR-013. Pittsburgh, PA: Software Engineering Institute, August 1994.

Highsmith, James A. III. *Adaptive Software Development: A Collaborative Approach to Managing Complex Systems.* New York: Dorset House, 1999.

Hofmeister, Christine, Robert Nord, and Dilip Soni. *Applied Software Architecture.* Reading, MA: Addison-Wesley, 2000.

Hohmann, Luke. *Journey of the Software Professional: A Sociology of Software Development.* Upper Saddle River, NJ: Prentice Hall PTR, 1997.

Hollenbach, Craig, Ralph Young, Al Pflugrad, and Doug Smith. "Combining Quality and Software Improvement." *Communications of the ACM* 1997:40(6)41–45.

Hooks, Ivy. *Guide for Managing and Writing Requirements.* 1994. Available at *ivyh@complianceautomation.com.*

Hooks, Ivy. *Managing Requirements.* 1994. Available at *http://www. complianceautomation.com/.*

Hooks, Ivy. *Writing Good Requirements: A One-Day Tutorial.* Boerne, TX: Compliance Automation, 1997.

Hooks, Ivy. *Why Johnny Can't Write Requirements.* 1990. Available at *http:// www.complianceautomation.com/.*

Hooks, Ivy. *Writing Good Requirements.* 1994. Available at *http://www. complianceautomation.com/.*

Hooks, Ivy F., and Kristin A. Farry. *Customer-Centered Products: Creating Successful Products Through Smart Requirements Management.* New York: AMACOM, 2001.

Humphrey, Watts S. *Introduction to the Team Software Process.* Reading, MA: Addison-Wesley, 2000.

Humphrey, Watts S. *Why Don't They Practice What We Preach?* 1998. Available at *http://www.sei.cmu.edu/publications/articles/sources/practice. preach/index.html.*

Humphrey, Watts S. *Introduction to the Personal Software Process.* Reading, MA: Addison-Wesley, 1997.

Humphrey, Watts S. *Managing Technical People: Innovation, Teamwork, and the Software Process.* Reading, MA: Addison-Wesley, 1997.

Humphrey, Watts S. *A Discipline for Software Engineering.* Reading, MA: Addison-Wesley, 1995.

Humphrey, Watts. *Managing for Innovation: Leading Technical People.* Englewood Cliffs, NJ: Prentice-Hall, 1987.

Inmon, W. H., John A. Zachman, and Jonathan G. Geiger. *Data Stores, Data Warehousing, and the Zachman Framework: Managing Enterprise Knowledge.* New York: McGraw Hill, 1997.

Institute of Electrical and Electronics Engineers (IEEE). *IEEE 1220, IEEE Trial-use Standard for Application and Management of the Systems Engineering Process.* New York: IEEE, 1994.

Institute of Electrical and Electronics Engineers (IEEE). J-STD-016-1995. *Standard for Information Technology Software Life Cycle Processes Software Development Acquirer-Supplier Agreement* [issued for trial use]. New York: IEEE, 1995.

Institute of Electrical and Electronics Engineers (IEEE) Software Engineering Standards Committee. *IEEE Recommended Practice for Software*

Requirements Specification. Los Alamitos, CA: IEEE Computer Society Press, 1993.

Institute of Electrical and Electronics Engineers (IEEE) Standards Department. "Guide for Developing Software Requirements Specification." In: Thayer, R. H., and M. Dorfman, eds. *Software Requirements Engineering.* Los Alamitos, CA: IEEE Computer Society Press, 1997:206–232.

Integrated Capability Maturity Model (CMMI) Web page. Available at *http://www.sei.cmu.edu/cmmi/.*

International Council on Systems Engineering (INCOSE) Position on Capability Models and the Capability Maturity Model Integration (CMMI) Effort, April 18, 1999, INCOSE/cmms/cmms.integration.html. *INSIGHT* 1999:2(2)19–20. Also available at *http://www.incose.org.*

International Function Point Users Group (IFPUG). *Function Point Counting Manual.* Westerville, OH: IFPUG, 1999. You may also contact IFPUG at 609-799-4900 or at *http://www.ifpug.org/.*

Jackson, Michael. *Software Requirements & Specifications.* Wokingham, UK: Addison-Wesley, 1995.

Jacobson, Ivar, Magnus Christerson, Patrik Jonsson, and Gunner Overgaard. *Object-Oriented Software Engineering: A Use Case Driven Approach.* Harlow, UK: Addison-Wesley, 1992.

Jacobson, Ivar, Martin Griss, and Patrik Jonsson. *Software Reuse: Architecture, Process and Organization for Business Success.* New York: ACM Press, 1997.

Jirotka, Marina, and Joseph A. Goguen. *Requirements Engineering: Social and Technical Issues.* San Diego, CA: Academic Press, 1994.

Jones, Capers. *Software Assessments, Benchmarks, and Best Practices.* Reading, MA: Addison-Wesley, 2000.

Jones, Capers. *Software Quality in 2000: What Works and What Doesn't.* January 18, 2000. Briefing available from Software Productivity Research, Inc., at *http://www.spr.com.*

Jones, Capers. *Estimating Software Costs.* New York: McGraw Hill, 1998.

Jones, Capers. *Positive and Negative Factors That Influence Software Productivity.* Version 2.0. Burlington, MA: Software Productivity Research, October 15, 1998. Also available at *http://www.spr.com.*

Jones, Capers. "Software Project Management in the 21st Century." *American Programmer* 1998:11(2)24–30.

Jones, Capers. *Software Quality: Analysis and Guidelines for Success.* Boston: International Thomson Computer Press, 1997.

Jones, Capers. *What It Means to Be "Best in Class" for Software.* Version 5. Burlington, MA: Software Productivity Research, February 10, 1998.

Jones, Capers. *Assessment and Control of Software Risks.* Englewood Cliffs, NJ: Prentice Hall, 1994.

Kalakota, Ravi, and Marcia Robinson. *e-Business: Roadmap for Success.* Reading, MA: Addison-Wesley, 1999.

Kaminski, Paul. *Reducing Life Cycle Costs for New and Fielded Systems.* Memorandum. Ft. Monmouth, NJ: Under Secretary of Defense (Acquisition and Technology), December 4, 1995.

Kaplan, Craig, Ralph Clark, and Victor Tang. *Secrets of Software Quality.* New York: McGraw-Hill, 1995.

Kar, Pradip, and Michelle Bailey. *Characteristics of Good Requirements.* Presented at the 6th INCOSE Symposium, 1996. Available at *http://www.complianceautomation.com/.*

Karlsson, Joachim, and Kevin Ryan. "A Cost-Value Approach for Prioritizing Requirements." *IEEE Software* 1997:14(5)67–74.

Kazman, Rick, and S. Jeromy Carriere. "Playing Detective: Reconstructing Software Architecture from Available Evidence." *Journal of Automated Software Engineering* 1999:6(2)107–138.

Korson, Timothy. *The Misuse of Use Cases (Managing Requirements).* 2000. Available at *http://www.korson-mcgregor.com/publications/korson/Korson9803om.htm.*

Kroeger, Otto, and Janet M. Thuesen (contributor). *Type Talk at Work: How the 16 Personality Types Determine Your Success on the Job.* New York: Dell Publishing, 1993.

Kulak, Daryl, and Eamonn Guiney. *Use Cases: Requirements in Context.* New York: ACM Press, 2000.

Leffingwell, Dean. *Calculating Your Return on Investment from More Effective Requirements Management.* 1997.

Leffingwell, Dean, and Don Widrig. *Managing Software Requirements: A Unified Approach*. Reading, MA: Addison-Wesley, 2000.

Litton PRC. *Phoenix Software Process Improvement Reference Guide*. 3rd ed. McLean, VA: Litton PRC, April 1996.

Litton TASC. *Guidelines for Writing Quality Requirements*. McLean, VA: Litton TASC, 1998.

Lubars, Mike, Colin Potts, and Charles Richter. "A Review of the State of Practice in Requirements Modeling." In: *Proceedings of IEEE International Symposium on Requirements Engineering*. Los Alamitos, CA: IEEE Computer Society Press, 1993:2–14.

Maguire, Steven A. *Debugging the Development Process*. Redmond, WA: Microsoft Press, 1994.

Marchegiani, Dan. *Requirements Engineering—A Tool-Based Requirements Engineering Process*. Presented at the Litton Industries Software Technology Management Conference. Dana Point, CA: February 28–March 2, 2000.

Markert, Charles. *Partnering: Unleashing the Power of Teamwork*, Burke, VA: Mediate-Tech, 1998. Also available from the author at *markert@erols.com*.

Martin, James. *Rapid Application Development*. New York: Macmillan Publishing, 1991.

Martin, James N. *Systems Engineering Guidebook: A Process for Developing Systems and Products*. Boca Raton, FL: CRC Press, 1996.

May, Elaine L., and Barbara A. Zimmer. "The Evolutionary Development Model for Software." *Hewlett Packard Journal* 1996:47(4)39–45.

McConnell, Steve. "The Software Manager's Toolkit." *IEEE Software* 2000: 17(4)5–7.

McConnell, Steve. *After the Gold Rush: Creating a True Profession of Software Engineering*. Redmond, WA: Microsoft Press, 1999.

McConnell, Steve. *Software Project Survival Guide*. Redmond, WA: Microsoft Press, 1998.

McConnell, Steve. "The Power of Process." *IEEE Computer* 1998:31(5) 100–102.

McConnell, Steve. *Rapid Development*. Redmond, WA: Microsoft Press, 1996.

McConnell, Steve. *Code Complete*. Redmond, WA: Microsoft Press, 1993.

Meadow, Andy. *CMM Integration (CMMI) Wall Chart*. McLean, VA: Litton PRC, September 2000.

Nasr, Eman. *The Use Case Technique for Requirements Engineering*. 1999. Available from the author at *eman.nasr@cs.york.ac.uk*.

O'Connell, Fergus. *How to Run Successful High-Tech Project-Based Organizations*. Boston, MA: Artech House, 1999.

O'Connell, Fergus. *How to Run Successful Projects II—The Silver Bullet*. 2nd ed. New York: Prentice Hall, 1996.

Oliver, David W., Timothy P. Kelliher, and James G. Keegan, Jr. *Engineering Complex Systems with Models and Objects*. New York: McGraw-Hill, 1997.

Palmer, James D. "Traceability." In: Thayer, R. H., and M. Dorfman, eds. *Software Requirements Engineering*. Los Alamitos, CA: IEEE Computer Society Press, 1997:364–374.

Paulk, Mark C. *The "Soft Side" of Software Process Improvement*. Pittsburgh, PA: Software Engineering Institute, Carnegie-Mellon University, 1999.

Paulk, Mark C. "Using the Software CMM with Good Judgment." *Software Quality Professional* 1999:1(3)19–29.

Paulk, Mark C. "Using the Software CMM with Good Judgment: Small Projects & Small Organizations." Presented at the Society for Software Quality (SSQ) Roundtable 1998. Washington, DC. January 26, 1998.

Paulk, Mark C., et al. *The Capability Maturity Model: Guidelines for Improving the Software Process*. Reading, MA: Addison-Wesley, 1995.

Paulk, Mark C. *A Comparison of ISO 9001 and the Capability Maturity Model for Software*. Technical report CMU/SEI 94-TR-12. Pittsburgh, PA: Software Engineering Institute, Carnegie-Mellon University, July 1994.

Paulk, Mark C., Bill Curtis, Mary Beth Chrissis, and Charles V. Weber. *Capability Maturity Model for Software*. Version 1.1. Pittsburgh, PA: Software Engineering Institute, Carnegie-Mellon University, 1993. Also available at *http://www.sei.cmu.edu/publications/documents/93.reports/93.tr.024.html*.

Paulk, Mark C., Charles V. Weber, Suzanne M. Garcia, Mary Beth Chrissis, and Marilyn Bush. *Key Practices of the Capability Maturity Model*. Version 1.1. Pittsburgh, PA: Software Engineering Institute, Carnegie-Mellon

University, 1993. Also available at *http://www.sei.cmu.edu/publications/ documents/93.reports/93.tr.025.html.*

Perry, William. *Effective Methods for Software Testing.* New York: John Wiley & Sons, 1995.

Petroski, Henry. *To Engineer Is Human.* New York: St. Martin's Press, 1992.

Petrozzo, Daniel P. *The Fast Forward MBA in Technology Management.* New York: John Wiley & Sons, 1998.

Poston, Robert M. *Generating Test Cases from Use Cases Automatically.* Presented at the National SEPG99 Conference. Atlanta, GA. March 1999.

Poston, Robert M. "Counting Down to Zero Software Failures." In: Poston, Robert M. *Automating Specification-Based Software Testing.* Los Alamitos, CA: IEEE Computer Society Press, 1996:224–231.

Pressman, Roger S. *Software Engineering: A Practitioner's Approach.* 4th ed. New York: McGraw Hill, 1996.

Putnam, Lawrence H., and Ware Myers. *Measures for Excellence: Reliable Software on Time, Within Budget.* Upper Saddle River, NJ: Yourdon Press, 1992.

QSS, Inc. *Writing Better Requirements.* Course slides. Mt. Arlington, NJ: QSS, Inc., 1999. Also available at *http://www2.telelogic.com/doors/products/.*

Ramaswami, K. V. *Process & Quality, Global Technology Operations— Software, Applications of QFD.* 2000. C Tower, 6th floor, Golden Enclave, Airport Road, Wipro GE Medical Systems, Bangalore India 560 017. Also available at *http://www.gemedicalsystems.com/.*

Raphael, Rich. *Risk Process and Risk Management Program.* McLean, VA: Litton PRC, 1999.

Rechtin, Eberhardt. *Systems Architecting of Software Structures, or Why Eagles Can't Swim.* Presented at the Software Technology Management Conference. Dana Point, CA. February 29–March 2, 2000.

Rechtin, Eberhardt. *Systems Architecting of Organizations: Why Eagles Can't Swim.* New York: CRC Press, 1999.

Rechtin, Eberhardt, and Mark W. Maier. *The Art of System Architecting.* New York: CRC Press, 1997.

Revelle, Jack B., John W. Moran, and Charles Cox. *The QFD Handbook.* New York: John Wiley & Sons, 1997.

Robertson, Suzanne, and James Robertson. *Mastering the Requirements Process.* Harlow, UK: Addison-Wesley, 1999.

Roetzheim, William H. "Estimating Software Costs." *Software Development Magazine* 2000;20(8):66–68.

Roetzheim, William H. *Project Failures—Mismanaged or Poorly Planned?* 1999. Available at *http://www.marotz.com/journal/mar99/article3.htm.*

Rosenberg, Linda. *Writing High Quality Requirement Specifications.* Tutorial presented at the 12th International Software Quality Week (QW'99). San Jose, CA. May 24–28, 1999.

Royce, Walker. *Software Project Management: A Unified Framework.* Reading, MA: Addison-Wesley, 1998.

Rumbaugh, James. "Getting Started: Using Use Cases to Capture Requirements." In: Thayer, R. H., and M. Dorfman, eds. *Software Requirements Engineering.* Los Alamitos, CA: IEEE Computer Society Press, 1997: 123–127.

Rumbaugh, James, Ivar Jacobson, and Grady Booch. *The Unified Modeling Language Reference Manual.* Reading, MA: Addison-Wesley, 1998.

Sabourin, Robert. *I Am a Bug.* Quebec: Robert Saborin, 1999. Address inquiries to *rsabourin@amibug.com.*

Schneider, Geri, and Jason P. Winters. *Applying Use Cases: A Practical Guide.* Reading, MA: Addison-Wesley, 1998.

SECAT LLC. *An Organizational Leader's Pocket Guide to Measuring Systems Engineering Success.* 1998. Available at *http://www.secat.com.*

SECAT LLC. *A Program Manager's Pocket Guide to Measuring Systems Engineering Success.* 1998. Available at *http://www.secat.com.*

SECAT LLC. *A Systems Engineer's Pocket Guide to Measuring Systems Engineering Success.* 1998. Available at *http://www.secat.com.*

SECAT LLC. *Micro Assessment Kit and Pocket Guide Information.* 1998. Available at *http://www.secat.com.*

Senge, Peter M. *The Fifth Discipline: The Art and Practice of the Learning Organization.* New York: Doubleday, 1990.

Senge, Peter, Art Kleiner, Charlotte Roberts, Richard Ross, George Roth, and Bryan Smith. *The Dance of Change.* New York: Doubleday, 1999.

Shea, Virginia. *Netiquette.* 1994. Available at the Netiquette home page at *http://www.albion.com/netiquette/index.html.*

Six Sigma Qualtec. *QI Story: Tools and Techniques, A Guidebook to Problem Solving.* 3rd ed. Tempe, AZ: Six Sigma Qualtec, 1999. Copies can be ordered by calling 480-586-2600.

Smith, Preston G., and Donald G. Reinertsen. *Developing Products in Half the Time.* 2nd ed. New York: John Wiley & Sons, 1998.

Software Acquisition Best Practices Initiative. *The Program Manager's Guide to Software Acquisition Best Practices.* April 1997. Available at *http://www.spmn.com/.*

Software Engineering Institute (SEI). *The Architecture Tradeoff Analysis Method.* 1999. Available at *http://www.sei.cmu.edu/activities/ata/ATAM/tsld004.htm.*

Sommerville, Ian. *Software Engineering.* 5th ed. Reading, MA: Addison-Wesley, 1995.

Sommerville, Ian, and Pete Sawyer. *Requirements Engineering: A Good Practice Guide.* New York: John Wiley & Sons, 1997.

Sommerville, I., P. Sawyer, and S. Viller. "Viewpoints for Requirements Elicitation: A Practical Approach." In: *Proceedings of the 1998 International Conference on Requirements Engineering (ICRE'98), April 6-10, 1998, Colorado Springs, CO.* New York: IEEE Computer Society Press, 1998:74–81. Also available at *http://computer.org/proceedings/icre/8356/8356toc.htm.*

Stapleton, J. *Dynamic Systems Development Method: The Method in Practice.* Harlow, UK: Addison-Wesley, 1997.

Starbuck, Ronald. "How to Control Software Changes." *Software Testing and Quality Engineering (STQE) Magazine* 1999:1(6)18–21.

Stevens, Richard, and Gary Putlock. "Improving Requirements Management." *INSIGHT* 1997:166–9.

Stone, Douglas, Bruce Patton, and Sheila Heen. *Difficult Conversations: How to Discuss What Matters Most.* New York: Penguin Books, 1999.

Strassmann, Paul A. *The Squandered Computer: Evaluating the Business Alignment of Information Technologies.* New Canaan, CT: The Information Economics Press, 1997.

"Tales of Terror." *Software Development Magazine* 2000:8(10)34–38. Also available at *http://www.sdmagazine.com.*

Terninko, John. *Step-By-Step QFD: Customer-Driven Product Design.* Boca Raton, FL: Saint Lucie Press, 1997.

Thayer, R. H., and M. Dorfman, eds. *Software Requirements Engineering.* 2nd ed. Los Alamitos, CA: IEEE Computer Society Press, 1997.

Thayer, Richard H., and Mildred C. Thayer. "Software Requirements Engineering Glossary." In: Thayer, R. H., and M. Dorfman, eds. *Software Requirements Engineering.* 2nd ed. Los Alamitos, CA: IEEE Computer Society Press, 1997:441–480.

The Atlantic Systems Guild, Inc. *Volere Requirements Specification Template.* 1999. Available at *http://www.atlsysguild.com/GuildSite/Robs/Template.html.*

The Chief Information Officers (CIO) Council. *Federal Enterprise Architectural Framework.* Version 1.1. September 1999. Available at *http://www.itpolicy.gsa.gov/mke/archplus/archhome.htm.*

The Open Group. *The Open Group's Architectural Framework (TOGAF).* Version 5. Available at *http://www.opengroup.org/public/arch/.*

The Standish Group. *The CHAOS Report.* Dennis, MA: The Standish Group International, 1995.

The Standish Group International, Inc. *A Special COMPASS Report: Requirements Management Tools.* Dennis, MA: The Standish Group International, 1998.

The Standish Group International, Inc. *Sample Research Paper: Unfinished Voyages.* Dennis, MA: The Standish Group International, 1996.

Thomsett, Rob. *Third Wave Project Management.* Upper Saddle River, NJ: Yourdon Press, 1993.

U.S. Department of Defense (DoD), Defense Standardization Program Office. *Communicating Requirements.* SD-16. Ft. Belvoir, VA: November 1998. Available at *http://www.dsp.dla.mil.*

Vienneau, Robert. "A Review of Formal Methods." In: Thayer, Richard H., and Merlin Dorfman, eds. *Software Requirements Engineering.* 2nd ed. Los Alamitos, CA: IEEE Computer Society Press, 1997:324–335.

Vischer, Jacqueline. "Will This Open Space Work?" *Harvard Business Review* 1999:17(3)28–40.

Wallace, Delores R., and Laura M. Ippolito. "Verifying and Validating Software Requirements Specifications." In: Thayer, Richard H., and Merlin Dorfman, eds. *Software Requirements Engineering.* 2nd ed. Los Alamitos, CA: IEEE Computer Society Press, 1997:389–404.

Walton, Mary. *The Deming Management Method.* New York: Putnam Publishing, 1986.

Webster, Bruce F. *Pitfalls of Object-Oriented Development.* New York: M&T Books, 1995.

Weinberg, Gerald M. *Quality Software Management. Vol. 4, Anticipating Change.* New York: Dorset House, 1997.

Weinberg, Gerald M. "Just Say No! Improving the Requirements Process." *American Programmer* 1995:8(10)19–23.

Weinberg, Gerald M. *Quality Software Management. Congruent Action. Vol. 3.* New York: Dorset House, 1994.

Weinberg, Gerald. *Becoming a Technical Leader: An Organic Problem-Solving Approach.* New York: Dorset House, 1986.

Weinberg, Gerald M. *The Secrets of Consulting.* New York: Dorset House, 1986.

Weinberg, Gerald M., James Bach, and Naomi Karten, eds. *Amplifying Your Effectiveness.* New York: Dorset House, 2000.

Weller, Edward F. "Practical Applications of Statistical Process Control." *IEEE Software* 2000:17(3)48–55.

White, M. Sue. "Requirements: A Quick and Inexpensive Way to Improve Testing." In: *Test Techniques Newsletter.* San Francisco, CA: Software Research, December 1994. Available at *http://www.soft.com/News/TTN-Online/ttndec94.html.*

Whitten, Jeffery L., Lonnie D. Bentley, and Kevin C. Dittman. *Systems Analysis and Design Methods.* 5th ed. Boston, MA: McGraw-Hill, 2000.

Whitten, Neal. "Meet Minimum Requirements: Anything More Is Too Much." *PM Network* September 1998:12(9)19.

Whitten, Neal. *Becoming an Indispensable Employee in a Disposable World.* Amsterdam: Pfeiffer & Company, 1995.

Whitten, Neal. *Managing Software Development Projects: Formula for Success.* 2nd ed. New York: John Wiley & Sons, 1995.

Wiegers, Karl E. "Habits of Effective Analysts." *Software Development Magazine* 2000:8(10)62–65.

Wiegers, Karl. "10 Requirements Traps to Avoid." *Software Testing and Quality Engineering Magazine* 2000:2(1)34–40. Also available at *http://www.stqemagazine.com/featured.asp?id=8.*

Wiegers, Karl E. "Automating Requirements Management." *Software Development Magazine* 1999:7(7)S1–S5.

Wiegers, Karl E. "First Things First: Prioritizing Requirements." *Software Development Magazine* 1999:7(9)24–30.

Wiegers, Karl E. "Process Improvement That Works." *Software Development Magazine* 1999:7(10)24–30.

Wiegers, Karl E. *Read My Lips: No New Models.* Presented at the 4th International Conference on Practical Software Quality Techniques (PSQT'99 South). San Antonio, TX. June 7–11, 1999.

Wiegers, Karl E. *Software Requirements.* Redmond, WA: Microsoft Press, 1999.

Wiegers, Karl E. *Creating a Software Engineering Culture.* New York: Dorset House, 1996.

Wieringa, R. J. *Requirements Engineering, Frameworks for Understanding.* New York: John Wiley & Sons, 1996.

Wiley, Bill. *Essential System Requirements: A Practical Guide to Event-Driven Methods.* Reading, MA: Addison-Wesley, 2000.

Williams, Louise. *SPI Best Practices for Small Projects.* Presented at the Society for Software Quality (SSQ) Roundtable 1998. Washington, DC. January 26, 1998. Also available at *http://www.quality.org/SSQ98.html.*

Wood, Jane, and Denise Silver. *Joint Application Design.* New York: John Wiley & Sons, 1989.

Writing Effective E-mail. Available at *http://www.delta.edu/~anburke/emtips.html.*

Young, Ralph R. *Requirements Plan for the ISC2 Project*. McLean, VA: Litton PRC, 1999.

Young, Ralph R. *Object Orientation in a Requirements Tool*. Presented at the PRC Spring Technical Seminar. McLean, VA: May 6, 1998.

Young, Ralph R. "Process in Action—Deployment of PRC's Requirements Process." *Technology Transfer* 1998:10(6)10–12.

Young, Ralph R. *The Value of an Organizational Requirements Working Group*. Presented at the Third International Conference on Practical Software Quality Techniques (PSQT98). Minneapolis, MN: October 1998.

Young, Ralph R., and Hal Miller. "PSP: A Strategic Opportunity for Litton Industries." *Technology Transfer* 1999:11(4)8–10.

Young, Ralph R., Leo Brennan, and Bart Hodgson. "Description and Themes of BPR, the Requirements Process, and Partnering." In: Pohlmann, Lawrence D., ed. *Systems Engineering: People, Processes, Technology, and Systems. Proceedings of the International Council on Systems Engineering (INCOSE) Mid-Atlantic Regional Conference (MARC)*. McLean, VA: INCOSE, 2000:14.1-1 to 14.4-6.

Young, Ralph R., and Matt Noah. *Requirements Management Process Implementation Support*. Briefing presented at PRC's Fall 1998 Executive Sponsor Status Review. McLean, VA. September 9, 1998.

Yourdon, Edward. *The Complete Software Developer's Guide to Surviving "Mission Impossible" Projects*. Englewood Cliffs, NJ: Prentice-Hall, 1997.

Zultner, Richard E. *Software Quality Function Deployment: The First Five Years—Lessons Learned*. Princeton, NJ: Zultner & Company, 1993.

Zultner, Richard E. "TQM for Technical Teams." *Communications of the ACM* 1993:36(10)78–91.

Zultner, Richard E. "QFD for Software: Satisfying Customers." *American Programmer* 1992:5(2)28–41.

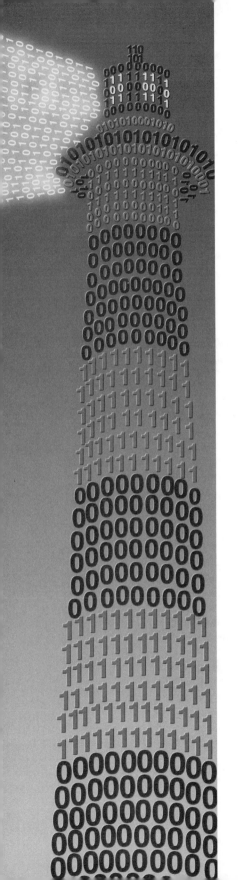

Author Index

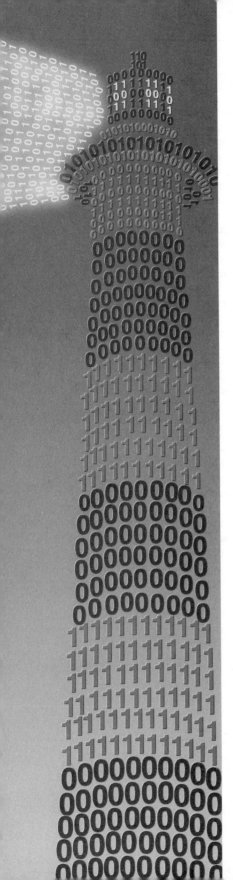

Subject Index

Register

Your Book

at www.aw.com/cseng/register

You may be eligible to receive:

- Advance notice of forthcoming editions of the book
- Related book recommendations
- Chapter excerpts and supplements of forthcoming titles
- Information about special contests and promotions throughout the year
- Notices and reminders about author appearances, tradeshows, and online chats with special guests

Contact us

If you are interested in writing a book or reviewing manuscripts prior to publication, please write to us at:

Editorial Department
Addison-Wesley Professional
75 Arlington Street, Suite 300
Boston, MA 02116 USA
Email: AWPro@aw.com

Addison-Wesley

Visit us on the Web: http://www.aw.com/cseng

CD-ROM Warranty

Addison-Wesley warrants the enclosed disc to be free of defects in materials and faulty workmanship under normal use for a period of ninety days after purchase. If a defect is discovered in the disc during this warranty period, a replacement disc can be obtained at no charge by sending the defective disc, postage prepaid, with proof of purchase to:

Editorial Department
Addison-Wesley Professional
Pearson Technology Group
75 Arlington Street, Suite 300
Boston, MA 02116
Email: AWPro@awl.com

Addison-Wesley makes no warranty or representation, either expressed or implied, with respect to this software, its quality, performance, merchantability, or fitness for a particular purpose. In no event will Addison Wesley, its distributors, or dealers be liable for direct, indirect, special, incidental, or consequential damages arising out of the use or inability to use the software. The exclusion of implied warranties is not permitted in some states. Therefore, the above exclusion may not apply to you. This warranty provides you with specific legal rights. There may be other rights that you may have that vary from state to state. The contents of this CD-ROM are intended for personal use only.

More information and updates are available at:
http://www.awl.com/cseng/titles/0201709120